*Voice
and
Speech Training
in the
New Millennium*

Voice
and
Speech Training
in the
New Millennium

Conversations
with
Master Teachers

Nancy Saklad

APPLAUSE THEATRE & CINEMA BOOKS
An Imprint of Hal Leonard Corporation

Published in 2011 by Applause Theatre & Cinema Books
An Imprint of Hal Leonard Corporation
7777 West Bluemound Road
Milwaukee, WI 53213

Trade Book Division Editorial Offices
33 Plymouth St., Montclair, NJ 07042

Printed in the United States of America
Book design by Lynn Bergesen

Library of Congress Cataloging-in-Publication Data

Saklad, Nancy.
   Voice and speech training in the new millennium : conversations with master teachers / Nancy Saklad.
      p. cm.
   ISBN 978-1-61774-058-9 (pbk.)
   1. Acting. 2. Voice culture. I. Title.
   PN2071.S65S36 2011
   792.02'8—dc22

                                                    2011013156

www.applausepub.com

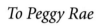

To Peggy Rae

Contents

 *Preface*

Speech is civilization itself.
—Thomas Mann

My intention in writing this book was to create a record of vocal training as it stands today in the US just over a decade into the twenty-first century. *Voice and Speech Training in the New Millennium: Conversations with Master Teachers* takes the reader on a tour through the theories, practices, pedagogy, personal histories, and innovations of twenty-four of the foremost teachers in the field, many of whom have inspired more than one generation of actors, teachers, and voice professionals. Each has contributed to the advancement of the discipline with a conviction that is fundamental to producing the kind of change that is propelling voice and speech work to an integral position in American actor training.

I have been fortunate to study with exceptional master voice and speech teachers. Several of them I studied with intensively to experience the shifts in voice, body, and awareness that can accompany total immersion. These teachers were magicians of the genuine sort, who waved their magic "voice and speech wands" and brought about essential transformation. They shed light on the work, not surprisingly, with their brilliant thinking.

My interest in voice and speech training began in 2000. I had been teaching acting and directing at the college level for about ten years and had some free time one summer, so I decided to take a voice class to broaden my horizons. This particular class was appealing because it offered intensive study and was unlike the sit-down, rote drillwork I had been exposed to in my college days.

During one of the class sessions, I experienced a sudden and profound muscular release that expanded my breath capacity considerably. My body, like an infant expressing powerful unrestricted emotion, responded first with a burst of laughter, which shortly turned to tears, and finally surrendered to a very deep, fully released breath. It was fluid and effortless. I remember feeling my focus was divided in two: one part of me was experientially engaged in the release, while the other part watched and analyzed. A colleague aptly described this aspect of the process. She said I had assumed the roles of teacher and student simultaneously. Then, through this dual lens of awareness, I noticed a pattern in my breathing that revealed the source that had been impeding the full breath. When overcome with emotion, I held my breath! It was a simple as that. In a moment I realized how life's daily habits embed habitual holding patterns in the muscles involved in breathing, and how frequently we hold our breath in response to powerful emotion. My understanding of breathing would change forever. When released, the body no longer resists itself and so contributes more completely to the actor's expressivity through voice, speech, and movement. The voice changes when the actor's body is free, becoming more healthy and vibrant. Vibration is a remarkable self-to-self feedback system for the actor, and also informs the audience of the vitality of the actor's presence. Finally, when the actor experiences a change in deeply patterned behavior, he or she is reminded of the beauty of experiencing the breath, the body, and the moment anew.

That experience whetted my appetite for more voice and speech training. I have since shifted my primary interest in teaching to voice and speech work. I currently teach a three-course sequence of voice and speech classes at a midsize Liberal Arts University. My training in voice and speech has enriched how I teach acting and how I direct. I listen and observe more closely. My classes and productions are richer as a result. I also coach, train, and consult with professional actors, theatre companies, and ESL students. Since studying intensively in 2000, I have worked with a variety of master teachers to expand my understanding of what voice and speech training is from multiple perspectives. This work has become the work I care to do for a lifetime. At the center of it all is a journey that has led to the writing of this book.

Acknowledgments

Claudia Gross, Clancey Watkins, Anita Gonzalez, Dan Kempton, Paul Kassel, Russ Dembin, Maureen Kaddar, Angela Eckhert, Phillip Douglas, Janet Shapiro, Shane Ann Younts, Liza and Kate Williams, Bernice Richman, Arnold Saklad, Joe Goscinski, Anne Drakopoulos, Robin Albert, Rick Gremlitz, Joseph Batcheller, Lucille Rubin, all of the teachers in this book, and especially my students, past and present.

Introduction

The purpose of voice work is to elevate the human spirit through language.

—Louis Colaianni

Persuasive Legacies

The soul of communication is the desire to persuade, and it is within our nature to strive to persuade ever more effectively. Actors, in order to become increasingly more persuasive, develop their instruments and hone their skills.

Voice and speech training has long been a part of the fabric of actor training and the training of those whose task it has been to persuade through the voice—primarily actors, politicians, lawyers, and other public speakers. The renowned ancient Greek orator Demosthenes (384–22 BC) had a speech impediment as a young boy. According to contemporary writers, he supposedly devised a series of exercises that might help him overcome it. Some say that he spoke with a mouthful of stones to improve his articulation. Whether this is truth or fiction, Demosthenes ultimately spoke well enough that he proceeded to become ancient Greece's greatest orator. Much later, in the early twentieth century, another proponent of voice and speech, G. Bernard Shaw, described a similar measure in his play *Pygmalion* involving the use of marbles in place of stones. Today an actor might substitute these measures with the use of a bone prop or a cork, or even imaginative play, to make the articulators more agile and more available to an increased range of linguistic detail.

Since the days of ancient Greece, Western voice and speech training has evolved in response to theatrical convention and venue, acting and oratorical styles, a knowledge of the physical instrument, technological advancements, and the fashions and predilections of the day. What follows is an abridged timeline through which the reader can explore the shifting relationship of acting training and voice and speech training. By examining a brief history of the interplay of developments in both of these areas, it will become apparent how these two components of the discipline have urged one another forward over the years. In looking back, perhaps we can distinguish a sense of direction, and so understand the role of today's voice and speech training more clearly. We begin in the mid–nineteenth century when elocution teachers wrote prolifically about their art.

Elocution Training in the Nineteenth Century

> "The systematic practice of elocution requires attention, in the first place, to the acquisition of correctness of enunciation, volume, pliancy of voice, vigour of organ, and purity of tone, on the scale of public reading or speaking."
> —William Russell, *The American Elocutionist*

In the mid–nineteenth century, American actors learned their craft through apprenticeship, observation, and elocution training, which dictated the use of gesture as well as inflection patterns, range, "appropriate" tempos, "force," and even breathing. While perhaps foreign to a modern-day audience's ear, elocution excluded subtlety, and was synonymous with the imitative acting style of the day. This form of voice and speech training was not typically concerned with the actor's vocal or gestural authenticity. Instead, elocution invited the listener to enjoy the "correctness" and "beauty" of the speaker's tone, pronunciation, style, and gesture.

In his article "Standard Speech: The Ongoing Debate," Dudley Knight describes an audio recording of famed theatrical couple E. H. Sothern and his wife, Julia Marlowe, at the turn of the century. Knight indicates that their speech and vocal patterns, particularly those of Marlowe, were reminiscent of the lessons of the early prominent American elocution teacher James Murdoch and *his* acclaimed teacher, James Rush. Knight describes the essence of the sound of the voices in this way: "It was a pattern that mandated the extreme extension of vowel sounds, often with a tremulous dying fall of intonation when a word was to be emphasized." The magnitude of the speakers' elocutionary style is quite aptly described by Knight. Upon examination of the multitude of elocution manuals and recorded material available from this time, what becomes apparent is that elocution training was intended to communicate what seemed to be a kind of spoken music that revealed the character's state of being, as well as pleasing tone, clear articulation, and so forth. Both Rush and Murdoch's teachings instructed acting through the voice. Murdoch, in his book

Orthophony: or Vocal Culture in Elocution, refers to a piece of instruction he calls "The Slide of Emotion," which he describes this way: "Strong emotions are expressed by the 'downward slide' [of pitch] except surprise—and earnest, or impassioned interrogation—which usually adopt the 'upward slide' of the 'fifth' or the 'octave.'" Rush, too, describes how musical intervals ascribed states of being in *The Philosophy of the Human Voice*: "The rising radical and vanishing fifth, like that of the octave, is interrogative; and emphatically expresses wonder, admiration and congenial states of mind when they embrace a slight degree of inquiry or doubt." Vocal variables—pitch, tempo, force, rhythm, and inflection—were like instruments to be played to evoke mood; to assign emphasis; and, as in the case of Sothern and Marlowe, to suggest the character's emotional quality or state of being.

The nineteenth-century listener's ear was discerning and so prized "good" sounds and "appropriate" sounds. In *The American Elocutionist*, author and orthophonist* William Russell, who also worked with Rush and Murdoch, states that nasal tones were bad and guttural tones inappropriate, but when combined, the two were considered "doubly injurious." Every tone, every inflection, and even gestures were dictated from any number of textbooks on the subject. Many believed that a definite rule was indispensable to effective instruction. Elocution manuals indicate that much of the training took the form of technical instruction—consonant drills, vowel drills, diphthong drills, musical scales and intervals, breathing exercises, how to deliver the text, when to pause, at which tempo to speak, how much force was to be used, and so on. Instruction could be very specifically detailed. In the following case in point on "passionate utterances," Rush offered this meticulous description of phrasing:

> There are particular states of mind which over-rule the occasions and grammatical properties of pausing, thereby producing notable rests after very short phrases, and even after every word of a sentence, without reference to the connections of syntax. I use the term Broken Melody, to signify those interruptions in utterance, which the excess of certain passions sometimes creates.

The elocutionists, as Rush demonstrated, elicited an acting outcome through mechanical and imitative methods. Elocutionary practice, as

---

* An orthophonist was someone who trained the vocal organs.

complex in its observation of verbal and gestural communication as it was, did not accommodate the unique expression of "the self." It was a highly structured, prescriptive art form, and because there was no systematized approach to acting training in western culture at the time, elocution served as both acting and vocal guide for nineteenth-century actors the likes of Sothern and Marlowe; Booth, Bernhardt, and Terry; and many more.

François Delsarte

Meanwhile François Delsarte, recognized as one of the most significant nineteenth-century European acting teachers, devoted himself to the investigation of the relationship between emotion, physical behavior, and language. Delsarte studied human postures, gesture, and even breathing, in order to formulate "scientific principles" in the area of human expression. In his book *The Delsarte System*, he codified a series of gestures and poses so they could be replicated by the actor to convey a range of emotions and attitudes. According to *The Essential Delsarte*, each gesture united with a vocal quality or variable to establish an impression of the character's state of being: "The deep voice with the eyes open, expresses worthy things...The deep voice with the eyes closed, expresses odious things." In creating this work, Delsarte became the first to systematize an approach to acting training. His lauded complementary *System of Oratory* outlined many areas of the voice and included much instruction on how to develop the voice as an emotionally expressive tool.

While perhaps naïve by contemporary standards, Delsarte's work was methodical in nature and highly detailed, with a foundation in some knowledge of anatomy and much observation of human behavior. In fact, his work considered by some to be a precursor to the turn-of-the-century James-Lange theory, in which William James and Carl Lange claim that one's emotions occur simultaneously with physiological changes in the body that could be induced by action or gesture. In this case, the action gives rise to the emotion without the added stimulus of the actor's imagination. Delsarte's many postures and gestures may have been intended to evoke not only feeling in the audience but a feeling response in the actor as well. If this were so, then Delsarte's early psychophysical exploration might make him a forerunner to Michael Chekhov. Regardless, for a while his system of acting training won him great popularity in Europe that would eventually spread to the US as well.

In 1871 Delsarte's only American student, Steele MacKaye, brought his teachings to the United States, and in 1884 MacKaye founded the first professional American acting school, later to become the American Academy of Dramatic Art. Delsarte's work was initially very well received through MacKaye's teachings. He had intended that his method would deepen the actor's connection to emotional truth. To the contrary and quite regrettably, his work was misrepresented by those who taught it without having studied with him directly, and so was scoffed at and labeled "pseudo-scientific." Eventually and inevitably, Delsarte's acting system faded in popularity, yet elocution training remained.

Samuel Silas Curry and Anna Baright

Not every nineteenth-century voice and speech teacher adhered to the rigor of elocutionary practice. Samuel Silas Curry opposed the mechanical style of elocution training, and in 1879, he and his wife, Anna Baright Curry, created their own school in Boston. At one time called the School of Elocution and Expression, the name was eventually changed by Curry to simply the School of Expression. Curry and Baright believed in a holistic education. The couple contributed to the development of voice and speech training by recognizing and promoting the notion that expression moved from within outward. Curry, in his book *Foundations of Expression*, states very directly: "Every action of face or hand, every modulation of the voice, is simply an outward effect of an inward condition. Any motion or tone that is otherwise is not expression."

While clear about the creative impulse stemming from within, Curry also had a distinct point of view on externally imposed mechanical rules for the actor/speaker: "Mechanical rules, such as, 'Pause before a preposition or relative pronoun,' and the like are useless. They are, moreover, vicious because they concentrate the student's attention upon accidentals, and may prevent genuine thinking." He wrote,

> What is it that determines the number of times we breathe? The thinking. One who breathes abstractly always breathes too seldom. Individualize ideas, concentrate attention on each successive idea and receive a definite impression; then the rhythm of thinking will determine the rhythm of breathing.

The teaching of a connection between breath and thought was new and challenged the established elocutionary practice. A fresh, more naturalistic style of acting was starting to make its presence known.

Curry and Baright were visionaries committed to the school's aim as a course of self-discovery and self-study, and to the creation of a new method of vocal expression. In 1943 the Curry School became Curry College, a liberal arts school, and today maintains many of its founding principles. And interestingly enough, Curry had studied with McKaye in the United States and Delsarte abroad.

Stanislavsky and the Moscow Art Theatre

The next significant development in acting training in the US occurred in 1923, when Stanislavsky brought the Moscow Art Theatre to New York. Stanislavsky had devoted his life to developing an approach to acting that gave the actor a means of achieving truth through "the reality of doing" instead of merely *pretending* to do or assuming an emotional affect—an approach that also considered the psychological realm of the character through the use of the actor's imagination. He searched for ways to approach the actor's inner life. According to Stanislavsky, actors would ask themselves, "What would I do if I were the character under the imaginary circumstances of the play?" The fruit of his labors was a system of realistic acting that took American audiences by storm. Ultimately, Stanislavsky accomplished what it seems Delsarte had unsuccessfully tried to do. He systematized a method for what was then understood as realistic acting.

And as for voice and speech training early in the twentieth century, American actors who performed in classical plays were instructed to speak with an English accent in order to communicate the idea that the actor's speech, like the playwright's language, was elevated. Actors in early American talking pictures also used this accent. The hope was that this new dialect would become, according to its creator William Tilly, the dialect for English speakers worldwide. Aptly, it was named World English.

The Truth of the Moment and the Truth of the Matter

During the 1930s, as American acting training continued to grow, new methods piggybacked on Stanislavsky's groundbreaking system. The work became even more internally focused with the innovations of members of the Group Theatre, led by Harold Clurman, Cheryl Crawford, and Lee Strasberg. The Group was much inspired by Stanislavsky, and used his work as a basis for the development of their own. Elocution, still the principle vocal training of the day, was becoming increasingly ill-partnered with this new, more naturalistic, impulse-based acting style.

Skinner, McLean, and Tilly

In 1942, Edith Skinner added a new dimension to speech training for the stage when her book *Speak with Distinction* was published. Skinner was descended from a formidable speech-training line led by William Tilly (1860–1935) who, in addition to developing World English, was especially regarded for his fervent promotion of the International Phonetic Alphabet (IPA). Tilly advocated that certain phonemes were superior to others. In World English, the use of r-coloring was minimized as a case in point. World English was supposedly free of regionalisms (though some have said World English had a New England flavor, probably due to the reduction of r-coloring and also the use of the more retracted "Italian *a*" in place of the "short or flat *a*"), and was appropriate for the "cultured" English-speaking sect everywhere. Later to be called Good American Speech, a modified version of World English became the standard on stage and screen. Tilly's student, speech and diction specialist Margaret Prendergast McLean, had written *Good American Speech* in 1927, which was based on Tilly's teaching ideology for World English. In the late 1930s, McLean ventured to Hollywood to teach at Maria Ouspenskaya's acting school, where she imparted Good American Speech to Hollywood actors. Skinner, who had been McLean's student, maintained Good American Speech principles when she wrote *Speak with Distinction*. The book became the articulation and pronunciation bible and IPA handbook for scores of actors for almost seventy years. While Good American Speech sharpened a number of articulation skills, it also prized itself above the abundance of other dialects that reflected the many regions in the US, and so placed limits on the actor's range of expressiveness. The sense and spirit of Tilly's World English would carry on through Skinner's work. Together, Skinner, McLean, and Tilly changed the sound of American theatre and film mid-century. Classical plays in the US at that time were performed with the accent prescribed by *Speak with Distinction*. Actors who studied Skinner's method were said to possess exquisite skill in articulation and were said to have sounded, not surprisingly, very much alike.

The Method—Inside or Out?

Later, in the 1950s, a decade after the Group Theatre disbanded, Lee Strasberg, then artistic director of the Actor's Studio, continued to pursue his inwardly focused, psychologically driven system of acting training, which he called "The Method." Now the question Method actors asked themselves was, "What inner resources and memories can I draw upon to satisfy the demands of the role?" Emotional recall and affective-memory exercises drew actors deep within themselves as they searched for a meaningful connection to the imaginary world of the play. Many American actors who studied the Method struggled to find a way to sustain the "truth of the moment" while simultaneously honoring vocal technique. For a while many Method actors discarded their vocal training altogether, believing it to be detrimental to their acting process. How could they focus on forming perfectly shaped vowels while connecting with an emotionally charged memory and its ensuing expression? How could they adopt Good American Speech, which was not their native pronunciation, and still maintain a sense of truth? One might think a naturalistic acting style would not require much vocal work. Quite ironically, as time would reveal, this new naturalistic acting style required a more in-depth approach to voice and speech training rather than none—one that considered the actor's inner life as connected to the totality of his or her being.

Vocal Visionaries

Eventually a breakthrough in voice and speech training came to rescue those who felt disillusioned with the disparity between the demands of naturalistic acting technique and methods of voice and speech training that did not seem to honor the actor's impulse. Arthur Lessac, Cicely Berry, Robert Neff Williams, and Kristin Linklater proposed new avenues of training and hope for the actor. The gulf between approaches to naturalistic acting styles and truthful expressive voice and speech training began to narrow. While perhaps lesser known, Robert Neff Williams was an early pioneer of voice/speech/text and acting integration. This quote is from an unpublished workbook of his:

> The actor's diction and voice should serve the language, ideas, emotions, style, and world of the play. It should not call attention to itself as voice and diction which is especially grand or awkward or beautiful or unclear, or to the personal idiosyncrasies of the actor rather than those of the character being played.

Lessac, Berry, and Linklater also offered vocal techniques that were well suited to the actor's process. They addressed the work from a holistic perspective. In *Body Wisdom: The Use and Training of the Human Body* Lessac writes:

> The craft of acting also demands an integration and instinctive coordination of voice, movement, awareness, emotion and perception with the spoken language; as such it deals with the human potential itself. It requires a training that respects and listens to the body-whole—the entire human organism.

Peter Brook wrote in his forward to *Voice and the Actor*, "Cicely Berry never departs from the fundamental recognition that speaking is part of a whole: an expression of the inner life... She would never try to separate the sound of words from their living context. For her the two are inseparable." As Patsy Rodenburg states in *The Right to Speak*, "Cicely Berry almost singlehandedly made the work both respectable and exciting for actors." *The Educational Theatre Journal* describes Linklater's work as "a radical breakaway from the old formal methods... an invaluable resource... essential." In 1967, Lessac published *The Use and Training of the Human Voice*. In 1974, Berry published *Voice and the Actor*, and Linklater's *Freeing the Natural Voice* was published in 1976.

In a couple of decades, another generation of texts was born. In 1992 Patsy Rodenburg wrote *The Right to Speak* and, subsequently, *The Need for Words* in 1993. With these texts came an extraordinary examination of the origins of vocal habits and the power of the word. Catherine Fitzmaurice's article "Breathing is Meaning" in *The Vocal Vision* (1997) outlines the principles behind her unique breath work, "Destructuring," and "Restructuring," which provide a means of efficient deep release of the muscles of the breathing mechanism, and also reliable, repeatable support, respectively. Also in *The Vocal Vision* is Dudley Knight's article called "Standard

Speech: The Ongoing Debate." Knight challenges the continued use of Standard Speech as anything but a dialect. He also wrangles with Tilly, McLean, and Skinner for the propagation of World English, Good American Speech, and a century of practice. Knight proposes a radical new approach to speech work that celebrates diversity of sound in its infinite possibilities, honoring the multitude of accents and dialects.

Building upon the foundation provided by Lessac, Berry, Linklater, Rodenburg, Fitzmaurice, and Knight, yet another generation of voice and speech teachers expanded the field by creating or adapting new bodies of work, with fresh visions of how voice and speech contribute to the performance curriculum. Here are a few examples: Phil Thompson joined forces with Dudley Knight in the development of their revolutionary approach to speech and dialect work. Other teachers have incorporated various educational models and learning strategies, such as Louis Colaianni, whose phonetics work was inspired, in part, by the early childhood teaching techniques of Maria Montessori, best known for her Montessori method of education; and by Rudolph Steiner's eurythmy, an expressive movement form sometimes referred to as "visible speech." Colaianni has published several books, including *The Joy of Phonetics and Accents*, and is the creator of pillows in the shape of phonetic symbols, used as a teaching tool. Robert Barton turned to Neuro-Linguistic Programming (NLP) as a model to identify and accommodate various learning styles. Rocco Dal Vera adopted Alba Emoting as a tool for unifying voice, emotion, and the breath. Rocco and Robert teamed up to write *Voice, Onstage and Off*, which uses a clever interactive DVD for the voice student. The DVD and book are quite comprehensive and easily accessible. Given the technological component, the book practically teaches itself. Many of the master teachers' techniques satisfied the actor's desire for the much sought-after internal sensations and impulses of acting work, and continue to fill in other missing pieces in the voice work canon while ensuring safe vocal production and dynamic speech and text work.

Characteristics of an Age of Synthesis

Voice and speech training has undergone a substantial makeover since the mid–nineteenth century. In just the past four decades, a confluence of innovative thinking has produced a collective body of voice work that is today a much more complementary fit with contemporary acting training than the early Method actors experienced. In fact, frequently voice and speech work takes the initiative in deepening the actor's work. The delineation between what is acting training and what is voice training might seem less clearly drawn these days. Phil Thompson characterizes the work this way: "We walk right up to the boundary of physical resistance [in an actor] to an emotional life and we invite students to cross that boundary, and we do it in a way that is unrelated to a specific role, even to the actor's identity as an actor." Strasburg, as well as fellow acting teachers Sanford Meisner, Stella Adler, and Michael Chekhov, each endeavored to do this. They sought to break down tension-creating habits that interfered with the actor's creativity and truth, and with the full expression of his or her instrument.

While it is difficult to define an era without having some hindsight, several voice and speech training features of this one stand out. One clear attribute is the wealth and diversity of options for studying voice and speech, ranging from the traditional, such as a Skinnerian approach to speech work—still widely used today—to the contemporary, such as Louis Colaianni's use of phonetic pillows as a vehicle for a hands-on journey to learn the IPA and explore the richness of a multitude of phonemes and accents.

Additionally, one finds clear shifts in ideology about the actor's physical and psychological being. One of the most fundamental changes has been the rejection of the Cartesian theory of a mind/body split and the adherence instead to a whole-body approach to voice work. Kristin Linklater refers to this in her interview, and many of the master teachers emphasize the importance of addressing the actor holistically. Much of today's training engages the actor's total being: physical, vocal, emotional, and psychological. Eastern approaches to muscular release, such as yoga and shiatsu, are used alongside western approaches, such as Alexander and Feldenkrais.

A new aesthetic has emerged with the speaking of heightened text. Language is not merely spoken for its musicality, as Cicely Berry points out in her interview and in her latest book, *From Word to Play*, but is *embodied*. Less emphasis is placed on a "correct" or "good" sound; instead, the "expressive, intelligible transference of thought and feeling" is valued, as described by Catherine Fitzmaurice. Spoken-language expectations continue to evolve to appeal to the sensibilities of the modern audience and current trends in acting style. Shakespeare's text is thought to be valued not only for its poetic form, but for the beauty of the truths it has maintained for so many years. Andrew Wade offers direct advice to student actors about how to access the richness and clarity of Shakespeare's language.

Breathing has garnered much attention. Jane Boston and Rena Cook recently edited *Breath in Action*, which contains a collection of essays on breath written from a variety of perspectives, ranging from scientific to artistic. Most believe that breath release and support are key ingredients for sustained vocal health. Viewpoints on breath support tend to follow one of two philosophies: one emphasizes the conscious engagement of certain lower torso muscle(s), while the other relies upon the actor's intention and the importance of his or her character's need to stimulate support.

The study of dialects is gaining momentum, especially for use in film. Gillian Lane-Plescia's dialect work comes in the form of CDs, each with a guide booklet, and presents the actor with a variety of authentic speakers from whom to fashion a dialect for a role. The International Dialects of the English Archives (IDEA) is a website that also offers a range of authentic English-speaking dialect samples. Dudley Knight and Phil Thompson have some interesting ideas about how to approach accents as well.

Voice science and technology have deepened our understanding of the vocal mechanism and its processes, leading to techniques for safe theatrical use and improved vocal health. David Carey discusses how technology has deepened his understanding of vocal anatomy and physiology. Eric Armstrong, voice and speech teacher from York University, and Phil Thompson have started sending weekly podcasts over the Internet that they've cleverly called "Glossonomia." They deliver an abundance of knowledge on one or two phonemes each week. Each podcast is a complete and entertaining lesson.

Today acting training and voice and speech training continue to crisscross. Here are some of the places where they intersect: both seek a connectedness of self to self, and of self to other, to the moment and to the audience; both seek clear communication and connectedness to the text and the imaginary world of the play; both emphasized the importance of the actor's groundedness, healthy alignment, strength, dexterity, stamina, physical freedom, and an expansive range of expressiveness.

Finally, many believe that both acting and voice and speech training seek to contextualize the work as constituting an integral part of the whole body of the *actor's* work. Voice, movement, and acting instruction are recognized as fundamental to the actor's training process.

In colleges, universities, and conservatories, voice and speech classes have become a staple in most theatre programs. Many major programs now hire at least two full-time voice professionals. Teacher certification programs have produced new generations of savvy voice and speech teachers, and organizations such as the Voice Foundation and the Voice and Speech Trainers Association (VASTA) have contributed significantly to the growth of the field, with conferences, publications, and grant funding.

In the midst of a very fast-paced world, with its "gotta get a quick fix" mentality, teachers run to keep up with the changing needs of the students. The world, it seems, turns faster and faster, creating resistance for the unhurried metamorphosis that is the voice and speech training process. It requires time—"repetition" as Patsy Rodenburg says—tremendous hard work, courage, and much patience.

VASTA

The advancement of the voice and speech field in North America is due in large part to an organization called the Voice and Speech Trainers Association, otherwise known as VASTA. In 1986 a small group of voice and speech teachers—Mary Corrigan, Dorothy Runk Mennen, Carol Pendergrast, Lucille Rubin, and Bonnie Raphael—formed VASTA to create an identity for, and promote the advancement of, the voice and speech training profession. Through VASTA, voice and speech teachers find a forum for sharing ideas and for networking. Members receive a newsletter and a copy of the *Voice and Speech Review*. Also of interest is VASTAvox, an online community that gives members a place to share their thoughts and concerns about voice and speech training. In 1987 VASTA presented its first conference. Since then the organization has presented a conference annually featuring prominent guests from the field, many of whom you'll find in these pages. In little more than two decades, the organization has grown to nearly 500 active members with eighty international members from twelve countries, and intends to continue to expand by reaching out to the international community. Today, voice and speech work is recognized by many theatre institutions as an integral, valued part of the actor's training, thanks in large part to VASTA and the vision and hard work of its membership and the twenty-four master voice and speech teachers included in this book.

The Work Today

The teachers included in this book espouse a comparatively unified set of objectives for actor training in voice and speech. They advocate audible, intelligible speech and the development of an instrument that is flexible, and free of habitual tension. They espouse healthy, safe usage of the voice. They seek to develop the actor's ability to vitalize spoken language for the stage, television, and film, while revealing clarity of thought and a full range of human expressiveness. They endeavor to direct the actors' focus toward an inward listening, so that they may know their instrument and self, and how to apply their tools. These teachers also direct the actors' attention towards an outward listening so that their work may be fueled by the presence of other actors, their environment, and the audience. They are the messengers of reliable, repeatable technique.

What is most notable about these master teachers is that each has devised his or her own unique vision of how to accomplish this mission— be it Nancy Krebs and Deb Kinghorn, who preserve Arthur Lessac's work to the letter; or Catherine Fitzmaurice and Kristin Linklater, whose opposing perspectives on the use and function of abdominal muscles in speaking inspires spirited debate; or Richard Armstrong, whose Roy Hart work invites his students to journey through what he believes is a universal and fundamental need to discover oneself through sound. There's Nancy Houfek, who heads the MFA vocal pedagogy program at the American Repertory Theatre, who took over for Bonnie Raphael who is now at the University of North Carolina at Chapel Hill; and Linklater teachers Natsuko Ohama and Fran Bennett, who both have active acting careers; and Saul Kotzubei, whose work integrates Fitzmaurice Voicework® with an approach to acting work. Andrea Haring currently runs the Linklater Center in NYC, and Susan Sweeney and Jan Gist, like many of the master teachers included here, are very active voice, speech, and text coaches. Each master teacher adds depth and dimension to the pedagogical land-scape as it exists today.

How the Book and Interviews Are Organized

As you will see, the interviews have been arranged in alphabetical order. Many of the interview questions are repeated from interview to interview to allow the reader to draw comparisons between philosophies and methodologies. Each interview begins with the teacher's background, mentors, and training. The middle section of each interview has two parts: "The Voice and Speech World of Today," which is a survey of opinions about training today, followed by a section called "Practical Considerations," which covers the teacher's practices in the various areas of training. The final section of each interview is called "Moving into the Future" and offers the student actor and new teachers a few words of wisdom about crossing the threshold into the professional arena.

The final interview takes on a form that is unique to the rest: master teacher Robert Neff Williams and I are joined in the interview by associate arts professor Shane Ann Younts. Younts was Williams's student about twenty-five years ago and is currently the head of the voice/speech/text department in the graduate acting program at NYU. Our three-way conversation of their shared history led to tales about Robert coaching Alfred Lunt and Lynn Fontanne, among others. Robert was a pioneer. His story as a voice and speech teacher spans about sixty-five years, and reveals professional associations with Evangeline Machlin, Edith Skinner, the Neighborhood Playhouse, and the Pearl Theatre in NYC, to name a few. In the spring of 2010, at age eighty-nine, Robert retired from the drama division at Juilliard (though he tells me he returns there to work on particular projects from time to time). He had been a member of the faculty since the early 1970s. His legacy carries on through Professor Younts, who devotedly teaches his material, as do a number of her students as well. I could think of no better way to draw the interviews to a close.

And so ...

Obviously, more master voice and speech teachers exist than was possible to include in the limited pages of one book. What you will find here is a noteworthy selection of the ideas and practices of some of the most highly regarded professionals in the field, each with persuasive points of view and recognized methods of training. Amidst their similarities and differences in approach is a unified spirit and acknowledgement that voice work is of fundamental importance to the actor's training process and has the potential to resonate profoundly with the actor and with the audience.

Voice and speech work can be a comprehensive means of guidance that harmonizes the seemingly disparate components of actor training. As Jan Gist said to me at the end of her interview, "The voice teacher has the potential to be the shaman of the theatre." Voice and speech training can lead the student holistically into the heart of actor training. It has been a pleasure and an honor to interview these master voice and speech teachers.

Richard Armstrong

Richard Armstrong's distinction as teacher, director, and performer is recognized throughout the world. A pioneer of the extension of the human voice, his unique abilities have taken him to over thirty countries, and have inspired a whole generation of performers and their work. He has been part of the music theatre faculty at the Banff Centre, Canada, since 1985. He is currently associate arts professor for New York University's experimental theatre wing at the Tisch School of the Arts, and teaches for theatre companies, universities, and opera schools around the world.

Photo by Cathy Crawford

Background

Nancy Saklad: You have offered a breadth of international training opportunities, Richard, crossing not only geographic boundaries but also that imaginary line that pretends to divide the singing voice from the speaking one. How has your work been affected by your journey?

Richard Armstrong: I guess it's impacted the work in the most obvious way, that my vision of the world is perhaps more open, more broad. It also is wonderful to have an approach that is needed, that other people want. I think this fundamental need to discover oneself through sound is worldwide. It's there wherever you go. In the '60s, at the beginning of this work I do, the group—later known as the Roy Hart Theatre—didn't travel much. We were based in England and then, from the mid–70s, in France. At that time, the research was very much about going inside yourself to find sound rather than looking for it elsewhere. Paradoxically, we would later discover that those same sounds existed around the world, like some of the more traditional Tibetan Monk sounds, for example. Everybody has them, but you tend to think they only exist in Tibet. I started to realize that world music, as it's known, is actually inside you. By the time we started traveling and touring, people would approach us after shows and say, "You must have been to Bali, or you must have been to Tibet, or you must have studied *cante jondo* in Spain," but we hadn't.

Saklad: Your name is often said to be synonymous with the Roy Hart Theatre in France. What was the theatre's mission, and what was your role with the company?

Armstrong: To be honest, I don't think there was any specific mission at the beginning. Like many small companies around the world, the work was born out of a need for transformation on the part of those concerned. In my own case, I was a painter and studied fine art in the '60s and had always done acting as a kind of parallel activity. But I found that the world of painting was sort of two-dimensional. It didn't seem to respond to the various things that were going on inside me at that time. Through a friend at university, I discovered this somewhat esoteric group in London who were working on vocal sound. I attended a meeting of this group in 1967, which didn't even have a name at this point. I found the work responded to a need I had for a more multidimensional, visceral physicality. I don't even think we thought about the physical and vocal work we did as training. It was just something we loved to do, and that we wanted to do. As to my role, I was above all a student, though I helped out with public relations and later contributed to the direction of the company. In 1969, when I was twenty-three, Roy Hart told me to begin teaching voice.

Saklad: Would you talk a little bit about Roy Hart and your relationship to him?

Armstrong: At this first meeting in 1967, he sat at a piano, though he never played it that first evening. There were about seventeen people sitting around the room talking. And they were talking about things that embarrassed me to no end at that time, like sex and relationships; I was twenty-one. What was most extraordinary to me was the quality of listening in the room. It's kind of a strange way to put it, but I heard this deep communication going on. Nobody talked at the same time as anybody else; it was wonderful. In fact nobody actually sang that night, though later I discovered that people did have lessons and they were working on a production. He anchored that listening through a gentle and persuasive kind of guidance, almost like a chairman. He died when I was twenty-nine, so I had eight years of very intense study and performance with him and with the group. Some of my most powerful memories of him are watching him teach and realizing that this was a great teacher.

Saklad: What was it about him that created this picture of greatness?

Armstrong: It comes back to the question of listening. I remember one evening I was watching him teach someone in the studio, and it was almost like the penny dropped—as we used to say in England. I suddenly realized that what he was doing was full emotional and body submission to the student. It wasn't intellectual submission. It was full, visceral serving of the student. The student was leading and he was following. He mostly taught—as I do—from the piano, but the piano became far more than a musical guide in his hands; it became almost like a moving sound-mirror of the lesson itself. He could be fierce at times or incredibly tender. Extra-ordinary results would appear—but he certainly wasn't looking for results. That was the thing I found most extraordinary about him.

Saklad: Did you study with any other teachers along the way?

Armstrong: I didn't at first. I was certainly very lucky that at age twenty-one, I found a context. It was not only Roy Hart himself. It was the whole context of the enquiry—the way that the work was developed and looked at. So I didn't spend a lot of time trying different things out. I only spent eight years with Roy Hart, but they were very important years. I believe that all the basic principles that guide me today I learned in some way in those years, the most notable being that the sound is the audible manifestation of who you are.

Saklad: That's a very powerful statement. I read a quote of yours where you describe the role of teacher as really in truth being the student. That seems to mirror what you're articulating about the listening.

Armstrong: Yes, my students, especially the ones that are paying a lot of money for tuition, when I say I don't actually know anything, look at me a little askance. But no, I believe it's an intensely practical way of looking at teaching. It's working from the privileged vantage point that the student has the answers already, which are waiting to be revealed or uncovered. Sadly, in so much teaching, the student is placed in a context of already being "wrong" and in need of correction.

Saklad: What aspects of the work most inspire you?

Armstrong: What we were just talking about—submitting, in a sense, to the student's process. The implication of that is that the work is always new, even though some things may reoccur. It's risky to talk about it because you can't guarantee that there's going to be a transformation. But I must have been doing something right for the last forty years because it does seem to work.

Saklad: I've seen it work. It's very powerful, very moving, and deeply human.

Armstrong: Thank you.

The Voice and Speech World of Today

Saklad: What features would you say distinguish the work you do in the field?

Armstrong: I hear from students—and certainly some of them are training either to be voice teachers or they may be voice teachers already—I hear that what they like is the work with sustained sound. You can call it singing if you wish, but it's the sound that is extended through time through a tone—and all the information that is in that tone, the story that is in that tone—which sometimes in their own training maybe they haven't explored. Other than that, I don't think it's anything more than what we've talked about, which is this question of the underlying uniqueness of everyone's voice, of encouraging everyone to find their own voice—not imposing knowledge. I don't doubt that I have some knowledge, but it's not something that I ever want to feel I impose on anybody, because I want them to make discoveries for themselves.

Saklad: Would you describe in a little more depth what you mean by extended voice?

Armstrong: It is an expression used currently to describe a more exploratory post–*bel canto* sound world in contemporary music, and sometimes the work I do as performer or vocal coach in such pieces will put me in the program as the "extended vocal specialist." And I always say, "No, I'm actually the 'normal voice nonspecialist.'" The term "extended voice" is a misnomer in a sense, because it implies that to work your full range is somehow outside what is normal. For example, a number of years ago I was thinking about *falsetto* and looked it up in the dictionary. To my astonishment I discovered it was described as "an unnatural sound, above the normal" or "artificially pitched." Well, there's nothing unnatural about it, and what is abnormal or artificial about using your full range? What is not normal is the fact that the average person on the street, particularly in North American/Western European white society uses so very little of their voice. The average person on the street uses an octave and a half, if they're lucky. Sometimes someone may stay within a half octave the whole of his or her life. So that is for me the shocking thing in a way, not whether someone can sing falsetto.

Saklad: What other myths about voice and speech training have you come across?

Armstrong: Probably the biggest myth that is propagated by many teachers is the idea that some people have got it and some people haven't—the idea that there are only good singers or bad singers. I think there are only human beings. Similarly with the question of the idea of singing in tune and the assumption that singing in tune is a desirable thing. Viewed from certain vantage points, yes it is. It has to do with harmony, it has to do with listening, but the information that you get from someone that doesn't do that is equally valuable.

Saklad: What are the greatest voice and speech obstacles that the student actor faces?

Armstrong: Fear is the really big one—fear, and the fact that much of the world is based on fear. Also, certainly in the singing world, it's the fact that much traditional training is based on the idea that you're already wrong— correction rather than discovery. That engenders tremendous fear.

Saklad: Where does vocal presence come from, and do you think it's teachable? I have a feeling this may be tied in to what you're talking about.

Armstrong: Yes, it really comes back to the same thing. That thing that we call vocal presence is already there in everybody. Whether it's audible or not, there lies the story, the intrigue. Clearly, in quite a lot of people it's not audible, but that doesn't mean to say it's not there. So my philosophy is, as I said earlier, that the student already has the answers, and it's just a question of trying to help them come to the surface. It doesn't always happen quickly, you know, sometimes it will take many years to help someone uncover the layers that conceal this thing that this question has called vocal presence.

Practical Considerations

Saklad: Your work really fully engages the body. What does the body need to produce optimal vocal work?

Armstrong: Courage. I think the courage to be implicated—you know, fully—head and body. I think it's fair to say that the people in the Roy Hart Theatre—going back forty years or more—the people that came to join Roy Hart in that research were not the most gifted. They were not the most talented. There were no auditions. Nobody was chosen because they did anything better than anyone else. If anything, quite a lot of the people that came along at the time that I did were people that had problems of one sort or another. They had issues that they were looking to find some kind of way of dealing with. So, I think that determination and courage are the most important things, combined with a sense of generosity.

Saklad: Do you think an understanding of anatomy deepens the student's relationship to his or her voice?

Armstrong: I think it really depends. I know that in my own case, in the training that I received, vocal cords were never mentioned. It's not that they are of no interest or value—of course they are—but sometimes there's too much focus on the mechanics and not enough on the mystery of what the voice is in its greater sense. The mechanics get too much attention.

Saklad: I know you approach voice work with lots of imagery. Would you describe some of the imagery you use?

Armstrong: It's hard to describe, because the images are reborn at every moment and they tend to get reborn in the function of what's happening. I'm thrilled if I can keep reinventing these images, which I seem to be able to. I don't know how, but it seems to be one of the facets we have as human beings to be able to reinvent the image. Going back to what we were talking about earlier—the teacher submitting to the student rather than the other way around—that process somehow brings the images with it. It's very hard to describe, and I'm reluctant to describe it because it sounds so mystical, but the images do actually come from the student. The process, which is hard to analyze but very practical, is that the submission on the part of the teacher—in this case, me—to the surrounding events, and in particular to the uniqueness of the individual before me, leads to the unexpected. It might have to do with what the student is wearing. It might be simple as a change in hairstyle. It could be just a little subliminal expression they come into class with that you notice wasn't there the day before. It might be something you overhear out of class. It might be something you notice down the corridor. The information comes from all kinds of sources.

Saklad: How do you address breath work?

Armstrong: Oh, it's fundamental, without a doubt. Most of the process that I try to engage in is an attempt to be spontaneous and conscious at that very same moment. It's a state to which I think we all aspire, not just in voice class but in our lives. And it's a state that I do believe we all know, but it's very elusive. Performers and nonperformers alike try to describe it and might say, "Yes, I had it a week ago last Wednesday walking down the street." It's that moment where you know what day it is. You know what year it is. You know what your name is. You know what you had for breakfast—in other words, the conscious aspects of this strange thing called existence. And yet at the same time, you're completely free, without limits. It's where mortality and eternity coincide. I believe actors search for that onstage, and find it by moments, or for seconds. You don't get it for the whole show. But you certainly recognize it when it happens, and in a way, I sort of feel that's why we keep doing these things. Well, I would apply exactly that to the question of breath. I am constantly trying to redefine, within the elusive nature of this thing called "conscious spontaneity," how you can breathe freely and spontaneously and yet at the same time know that you're doing it and how you're doing it. Usually that comes back to what you were asking about image. It has to do with the story. The in-breath I always say is like the prestory or the antestory; it's full of information about what's about to come out. It's not just a refueling. It's not just getting the gas for the car, and yet it is that. It's this very elusive, strange thing.

Saklad: What does it mean to support the voice?

Armstrong: Different things at different times to different people. In general, it means having some kind of conscious relationship to gravity, to the pull of the earth, allied with the need for action, our resistance to gravity, which we do all the time, otherwise nothing would ever get done! It's an elusive mixture of relaxation and strength. How do we combine the two so we are still in a state of freedom and liquidity? At the same time, both the words *support* and *voice* deserve a high degree of individual questioning, as if they can be code words for almost anything and change according to the specific context of the student's enquiry.

Saklad: How do you approach range and tonality, resonance, and other vocal qualities?

Armstrong: Well, I have strategies and games that get adapted according to who's there. With any group of students, I'm trying to contain all the information that I'm getting on all these levels—resonance, range, and so on—and then give it back to the students at the right moment, which may not even be that day. It may be a week later; it may be a year later. It's a strange set of circumstances that occurs in the teaching process, over which I personally find I don't really have much control once I've availed myself of the mood or the atmosphere. Those things will happen when they happen. And then even describing the games themselves wouldn't really be much help to anybody, because they're really the kind of blueprint, or the construction plan, that then gets discarded or adapted. They are not the building itself. As to the question of range, I think the fear of height and the fear of depth are two of the greatest human fears. Some people have more fear of going in one direction than the other. So I would approach range as a human manifestation first, with all the potential for fear or joy that that brings with it. I would also try to help people be at ease with having a wider range than they were encouraged to have. The students have known a time when their range was freer, which is when they were babies. They've known a time when they were not frightened of liquidity—when they were in the womb. The process of growing up reduces or represses that freedom, and therefore our vocal range.

Saklad: What role does listening play in voice and speech work?

Armstrong: The role is huge. It's fundamental like breath. As I said earlier, the power of my first encounter with Roy Hart's work had to do with the quality of listening in the room. The high level of animated consciousness was palpable. It's what brought me back to the studio the next time and the next and the next. What I love to help people generate in class is the idea that to make sound—whether it be speaking, singing, or anything in between—you need to listen. To make sound is to listen.

Saklad: At one time you were interested in healing as an aspect of the work. Are you still interested in it?

Armstrong: I've never not been interested in it. Although the idea of healing comes along with what I do, I don't set myself up as a healer. But there's no doubt that there is a huge therapeutic benefit in the work.

Saklad: Have you witnessed much of an evolution in voice and speech training over the course of your career?

Armstrong: Well, part of that evolution is the fact that from the '50s on there was such an incredible opening of sensibility to the body through music. In the '60s all hell broke loose around the world—women's liberation, gay liberation, you name it—the sexual revolution . . . Looking back, I feel that this climate explains the need we had to focus on the body and on the sound that came out of the body. From the '60s on there was this sense of transformation, of self-study. Out of that came Oprah. I'm not championing Oprah, but the idea of a mass marketing of the idea of transformation and self-study came from ever-multiplying personal searches. There's no doubt that things are very different today than they were forty years ago. I've also noticed, particularly in Europe—and I'm guessing it might have been the same here—that within this search, it was mostly women that were doing it. The majority of the students in workshops would be women, very often women of a certain age, who had grown up, maybe had a husband, maybe had kids, and then suddenly thought, "Who am I?" "Where am I?" In France, through the '80s and '90s, that definitely was true. I say Europe because I also taught a lot in Latin America, where there was a much bigger male presence. That's a whole other story.

Moving into the Future

Saklad: It has been said that you inspired a whole generation of performers and their work. Today, what advice would you give to voice and speech teachers at the beginning of their teaching career?

Armstrong: Don't do it for the money. Resist being a teacher. Wait. Listen. Wait. Listen. I mean, I do feel that many people do feel very quickly that they can teach something and they haven't really waited to live it in any way. Two years after graduation you'll suddenly get an email from a former student saying, "How did you become a voice teacher? I'm really looking for a way of supplementing my income." No. I don't think that's how it works. You have to fully embody what you are proposing, and that takes time and dedication. And be generous. I think a lot of people have forgotten how to be generous.

Saklad: What do you think the future holds for voice training? Where are we going?

Armstrong: I do feel people are more attentive to something as mysterious as the voice and more attentive to the body, to the sounds around them, than they were forty, fifty years ago. I would love to think that would continue and that it would embrace more of the world in general, in particular the part that contains the politicians and people that make war. I would hope that it would be on that level, perhaps not in my lifetime, but that the voice work that's being done would embrace that dimension of our existence that we often feel we have no control of. I do think, especially for the people that have power, you know, politicians, judges, etc. I don't know. I often think, "What would I do if I got a group of politicians in the room? They would probably never come..."

Saklad: I don't know—you're pretty persuasive—

Armstrong: In fifty years' time or one hundred years' time, maybe.

Saklad: Richard, what impact do you hope your work will have on vocal training at large?

Armstrong: I truly believe that the success of the work that I do almost depends on resisting it, on not wanting to have an impact. I had no thought of being a voice teacher when I was young. And the fact that it emerged from the way I was brought up and what happened to me feels to be a big part of what makes it work. Something of my reluctance to assume the role has been crucial to its success.

$\mathcal{R}obert\ \mathcal{B}arton$

Robert Barton is a professor emeritus of acting and continues to teach at the University of Oregon. He has performed in most of Shakespeare's plays, including the title role in a PBS production of *Hamlet*, and has directed half of them. His signature text, *Acting: Onstage and Off*, is now in its sixth edition. Robert also coauthored *Voice: Onstage and Off* with Rocco Dal Vera, and his book *Style for Actors* was the recipient of the Theatre Association's Best Book Award. Both of these texts have recently been published in new versions by Routledge. He has been honored as Outstanding Acting Coach by the American College Theatre Festival.

Photo by Cliff Coles

$\mathcal{B}ackground$

Nancy Saklad: What initially drew you to voice work, Robert?

Robert Barton: Well, voice was the first area in performance where I really received positive feedback. Once I survived puberty, people started saying, "I kind of like the way you sound. Would you read for us? Would you host this occasion?" So when that happens to you early on, when you get that level of encouragement, then I think, of course, you just get interested in the subject.

Saklad: Who were your mentors, and how have they influenced your work?

Barton: Well, I have no formal training whatsoever. In the early years of working for Shakespeare festivals, I was mentored by a number of more experienced Shakespearean actors who took me under their wing. Also, there is without question Rocco Dal Vera. When I was first recruited to write *Voice: Onstage and Off*, I was inclined to refuse, because I didn't feel like I had the full credentials, and Rocco literally showed up at my door. We instantly fell into complete rapport, and I realized, "I could do this with him." Rocco has deep-tissue voice knowledge. He's a constant inspiration to me.

The Voice and Speech World of Today

Saklad: How would you describe the features that distinguish your work in the field?

Barton: My work is all about trying to help people understand the fact that theatre, the art of acting within it, and the art of voice within it are not just limited to public performance. They are ways of helping us live our lives better, act our lives better, even speak our lives better. I think there's a profound usefulness that most people don't acknowledge in this art to simply living a more rich and fulfilled existence.

Saklad: Your work in the field has really traversed acting and voice and speech. Your books and articles reveal an interest in *how* we learn as much as *what* we learn. What is your current passion with voice and speech work?

Barton: Routledge has bought the rights to our book *Voice Onstage and Off* from Cengage, and that's incredibly exciting, because they're committed to a new revised edition with a huge electronic component, with the entire book being recorded. So the book's website will be something much more expansive than the book itself, with many more suggested activities. It has an incredible component that's available for teaching, called "the voice recipe," that Rocco has developed. The voice recipe is divided into nine ingredients: pitch, volume, rhythm, tempo, quality, articulation, pronunciation, word choice, and nonverbals. The idea is that there is a recipe for every person's voice. Well the website has a chef, and as the ingredients are being explained, the chef tosses them into the bowl. Then, there's an instance where you hear an actor speak a very famous line from an old movie, and if you guess the right tempo, you guess the right quality, etc., that ingredient will go into the bowl. If you get all the ingredients right, the picture of that actor comes up with a description of the film, and you hear the line again. So it's instant reward. It's a great, fun way, electronically, to teach the "ingredients" that make up everybody's voice. I've also done new training in Neuro-Linguistic Programming (NLP) this summer and plan to do a book on that, so that's also really exciting.

Saklad: What applications do you see for NLP in voice and speech work?

Barton: I think there are almost unlimited applications in terms of understanding where your student is coming from and being able to join him or her and relate. I think, unfortunately, many voice teachers have an enormous auditory component and many actors don't, especially in our culture. In fact, I think the auditory component in our lives is lessening. The way I explain it to my students is if you have high auditory learners— and let's say they're having trouble pronouncing a word—you just *tell* them the note and they usually get it. With someone who is a high visual learner, you actually have to *show* that person what it looks like. And for a kinesthetic, helping realize how the difference *feels*. There's an old adage of teaching: "If it doesn't work, then you try something else," but sometimes we draw blanks. NLP provides you this kind of tool to be able to enter the person's world, and once you've done that, you'll have much more opportunity to lead them where you want them to go.

Saklad: Do you find there are trends in the lay person's voice and speech that become obstacles in the training of today's student actors?

Barton: Well a few years ago, "upspeak" was an epidemic that seems to have passed. Now, of course, it's the intrusive "like"—"I'm like" and "He's like." I think more than anything else, the auditory component of life is lessening. People are spending all their time staring at a screen. They're emailing instead of speaking. They're texting instead of speaking. The SAT vocabulary scores are dropping radically. People are spending less time in conversation. So it means that in our field, we're dealing with a bunch of people who no longer have a lot of words at their disposal, who don't engage in the art of conversation, who don't prefer to communicate with the spoken word. That's a huge barrier for voice and speech teachers to have to deal with.

Saklad: Do you think voice and speech training plays a unique role in performance training?

Barton: Well it's the crucial final link, isn't it? I was reading an interview with the director of a recent revival of *Twelfth Night* in Central Park, and he was saying he walked two-thirds of the way out in the house and said, "I was reminded that I could no longer really see faces, and from this spot right here voice and vocal energy become all."

Saklad: Where does vocal presence come from, and is it teachable?

Barton: Oh, that's really tough... And what is presence? It's a certain charisma, a certain effortless ability to draw attention. I don't know that you could have vocal presence if you didn't have a pretty good set of pipes and a confident center to begin with. I think you can work someone towards it. You can certainly help them root the sound for support, and you can work with them psychologically on a sense of inner stillness and confidence. So I guess I would say yes and no to teachable.

Practical Considerations

Saklad: What do you think makes a good voice and speech teacher?

Barton: I think it's a very difficult combination of skill and empathy.

Saklad: Do you think students benefit by studying multiple approaches to the work?

Barton: Well, yes. In *Voice: Onstage and Off*, everything is about all the ways you could possibly approach something in voice and speech work. We offer a bunch of options. We have a chapter called "Selecting Your System," where we analyze the differences between Lessac, Linklater, Berry, Skinner, and Rodenburg. The idea is to make students good shoppers. I think at the beginning of your training, it's good to look at a lot of options. I also think at some later point in your training, it's good to simply sign on for a single approach and give yourself up to it and immerse yourself in it, but that often happens way too early and without enough knowledge of the other options that are available.

Saklad: What does the body need to produce optimum vocal work?

Barton: I would love to say that you need to be an athlete. You need to be toned—have cardiovascular fitness and endurance—but I don't think empirical evidence supports that. The world is full of the Richard Burtons, going back to the John Barrymores who abused their physical selves constantly and yet produced magnificent voice and speech work. What you ultimately need is really a freedom from blockage of passage of air or blockage of support. You don't need excess tension, and you need access to diaphragmatic breathing. So Alexander is really useful. Feldenkrais is useful—anything that can bring you into a state of alignment and get you in touch with the power of breath that you have. Otherwise, I think it's not really formulaic at all.

Saklad: You mentioned blockage of support. What does it mean to you to support the voice?

Barton: It's probably easier for me to describe what happens when you don't have it. High visuals, in NLP terms, don't have support at all. High visuals breathe only down to the upper chest, and they have incredible tension in the neck and shoulders. Their chin is often pulled down, their eyes are up, and they speak really fast and really breathy. There's a lot of breath all the time and there's no variety in what they do. They are the antithesis of breath support. I guess in a way you would say they think so fast and they breathe so high in their torso that there's no chance for support. There's no chance for chest resonance. They never get the air down. There's no chance for the diaphragm to be low and flat and supported. As we get more and more visual learners in our culture, unfortunately, their characteristics are an almost classic case study of every problem that is a voice teacher's nightmare.

Saklad: How do you approach tonality, resonance, and vocal qualities?

Barton: In our voice recipe, we've certainly acknowledged that of the nine ingredients, quality is the most important one. I had a call the other day from a friend I hadn't heard from in twenty years, and he says, "Robert," and that's all it takes. It's all about the quality. So we don't just analyze it in terms of the technical terms, but in abstract imagery as well. In my class we analyze what the voice recipe is for each of the people in the class. We start with the whole class being involved and then go into smaller groups where I circulate. "We're talking about so-and-so's voice recipe:

"What's the pitch component? What's the volume component?" etc. When we get to quality we ask, "What musical instrument is it closest to? What other sound effect that is not musical? What kind of fabric, colors, weather, texture?" The other thing about voice quality is that people don't understand what the classic qualities are. So I do a lot of, "These are the twenty classic voices. Here's a classic nasal voice. Here's a classic strident voice. Here's a classic husky voice: "<u>H</u>ey, <u>h</u>ot stuff, <u>h</u>ow's about <u>h</u>olding <u>h</u>ands?" The lines are always very evocative of what that personality would be, because I think in the beginning many people don't know what the various classic qualities are. So that helps very much to identify the archetypes of tonality in terms of giving choice.

Saklad: How would you describe the role of listening in voice and speech work?

Barton: Listening, of course, is crucial to good acting. I would say in class I ask my students to listen in a couple of ways. I ask them to constantly record themselves with a guideline of what they're listening for and usually with a form to fill out in terms of what they heard, because it takes them so long to make peace with the sound of their own voice in terms of recorded feedback, but it's helpful if they have a very specific focus. They do imitations of each other, so they have to listen to other people very carefully in order to nail that person's vocal life. They're assigned critique responsibilities. There are teams—this is the "pitch" team, this is the "tonality" team, this is the "volume" team. Everybody has to listen very carefully to you so they can learn from themselves and each other. In this case, actors are listening to themselves more than they ever have before, and they are listening to each other in ways that have probably never occurred to them before. For many it is as if the world of auditory awareness awakens in them for the first time.

Saklad: Do you teach the IPA?

Barton: I do. I use Louis Colaianni's *Joy of Phonetics* pillows. It's so fun and works so fast. It's very kinesthetic and it's very visual, beyond the obvious auditory component.

Saklad: Do you devote time to teaching vocal characterization?

Barton: I think vocal characterization for a specific role should be a part of any acting class. We characterize vocally, physically, psychologically.

The more character voices you have at your disposal, the more tools you have to characterize. So you can say, "What if I make this character loud, a little husky, except when she gets insecure, in which case her pitch goes up? etc." In other words, the more tools at the actor's disposal, starting out with classic voices and a lot of qualities for characterization, the more likely the actor is to make complex and interesting choices.

Saklad: How do you see scientific and/or technological advances influencing your work or the work at large?

Barton: Well, I'm kind of Mr. Science Guy when it comes to acting. NLP, of course, is very scientifically based. It's based on close observation of three great role models: Virginia Satir, Milton Erikson, and Fritz Pearls—three legendary therapists. I was Susana Bloch's first US theatre contact, introducing her and her scientific approach to recreating emotion to the Association for Theatre in Higher Education (ATHE) community. I think there will always be plenty of art in this art, but it can always use a little science.

Saklad: How do you feel about the use of microphones in the theatre?

Barton: Oh, I don't like it. Of course, I come from lots of outdoor Shakespeare festival work, and there's a certain pride that goes along with filling those cavernous spaces. On the other hand, there's great nuance that's possible in huge spaces with mics. I don't think we're going to fight it. So it seems to me that what you do as an actor is prepare yourself for both kinds of phenomena. And they are very different kinds of training, the same way voiceover is incredibly different from live acting—the same things, for example, that we do to punch a consonant in order to hear it in the theatre, would pop a mic. There are entirely different strategies, so I just choose to embrace microphones as one of the phenomena of modern life.

Saklad: Is there anything else that you think gets short shrift in the field?

Barton: I think for me, one of them is dialects. People don't consider dialects as vital as they need to be. I talked about my students awakening through the auditory world—dialects awaken, they *uber*-awaken, because suddenly you're aware of all the ways to manipulate sound. It isn't just about when in your future you're going to use that specific dialect. It's the fact that if you study in a class at least a half dozen of them—let's say, for example, the *r*—you probably weren't aware that you could roll it or trill it or tap it or make it guttural or uvular. You learn all those choices, and then you have them at your disposal. I also have to say they are incredibly fun. For years I taught with dialect-appropriate material, and I finally learned that people learned more and had a better time if I did completely the opposite. So when you're working on a scene for class, you have to pick the scene that is least compatible to your dialects: a German *Mary Poppins*, a Russian *Streetcar Named Desire*, a *Romeo and Juliet* in Cockney, etc. The showcase for that class is the most widely attended in our department. There's always a packed house and audiences on the floor laughing, but they're also listening, you understand, because the material is familiar to them, they know the way the line is usually done, and then they hear it in this incongruous context. What's better than that? The learning is sharper and everyone is having a great time.

Moving into the Future

Saklad: What advice would you give to voice and speech teachers at the beginning of their careers?

Barton: I would say don't do it alone. Get yourself at least two or three mentors. Network with veteran voice teachers at conferences. There will be problems you haven't anticipated, and at the risk at seeming self-serving, I would also say use a textbook in the beginning.

Saklad: What voice and speech advice would you give to performance students on the brink of their professional careers?

Barton: I would say always work out. Keep studying. Develop a voice and speech workout that's compatible with your physical workout, and if it's possible for you to multitask, then do that. Always do something, even if it's learning a new dialect each month or working on a voiceover demo tape, so that you never get rusty.

Saklad: In your lifetime have you witnessed much of an evolution in how voice and speech has been taught?

Barton: Yes, I think more than anything else, it's become more Gestalt, more kinesthetic, more time on the floor, more time leaping in the air, more time moving through space, less time sitting at a table, more voice connected to the entire body and to the entire psyche and embracing how important that is, and that we can't isolate them, or that we shouldn't isolate them unless we actually have to.

Saklad: What do you think the future holds for voice and speech training?

Barton: I think it's frightening because of the reasons we've spoken of—because of students coming in with less of a love of conversation and less of an ability to caress words and to have the sensual sense of language—so I think our challenges are going to be greater and greater.

Saklad: Robert, what impact do you hope your work will have on vocal training at large?

Barton: The column that I write for the *Voice and Speech Review* is called "Many Right Ways," and I would say that what I really hope is that I would be a part of freeing us from indoctrination, fighting the belief that certain systems are completely incompatible and they will never meet. No one is a voice god. No one has all the answers. There are many right ways to deal with any voice issue, and solutions can be highly personal. And ultimately I would hope that I contributed to the idea that studying voice can be fun, that it really doesn't have to be deadly, that it doesn't have to be incredibly slow, that it can be joyous.

Fran Bennett

Fran Bennett was head of acting/director of performance at CalArts School of Theater from 1996–2003. She earned a BS, MA, and credit toward a PhD at the University of Wisconsin, Madison. She was the voice and movement director for the Guthrie Theater in Minneapolis for twelve years, as well as an actress in the company. There she worked with the late Sir Tyrone Guthrie, Douglas Campbell, Mel Shapiro, Ed Payson Call, and Michael Langham. Bennett was trained by Kristin Linklater in her first voice-teacher training program and is a master voice teacher with Shakespeare and Company, based in Lenox, Massa-chusetts. She is also an associate director of the Company of Women created by Kristin Linklater and Carol Gilligan. She has led voice production workshops throughout the US and is also a professional actress working in theatre, TV, and movies. Fran is the recipient of the first AEA/AFTRA/SAG Diversity Honor Award. August 7, 2005, was named Fran Bennett Day by the mayor of Malvern, Arkansas. The governor of Arkansas proclaimed her an Arkansas Traveler.

Photo by Dick Wieand

Background

Nancy Saklad: Who were your mentors, Fran?

Fran Bennett: My first mentor was my mother. I was born in the South, and she insisted that I would not have a deep Southern accent. Instead I would speak English, not split verbs, and all sorts of other speaking habits she thought I might develop as a kid in the South. My second mentor was a woman whose name I can't remember. I was a teenager at the time and was passing by the local YWCA one day in Milwaukee, Wisconsin, where we had moved. I heard these voices coming from inside the building. I went in to inspect and discovered the voices were a verse-speaking choir. I sat and listened to these women. They were magnificent. They were speaking poetry in a group, and every now and then there would be a solo voice. So I asked the woman if I could join, but she said it was really only for adults. Finally, after I pleaded, she allowed me to join this group. We toured around the state doing poetry, and I soon became one of those soloists.

Saklad: You've vocal-coached for the Guthrie Theatre, Shakespeare and Company, and more. What roles did artistic directors Tyrone Guthrie, Michael Langham, and Tina Packer play in your work?

Bennett: Beginning in the Guthrie's third season in 1966, I was very fortunate to have worked with the late Tony Guthrie—an imposing, tall figure of a man. He was delightful. He would sit in my voice classes that met one on one. As for impact, I would say he pushed me hard because I had just recently been trained by Kristin Linklater. The Guthrie was my first voice-teaching job, so I was quite lucky. I had taught voice and speech and acting before at Fisk University in Nashville, Tennessee, but this was my first job with a company of actors who, incidentally, had also worked with Edith Skinner and Kristin. Tony expected a lot from all of us. For instance, he felt that a sonnet should be spoken on one breath, and we worked until we could do it. Later, beginning about the seventh season, I worked with Michael Langham. Michael was interested in the clarity of the text, but also the rapidity of the spoken text. I was learning as I was teaching. All these talented people came through the Guthrie. I was there for twelve years, so I worked with a lot of very talented people there. You also mentioned Shakespeare and Company. The director I worked with there was Tina Packer. I not only acted with Shakespeare and Company; I was, and am, one of their master voice teachers. I acted in one show directed by Tina, and another she directed with the Los Angeles Women's Shakespeare Company. Tina absolutely loves the Linklater voice work because Shakespeare and Company was built partly on Linklater work. So this was a continuation of the work that I always did, but with someone who understood and respected what I was doing.

Saklad: Your work at the Guthrie in the 1960s and '70s as the voice and movement coach was somewhat unprecedented. American regional theatres were not in the habit of hiring someone to serve as voice and movement coach for twelve years.

Bennett: Well, I don't know if they knew I was going to stay for twelve years. At the time when Kristin led her first teacher training and that first group of us was ready to go out, we acted in some scenes in New York. I think the artistic directors from all of the repertory theatres in the United States and Canada must have been in attendance, because this was a big deal in repertory theatre history. Each one of us was hired by repertory theatres. So there were other people that also went off to repertory theatres to work. I just happen to be hired by the most important one in America. The work I did at the Guthrie involved individual classes. In fact, it shocked me because at first I was doing group classes. Then the theatre began to hire actors who had studied voice before. Some of them had studied with Kristin and some with Arthur Lessac. These actors insisted on one individual voice class per week. So I had contractual obligations. I taught four individual classes per day. I taught a group class every day, and I did a warm-up before each show—that's matinee and evening shows. Now it made no difference whether I was in the show or not because I also had a contract as an actress with the Guthrie. I did a good deal of acting with them. Plus, I sat in on rehearsals, because directors would send me notes or would see me and say, "Come to the rehearsal." So my days there were very full with voice, with speech, and with movement, because I was the person who did it all. Both Canadians and American actors moved from Stratford, Ontario, to the Guthrie; and from ACT in San Francisco to the Guthrie. Anybody who was new was told they should make sure they took a class with me one on one. Maybe I had some influence in the field. I don't know. Stanley Silverman wrote the music for a production of *Oedipus* that Michael Langham directed. He said he had heard sounds coming out of my studio at the Guthrie and came in one day to observe. He ended up writing the music for *Oedipus* based on the exercises he saw me do in the voice work. In fact, he came to the voice class numerous times. He wrote music that was very high pitched and very low because he found that these actors had range. So Michael Langham who directed the production sent me a very nice item that Stanley had given him telling about his process in writing the music for *Oedipus*. But Michael thought that I should have it. I now have it framed in my study.

The Voice and Speech World of Today

Saklad: What features would you say distinguish your work in the field?

Bennett: I'm looking for the true voice and for the true person. I'm looking for honesty from the person speaking the text. I don't think you can have the truth until you've done an awful lot of voice work and opened yourself up and done the technical work that's involved in freeing yourself from habits—the habitual physical tightness. I studied a lot of voice before, not necessarily anybody's methodology; I'm sort of a mutt. But when I found Kristin's work I knew I'd found home. Her work was what I had been looking for. This was the freedom I had been looking for. It reached me deeply and still reaches me deeply. I do my voice work every day. This is something students do not understand. They say, "What? You've been teaching for a long time and you still work on your voice?" I tell them that's why I get up at 5:45 am so I can walk three miles a day. That takes care of my physicality, and then I work my jaw. I work my tongue while I'm doing other things in the morning. Then I work on my voice in the car going to CalArts, which is thirty-two miles from where I live. It connects me with me so that I am able to give of myself to my students and try to connect with them. This work is powerful work.

Saklad: What aspects of it most inspire you?

Bennett: The breath, the spine, and the connection of the breath to the spine—oh darling, all of it. It's the basic stuff I think that inspires me the most. I'm going to try and make a comparison here. I'd had a lot of movement work, which as far as I was concerned was watered-down dance work for actors. The late Peter Zeisler, without my knowledge, got me a Rockefeller grant to study with the late Litz Pisk, who was teaching movement at the Central School of Speech and Drama in London. This was work from a soul place—moving the joints and then exploring how to get more movement out of that joint. If I'm doing something with the shoulder and I add my elbow to it, that increases the movement. Then if I add my wrist, that increases the movement even more. It was movement for my body and my soul. So here's the comparison. Voice work is very much like that because it teaches me about me from the inside.

Saklad: What voice and speech myths abound?

Bennett: Students feel when they've completed their schooling they've completed their work on voice. That's one of the greatest myths I encounter. They've been in school for three years or four years. They've had two voice classes for each of those years, and they think they're finished. They don't realize that if they want to do any kind of performing that involves speaking, they should work on their voice and their bodies for the rest of their lives.

Saklad: How would you describe the current state of affairs of American actor training in voice and speech?

Bennett: It's much better now than it was years ago because I think school administrators are feeling the need for it. Small schools are now asking for voice and speech teachers. In fact they put it all together—voice, speech, movement, acting teachers. They want teachers to do it all and that's a good thing.

Saklad: What do you consider the greatest voice and speech obstacles that the student actor faces?

Bennett: Habitual problems they have not really taken care of while they were still in school. They might have started taking care of them when they were in training, but they don't necessarily continue. I don't think they realize that it takes a very long time and a lot of effort to get rid of habits.

Saklad: Where does vocal presence come from, and is it teachable?

Bennett: I think vocal presence comes from the desire to communicate. If I truly want to say something to you and I want you to understand me, I'm going to say it clearly. I'm going to do all those things that we talk about in the voice class. That is where my vocal presence lies. My physical presence is my vocal presence. And it is teachable.

Saklad: You've worked extensively in television and film. Has this work influenced how or what you teach?

Bennett: I tell my students that for camera work they're going to use the same techniques they learned for the stage, but since they're either going to be miked or there'll be a hanging mic, volume is not necessary, but vocal energy has to be there. I don't think I would have worked nearly as much as I have if I hadn't been diligent with voice work for my own acting. I've been very fortunate in terms of television. The relaxation of the body and mind, the connection to me, breath/thought from the voice work, has helped me really mind the script to find more of the subtleties and more of the humor. I've received many compliments from writers who've said, "I didn't know I wrote that. I didn't realize I wrote that in that character." I think a lot of that comes from the voice work. It also comes from going deeper and deeper inside myself, which of course is what I'm trying to get the students to do.

Practical Considerations

Saklad: Do you think students benefit by studying multiple approaches to the work?

Bennett: I think multiple approaches are fine after you've learned one and found out what appeals to you and works for you within that one. Then there's nothing wrong with learning from others. But I really think you have to do one thoroughly.

Saklad: What does the body need to produce optimal vocal work?

Bennett: The body should be healthy and free from tension. It should be agile and flexible. I always start working on the body first, because one's voice is going to take on and reflect what is going on in one's body.

Saklad: How do you address breath release work?

Bennett: Breath release work is initial and ongoing work that you do in any voice class. I find I do all sorts of things. One of my students I'm working with privately, a young professional actress, has been through a training school. She studied voice and speech and also movement. She is quite free physically. One of the reasons for that is when you work on your body, you can see results. When you work on your voice, you don't see results; you have to *feel* results. Now this woman was having problems with not having enough breath. She is a tiny person, and she's really got a tiny little voice. From her neck down she's quite free, but her neck is quite tight and her vocal apparatus lies there. When working with her on breath release we first worked on neck rolls. I introduced her to her jaw, which is also very tight, and we worked on that. I have not worked with her long enough on the jaw release yet to work on her tongue, but we have been working on breath. I will have her count "one, two"—it doesn't require a lot of breath. "One, two, three, four" requires a bit more breath, and so forth. I will do that with her hand on her belly. Then, when we get to a little longer breaths, her hand goes on her ribs to see that when she is speaking, her voice is riding out on her breath. She's making headway, but she does not take the work into her everyday life. Meanwhile, I've tried to implant the notion that the ingoing breath is the thought that she speaks on the outgoing breath. One actor I've been working with for about a year and a half does the work I assign for outside of class. Since he has done it, he's made great improvement. So she asked him who he was working with. Now this woman does not do enough work outside of class. She comes to me quite frustrated because she's taken five steps back, and I say, "What have you done since I last saw you?" She works for a half hour right before she comes to me. Now I tell her she's wasting her money, her time, as well as my time unless she wants to come every day—which is more money than she can afford. When I'm working on breath with my students at CalArts, after they've met their spine they meet their regular rate of breathing. One of the things I have them do is lie on the floor on their backs and place a hand lightly over their belly button and simply notice what's going on. We don't talk; I simply want them to be aware of what's going on. Then I might ask them to find a "huh" sound that doesn't take much breath. Then I might double the "huh" so it's two "huhs" on one breath, which takes a little more breath for two than it does for one. I'm giving them a neutral sound, a sound that needs no articulator—only breath, clear thought, and their body on which to resound. So I do different exercises depending upon the people I'm teaching.

Saklad: How do you teach support?

Bennett: Support is nothing more than breath. A breath is a thought. If I know I have a long thought and I've worked on my ribcage, have increased my capacity, and have vacuumed my lungs, then I've got a good capacity for breath. Your breathing will obey your brain if you've worked on it. I don't believe in controlling your breathing or in holding your ribcage out. If I have to do all of that then my thought is going to focus on holding my ribcage up and not what it is I'm trying to express.

Saklad: What role does listening play in voice and speech work?

Bennett: Listening comes from beginning acting classes where students are taught to listen to their partners. That should follow through to voice work. Listening affects the vocal response of the scene partner—tempos, rhythm, volume, pitch, etc. I want the students to avoid listening to the sound of their own voice. If I feel that there's something they need to hear, I ask them to record themselves. There's a young man who was in a BA class who speaks everything in a monotone. He was doing a scene in his acting class, and I sat in to make sure he was bringing the voice work into the acting. I had him picking up stacks of heavy chairs just to try to get some difference in inflection in what he was saying. It didn't work. He picked up the chairs but it did not affect how he spoke his text because he was not hearing his partner. At one point I even asked his partner to say his lines completely differently, which changed the meaning all together. The reply from the young actor was exactly the same. When you listen you are affected, and thus when you listen the voice is affected. He admitted that he hadn't heard any difference. I did not record him but rather sent him to a doctor to check his hearing.

Saklad: "When you listen the voice is affected." Such a simple statement but so true. How do you help your students connect imagery and the text?

Bennett: I send them off to art galleries. One thing that I instituted at CalArts, because I thought it was needed, was a class called Language. It was taught by a voice teacher who happened to be Irish and had a great sense of language. She loved poetry. She would ask the students to walk around the campus and come up with ideas of things they could write about. Sometimes she would pick a particular theme. Other times she left the subject matter open. This class of writing and reading aloud helped the students to read a script, to find the "want" and arc of a character and moment. The students who took that class were much more imaginative. You didn't have to give a lot of imagery to them; they brought it to you. I also tell them to go to music concerts. Go to the dance concerts. It helps them develop their imagination and their imagery when they work with text.

Saklad: How do you approach the teaching of range?

Bennett: We play with text in various pitch ranges. Some of them can actually be quite ridiculous, but the students can experience the stretch in case they ever need to do it in a role. Then they know how to expand themselves without harming themselves. The last months of a school year, my work concentrates on range. I work a lot on the ribs so they're open and flexible. It really makes sense to work on range and heightened text with an increased breath capacity.

Saklad: How would you describe the relationship between emotion and voice and speech work?

Bennett: Emotion is right there in voice work. Anytime you speak on breath you touch emotion. Every time I allow a breath in—if it's a deep breath—I'm touching emotion whether I acknowledge that or not. Which is why when young actors first learn to breathe deeply they may cry or laugh or do something out of the ordinary, because it's the first time in a very long time they've had a deep breath in their bodies. There is usually an "aha!" moment in the student meeting his or her breath.

Saklad: How do you see scientific and/or technological advances within or without the field influencing either your work or the work at large?

Bennett: People use microphones in small theatres. People use microphones in little square black boxes. Why? I don't know. In fact, our school uses mics a lot. I am forever saying the actor can fill this room. You don't need it. But they use them anyway.

Saklad: What would you tell an aspiring young actor to look for in a voice and speech teacher?

Bennett: First of all you have to find a person you can trust, and there has to be a mutual respect. I say that because when you study voice, you are putting yourselves into the hands of the other person. Voice is very subjective. When you work on your voice, you're really working on yourself.

Moving into the Future

Saklad: Have you witnessed much of an evolution in voice and speech training over the course of your career?

Bennett: Louis's Colaianni's work with phonetic pillows is about the newest thing in terms of speech. Catherine Fitzmaurice's Destructuring/

Restructuring voice-training approach is taught by many teachers in MFA programs. Lessac Madsen's Resonant Voice is a new approach to voice training.

Saklad: What advice would you give to performance students on the brink of their professional careers?

Bennett: If you've learned it, forget it. Go and do the job. If you haven't learned it, go back and learn it.

Saklad: What impact do you hope your work will have on vocal training at large?

Bennett: I don't really hope it will do anything at large. I just hope that the people with whom I'm working will continue working when they're no longer working with me. I try to give everybody a routine of work, and I hope they will continue to do it. But I don't know what effect that's going to have on anything at large. I am passionate about what I do. You know, I have a reputation of being—some have used the word "h-a-r-d." By the time they finish working with me, they say: "She's not hard. She's just passionate about what she knows. She loves her field, and she wants us to love it as much as she does and to do the work on ourselves." And that's really all I want.

Cicely Berry

Cicely Berry has been voice director at the Royal Shakespeare Company since she joined in 1969. At the RSC she has been deeply involved in the education work, and has also worked extensively in prisons. Her directing work includes a production of *Hamlet* for the National Theatre Education Department, and also *King Lear* for the RSC at the Other Place. Cicely is an artistic associate of Theatre for a New Audience in New York, and has worked regularly for a number of years with the *favela* group Nos Do Morro in Brazil. She has written four books for actors that cover all aspects of voice and text work. Her fifth and latest book, *From Word To Play*, is for directors, and focuses on ways to work with the text during the rehearsal period. She also made a series of videos called *Working Shakespeare* on the speaking of Shakespeare's text, featuring a number of well-known actors, including Helen Hunt and Samuel L. Jackson. In 1985 she was awarded the Order of the British Empire (OBE) award for services to the theatre.

Background

Nancy Saklad: I read that Gwyneth Thurburn was a mentor of yours.

Cicely Berry: Yes, she was the head of Central School of Speech and Drama, where I went to train as a teacher in 1946. The training was just wonderful. It was so complete, and she was the most amazing woman. She had an incredible view of the whole structure of language and speech and voice. Gwyneth was a very well-informed, well-read person with strong political views—a good socialist—which suited me, because I have always identified as leftwing. She ran the school with very good teachers and was a great inspiration to me.

Saklad: How did she inspire your work, Cicely?

Berry: She inspired me with her open and generous view of life. Her work was never narrowed down to the technical details of voice. She believed that one's voice was an integral part of oneself and needed to be opened up in order to express oneself fully.

Saklad: You've been with the RSC for forty years now. That's quite a career. What was it like in the early days?

Berry: Well the RSC was—and this was when Trevor Nunn was running it—the Royal Shakespeare Company was the first company ever to employ a voice person. Trevor thought that young actors didn't have enough experience with their voice work. I suppose I had been there six months working on the voice when I began to get involved in the productions. At the time there were three main directors. There was Trevor, John Barton, and Terry Hands. They were the three solid directors in the company and were so open to me. I would go into rehearsal and find where the actors were having difficulty finding their way into the style of the direction, or into the way that the specific director was working. This opened my eyes hugely; I mean, this was my introduction to the whole theatre business. Trevor was always going for the intimacy between characters and how they interacted and connected with each other. I remember the first production that I worked on with him was *Winter's Tale*, and it was very, very intense. John Barton sought out the structure of the language, finding the opposites in the language, finding the different forms of language, and getting actors to honor that. Terry Hands tended to do the histories and the strong epic plays, and in rehearsal always asked the actors to speak louder and faster to the end of the speech. Going into all these rehearsals, I began to see how difficult it was. This was my great opening, I suppose, which focused on how the actor owned integrity to a part and yet still took the direction that was being given. So that was when I started to evolve exercises that would help the actors keep their integrity—their own sense of what the truth was—and still honor what the director wanted.

The Voice and Speech World of Today

Saklad: What is it about the work that most inspires you today?

Berry: Because I work at the Royal Shakespeare Company, my focus is on Shakespeare, of course, and finding a way for the actor to inhabit the language in a way that means something very specific to that actor. That is something that always has to be worked on individually with the actor, because it will be different for each person. What I am interested in is getting actors to feel that they are *inside* the language, that the language is living in them and it's not something they have to do something with—they don't have to make it work right. If they are aware of their own voice coming from way deep in their center and finding the excitement of the language for themselves—not just the meaning, but finding how the language moves inside them—then they find a way of seeing that language. That's why I do a lot of exercises on text, getting a group to move around and find the movement of the thought and changing direction of thoughts, or things like that. The other day I was doing an exercise with the whole group. I recited Juliet's soliloquy that begins, "Gather apace you fiery footed steeds." I spoke each phrase one at a time, which they had to repeat, and as they did so they had to act what they spoke. In this way, through Shakespeare's imagery, they found something of what Juliet was feeling inside—how her blood was racing, her sexuality in fact. This way they inhabit the language in their bodies as well as their minds. That is what interests me.

Saklad: What would you say distinguishes your work from others in the field?

Berry: Well, all I care about is that people feel they want to inhabit the language from inside…and how they do that…It helps if they're relaxed, if their resonance is good and easy without feeling they've worked at it. They should feel the resonance—feel the vibrations inside them—so it informs how they speak the language. It's the language that matters to me. Theatre is with us to entertain, but it should ask questions. It should always provoke us to think more about our lives, and to change if necessary. It's like Edward Bond saying, "Do not leave the theatre satisfied. Leave the theatre hungry for change." That's what matters to me. It's a political matter, always.

Saklad: In addition to vocal coaching at the RSC, would you say that vocal training is also an aspect of your work there?

Berry: That's always part of it, yes. Training always has to be part of it because actors need to feel the whole of their voices, without effort, to ensure their instrument is ready for use. Once actors get tension in the upper torso, they're not anywhere near as likely to communicate what they want to an audience.

Saklad: How would you describe the current state of affairs of voice and speech training for actors?

Berry: I think it's in a very good place, actually. There are a lot of really ace teachers about, and I think they're all working very hard. Fashions in language really change so much. Writing also changes. I haven't said anything about modern writing, but I love working with modern writing because it is also difficult for the actor; you read someone modern like Beckett or even more modern than that, and what seem like very ordinary, casual speech rhythms are actually very deliberate. The commas and phrases are very specific, and the meaning is in the rhythm of those phrases. Once actors get hold of that idea they're fine, but it takes quite a bit of understanding and awareness for the actor to really grasp the specificity of punctuation, rhythm, and phrasing.

Saklad: How do you feel about the multitude of training approaches that are in use today?

Berry: I think everybody finds their own way. So long as the work gives actors confidence, increased ability, and an openness to the work, and as long as it works for them, it's fine. I don't make any judgment about that. I know what I like to do. I like to open up the voice, get it working open and free, and then work on the actor inhabiting the text. That's my thing. We touched on something earlier that I wanted to follow up on about working with different directors and in different styles. My husband was an American actor who came over to Great Britain in 1950. He trained at the Actor's Studio, so he was very much in touch with Stanislavsky's Method, and I became very interested, therefore, in finding ways of embracing both the English attitude—which focuses on making sense of things—and the American attitude, which is more about finding the emotion inside. It helped me very much to find the two things together. All language, everything that everybody says, is the character's way of surviving, and emotion is of less interest to me. It's how you survive to carry your life on and succeed that matters. Therefore, that's why language is so active all the time, because you're finding your way. Very seldom in a play do you give an end product of your thought. You're always thinking and discovering something new, and that's what interests me.

Saklad: What are some of the greatest voice and speech obstacles that actors face?

Berry: Well, reaching across the space is always something that they have to face, and it's so seldom through increased volume. It's always through an increased sense of the muscularity of the language that it communicates through distance. What are the greatest obstacles? Well, I think the principle one is this balancing between getting the language to sound as if the text is natural, while still allowing the audience to hear the language, because it's in listening to it that you get another understanding of it—that understanding is in the very *sound* of the language, however modern the text is. If the text is very broken up, it's in the broken-upness of it that we become aware of what the actual feeling underneath is, the thought underneath. So I think the obstacle is really hearing what the sound of the language is and getting that through to an audience. When you hear the Hostess speaking of the death of Falstaff it is very moving: "I put my hands upward and upward, and all was as cold as any stone." It is in the sound that we receive feeling. That is why it is very important in the training of actors to get them interested in speaking poetry, because this makes them aware of the rhythm and phrasing of the written word—how each phrase is a different length, and how one thought lifts through to the next with a slight rise in the voice—and how that rise continues to engage the hearers' expectations and makes them want to listen. Actors really have a hard time with that now. They want to keep it cool, but then a certain subtlety gets lost.

Saklad: Do you think voice and speech training plays a unique role in performance training?

Berry: Yes I do. I think it's deeply important. Part of the skill of the actor is to use the voice and the subtle changes that are possible in the voice to affect the listener, and unless they are aware, in a good way, of the possibilities they have, vocally that won't happen.

Saklad: Is the director usually in your working sessions while you're vocal-coaching?

Berry: Yes. I'm lucky with the RSC because I can go in at any time and suggest things to do and suggest exercises, and the same is true with Theatre for a New Audience in America.

Saklad: Your latest book, *From Word to Play*, is a testament to what you've been speaking about here. In it you talk about exercises you use called "displacement strategies," which you say are designed to free the actor. Would you describe how they work?

Berry: Actors do a simple task that doesn't require logical thought, such as drawing a picture, or I might ask them to draw the first house they lived in. By doing that, while they're speaking the language, they stop thinking about the literal meaning, and it takes them into a deeper world. They know the speech, so they know the meaning of it, but they let it happen in a unique way. Then they start to hear the sounds in the speech that are subliminal but that are part of the meaning all the time.

Saklad: Are the exercises that you just mentioned in both *Text in Action* and *From Word to Play*?

Berry: They're in all of them. They started with *Voice and the Actor* and then *The Actor and the Text* and *Text into Action*—very much so in that. I can remember how Trevor worked very quietly in order to get actors to be very specific about the emotion of the character. The danger in working this way was that the acting became very quiet and personal and so not ready to reach into a large space. So I found ways of getting them to keep it very intimate but actually reach across to the audience—which is partly technical. With Terry I used to make the actors draw pictures of very specific things they could see while they were speaking loudly. With John, to free the actors up, I used to chuck a whole load of books on the floor and get them to arrange them in order of height on a shelf above while they were honoring what he wanted them to honor. I started to do this back in the 1970s. Then of course Peter Brook joined with me on *A Midsummer Night's Dream*. Well he was my guru, as it were. Always has been, always will be. I suppose the two people who've had the greatest influence on me are him and Edward Bond, who's a writer.

Practical Considerations

Saklad: What advice would you give to an aspiring actor who was looking for a voice and speech teacher?

Berry: They need to find someone who is sound on all the areas of breathing and relaxation, and in putting that into action and giving them exercises to do and texts to work on, that will open up the voice and get them to realize what they've got in their voice.

Saklad: Do you think that students benefit from studying multiple approaches to the work?

Berry: Not particularly. I think they've got to find their own way of working where they feel comfortable and that they feel opens their voice up in the best way.

Saklad: What does the body need to produce optimal vocal work?

Berry: You need to be fit, and the main thing is to be able to open your ribs easily so you can feel the breath going right down into the center so you can feel the breath starting the sound from the center. The actor also needs muscularity.

Saklad: In *From Word to Play*, you describe listening as a collective act between the actor, the text, and the audience. Would you elaborate?

Berry: Listening is very important. Actors often feel they have to get a move on and move the language forward, partly because of the director, I think. Often, if the text is a piece of dialogue, I don't hear them hearing that last word that has been spoken to them just before they reply. They've learned the text, so they reply quickly. They know what the text means, but they're not replying to the precise word that is there, which takes them in a different direction. I do lots of exercises with actors doing dialogue repeating the last half line of what was said to them, or the last word, before they answer it. They get really surprised by it, because it takes them away from themselves and puts them in the language of the play. It creates a whole different energy, an arc.

Saklad: How do you describe the relationship between emotion and voice and speech work?

Berry: I don't know—you see, I don't like dealing with emotion. I don't deal with it at all.

Saklad: You mentioned that you look for the thought, and then the emotion is a byproduct—

Berry: Well, I think you look for the thought—you've always got to find a way to go forward, to survive, as it were. That's my bottom line. For instance, I'm answering you. I'm answering because I want to go further with you. If the emotion does come, it's because you can't stop it. It's like if you ask somebody to describe something from the past, their mother who died or something like that; if you ask someone to describe it, the actual words, just by speaking them, overwhelm you and you want to cry. But it's only because you want to describe something, because you want to *get* something through, that emotion can just take over. But I don't think you ever want to go for that.

Saklad: So you seek a truth in the language and something in the truth of the language—

Berry: —could be upsetting.

Saklad: How do you see scientific and/or technological advances within or without the field influencing your work or the work at large?

Berry: I think the use of the microphone is never good, because it distorts the voice and generalizes it. You're never going to get the truth of the character or of the actor through a microphone. The microphone takes something away from the bare truth of the character and the actor.

Moving into the Future

Saklad: What advice would you give to voice and speech teachers at the beginning of their professional careers?

Berry: They have to be true to what they believe. To do good basic voice work is the bottom line, which I learned from Gwyneth Thurburn all those many years ago. And nothing has changed my belief in the opening of the ribs, the relaxation of the chest, the vibration in the chest, the vibration of muscularity in the head, the feeling that the breath and the sound is coming from the center of you. That, to me, is where you start, and then you have to open out and listen to what the language is doing that the actor is working on, to be really aware of rhythms and how rhythms affect you as you hear them, and to get the actor very aware of the possibilities in language, the rhythm of the language, and how thoughts lift through. One of the difficulties today is that we tend to talk on the same pitch all the time, and in the theatre that doesn't interest an audience. You have to lift it just that half a tone to get people to hear and to hear the *spaces* in the language. Edith Evans used to call it a "poise." It's not a pause. It's something that lifts and makes the listener want to hear the next bit. You've got to always make them want to hear the next thing. I'm talking to you and I get to a moment in a thought and I just hold it because I'm not quite sure how to go on. So it's hearing that and hearing how language changes all the time.

Saklad: What advice would you give to students at the brink of their professional career regarding voice?

Berry: Well, literally to work on all the things I've already said. Really do the exercises so you can get comfortable with your voice. So that when you get nervous, the nervousness doesn't hinder the actual production of the voice. You can get through the nervousness but still have a basic resonance that you feel comfortable with that is yours, not something that is put on. They've got to do that, and they have to realize that it's something that has to be done every day. We do voice warm-ups every day in the company. That's how important we think voice work is for the actor and how important the actors themselves think it is.

Saklad: How would you describe the evolution of voice and speech training that has happened over the course of your professional career?

Berry: When I joined the Central School and trained as a voice teacher, actors were asked to make the language very musical. Later in 1970, when I joined the RSC, it was still the fashion when you spoke Shakespeare to find the music of the language. You'd hear wonderful examples of that in people like Gielgud, who was an amazing actor, and I don't mean to underestimate him at all, but since then we've progressed. Fashions of language are always changing. That's the bottom line. Now we don't want to hear Shakespeare spoken beautifully. We want to hear what it means to us now, today. Actors are always walking a tightrope between finding that roughness of today's world in the language, honoring a certain music in it, while also honoring the size of the imagery. And there *is* music there, still, that we will respond to. One still responds to the speeches of Martin Luther King, and that is through their music as much as anything. Unfortunately, most politicians have lost a sense of rhetoric in their language. Maybe Obama has it now a little bit.

Saklad: How has your own work evolved?

Berry: Well, it is always evolving. It evolves because of the necessity of the moment. When I first joined the RSC, we did a huge amount of opening up the ribs, getting the vibration in the chest, and finding the vibration in the head and in the whole body. I suppose there was much more emphasis on finding the structure and the musicality of the language. But as I've said, we want to make it more and more the language of *now*, because Shakespeare has so much to tell us about our own lives and the politics of our own culture. The language needs to be made to feel as though it is being spoken for now.

Saklad: You've given so many gifts to the voice- and speech-educator community. Is there anything on the horizon we might look forward to?

Berry: Not at the moment. *Word to Play* was really what I wanted to do all my life. So I think I've said it all in there.

Saklad: Cicely, what impact do you hope your work will have on vocal training at large?

Berry: Well, one always hopes that people will work on it, you know, and accept it. I think they do. You can't do any more than that. I put it all down and people choose it or not, as they do. I don't feel as though "this is the method and you've got to do it"—I don't feel that at all. Everybody's got to find their own way, I think.

Saklad: And you've chosen to address the actors' and director's work with Shakespeare—

Berry: Yes, that's important because I think Shakespeare is very important to us today. I think he's the greatest absurdist, and he makes a stink. And politically he's so clear, and politics is very important to me.

David Carey

David Carey is a senior voice tutor at the Royal Academy of Dramatic Art, London. Previously, he was principal lecturer in voice studies at the Central School of Speech and Drama, London. He trained in speech and drama at the Royal Scottish Academy of Music and Drama in Glasgow, and earned his degrees in English Language and Linguistics from both Edinburgh University and Reading University. A voice teacher for thirty years, he has worked nationally and internationally in higher education and the professional theatre, including four years as assistant to Cicely Berry at the Royal Shakespeare Company. In 2007, he was awarded a prestigious National Teaching Fellowship by the Higher Education Academy of England in recognition of his contribution to voice teaching. In 2008, he and his wife, Rebecca Clark-Carey, published their *Vocal Arts Workbook and DVD*.

Photo by Rebecca Clark-Carey

Background

Nancy Saklad: Who were your mentors, David, and how have they influenced your work?

David Carey: My first mentor was my mother. She taught me about poetry, storytelling, and what the expressive use of the voice was about. Then with my father, I would read for him while he learned his lines. I was unconsciously absorbing things to do with accent, expressivity, and language as well. Then professionally, as mentors, I would credit Jacqui Crago, who was one of my voice teachers from the Royal Scottish Academy of Music and Drama in Glasgow. She inspired me with her teaching and with a love of phonetics. Then subsequent to her, I would credit Ann Cattanach, who was also a teacher. She had trained at the Central School for Speech and Drama (as had my mother) and encouraged me as a first-time voice teacher. Then finally, I would credit Cecily Berry, because she was my first professional theatre mentor, and her work just inspired me. Cis was my great mentor.

Saklad: Have there been other influences that have inspired your work?

Carey: Kristin Linklater's work *Freeing the Natural Voice* was a great inspiration for me as a young teacher, in terms of the voice connection to the world of the imagination, the world of image, and the world of impulse. I could see a distinction between the British way into voice, which worked from building up technical skills and developing those in relation to expressing language and the imagination, and what I saw Kristin's work offering—which came out of a British context but flourished in an American context—which was about connecting the work to impulse and the psychological or psychophysical reality. I was interested in synthesizing between the different schools. We're all talking about the same thing. I've always been eclectic in my work, yet simultaneously I have a core that is centered in what is *human* about everything we do. We are bodies, we are minds, we are hearts, and we have desire. The work is about enabling all of those elements to be part of the artistic choice that the actor makes.

The Voice and Speech World of Today

Saklad: What features would you say distinguish your work in the field?

Carey: I've encouraged people to see and to appreciate what the different approaches offer and then to ask, "What's speaking to me as an individual teacher that I want to embrace because it will inform me?" So I'm a little bit of a magpie, and I encourage other people to be magpies, because that makes you more unique as a teacher. I think it's valuable to stay open and to continue learning.

Saklad: Your book with your wife, Rebecca Clark-Carey, *The Vocal Arts Workbook*, is practical and refreshing. What can you tell us about the book and your inspiration for it?

Carey: Rebecca and I both felt we wanted to write something about voice but wondered what we had to offer. What would be distinctive about what we might be able to write? And it became that sense of recognizing how to enter the world of voice both as a learner and as a teacher. So that was our inspiration, to look at the learner/teacher within the classroom situation.

Saklad: How would you describe the current state of affairs of actor training in voice and speech?

Carey: I think there is a great danger at the moment that voice and speech work can get diminished, because it's not necessarily seen as the core element of actor training. It has to be seen as part of the three elements of actor training: the body, the voice, and the imagination. If the actor is not functioning as a whole, skilled instrument and creative being, then the imagination won't actually be fully realized, and the audience may be excited but may not be moved, because they're not actually receiving vibration that is being released in a full, dynamic way. The body and voice need to be free for the imagination to be realized.

Saklad: Do you find substantive differences between American and British actor training in voice and speech?

Carey: Historically, America has tended to favor *systems* of training as opposed to Britain, which has tended to say, "Well, there is *the training*." There is no name attached to it. There is no Meisner. There's no Lessac. There's no Feldenkrais. There's just the training. There are great advantages to having systems, but it does tend to compartmentalize.

Saklad: If I understand you correctly, you might actually use, for example, a Lessac exercise towards developing resonant tone without actually using the full body of Lessac work.

Carey: Yes, I would, perhaps, working on resonance, use a range of approaches, one of which may well be Lessac or another approach. It's different strokes for different folks, because what works for one student doesn't work for the other. That's the danger of systematizing.

Saklad: Do you find there are trends in the lay person's voice and speech that become obstacles in the training of today's student actors?

Carey: What I've seen over the last fifteen to twenty years is a tendency for young people to sit on their vocal folds, which I call the "laid-back" usage. The voice drops down in pitch and becomes vocal fry. It actually isn't very strongly supported with breath. I've worked with a British accent just as much as with an American accent and see the same kind of quality. I noticed it affecting young male voices. It now also affects young female voices but in a different way. I hear young female voices that are very close to being damaged because there is no support. Speech habits can also be a barrier to the training of the actor. There is a tendency, certainly in Britain, for habits of articulacy to lack muscularity, to lack definition of consonant sounds, and therefore lack resonance and energy of vowel sounds. I think it has to do with energy. The actor must recognize that energy is not just about opening the instrument. It's about channeling and focusing that energy into consonants that have a fullness of tone, and vowels that have a definition of space and of quality. The purpose of the work is not only artistic, but also communicative; ultimately, it's about connecting to the audience.

Saklad: Do you think voice and speech training play a unique role in performance training?

Carey: As I mentioned earlier, I see it as one of the three cores of actor or performance training. The voice is one of, if not the primary, form of expressivity, of communication, of role, of character, of language, and of intention. So for that to be encompassed with a sense of artistry, with a sense of understanding and awareness, one needs training. The danger is that people see vocal training merely as technical skill, and the technique becomes disparaged. This happened in the 1960s and '70s, with the tendency to throw out technique because it wasn't thought of as truthful. I think perhaps there were certainly elements of technique that we had inherited since before the Second World War in the '40s, a kind of heightened speaking that didn't represent what film and television and contemporary acting required. But if you throw out technique just because it's not serving the style of acting that's contemporary, you're actually throwing out artistry. You're throwing out potential. You're throwing out development of the instrument and you're throwing out health. The more aware we are of how we use the instrument; of why we use the instrument; of how the instrument connects the body, the brain, the heart, the imagination, sensation in a holistic connection; the more we can be a living artist. Just because certain media requires an approach that seems naturalistic doesn't mean that we shouldn't be aware of what we're doing. It doesn't mean the process should be simply instinctive or unconscious. We can have an awareness of what we're doing. and this awareness can actually serve us in a positive way rather than be a barrier to truth in theatrical and artistic terms. Truth is different from reality. That's what a lot of young actors don't recognize. Truth can be bigger than realism or naturalism or whatever we want to call it, and vocal training can serve that.

Saklad: Where does vocal presence come from, and is it teachable?

Carey: I think vocal presence is one of those indefinable things, which to me relates to another indefinable thing, which is resonance. What is resonance? One can describe it scientifically, one can help people develop it, but to make it actually tangible is immensely difficult. It's something that we know we have an intimate connection to and which, if we allow it to express our inner selves and our lives, will communicate fully with people. If we don't use that awareness, if we don't use our connection to breath and release and openness and articulacy, then we will be denying our presence. Vocal presence is about recognizing ourselves in our voices, just as body presence is about recognizing ourselves, or our characters' selves if you like, fully investing in that and releasing and sharing it.

Practical Considerations

Saklad: What does the body need to produce optimum vocal work?

Carey: The body needs release. It needs appropriate relaxation, but it also needs appropriate energy. It needs muscular tone to be present. I work with Alexander technique and also with Alexander technique teachers. I find the technique has been a very important component of my work in terms of its ability to develop that conscious awareness of release, muscular tone, and appropriate use of muscularity from a physical point of view as well as a vocal point of view. I also have found, personally and professionally, that Tai Chi has been a very valuable component of my work, because it brings together awareness, energy, release, and flow. There are a whole lot of other body work components that I've had contact with in the past: Laban work, Feldenkrais work, and others that I've found a lot of connections with and like to make use of in appropriate ways. So the body for me is not separate from the voice. It's absolutely and totally connected, and you cannot work on the voice without working on the body. You can't work on the body without working on breath, so they're deeply connected.

Saklad: Do you think an understanding of anatomy deepens the students' relationship to their voice?

Carey: I believe so, yes, but I also think anatomy can present a barrier, because it can be about bits and pieces and separating things and not necessarily about seeing the totality of the body. Functional anatomy, rather than pure anatomy, or scientific or medical anatomy, is what's most useful for the acting student. I find it's not always helpful to name all of the muscles, but certain muscles, such as the transversus or intercostal muscles, or knowing about the larynx and how it functions—that's important. Students need to have some essential functional anatomy.

Saklad: And what about an imagistic understanding of the voice. Do you think that is helpful as well?

Carey: That's valuable too because people learn in different ways.

Saklad: How do you address breath work?

Carey: Breath work is the absolute essence of the voice. You cannot have a functioning voice without breath, obviously. So, the arc of it is about discovering how to open up the breath in a way that will serve the voice in a healthy instrument and in an imaginative way. That means working with an awareness of vocal anatomy and also working from the imagination, using imagery, and also using a sort of stimulus and response connection that if you have an insight, you breathe in. You don't breathe out when you think of something. You breathe in and then you express the thought. We have a neurological connection that informs how we breathe. We also have an ability to increase the size of breath that we take through muscular action. We possess an ability to support the breath through a connection to a specific set of muscles. We have an ability to extend the breath from a physiological point of view, but all of these things can also be tied into the imagination. So for me, what's important is finding ways of understanding and connecting the functional anatomy with impulse, thought, feeling, and imagination.

Saklad: What does it mean to support the voice?

Carey: For me, supporting the voice means having a muscular, energized underpinning to the breath. Essentially, the breath is being supported and not the voice. The idea is to support the breath so that the voice is released. That happens with the muscular energy and the abdominal muscles. I use the transversus, the lower obliques, the internal obliques, and also the pelvic floor muscles. That strength of muscular energy from the lower abdomen engages the support that then allows the muscles in the throat to release, because otherwise they will engage if you don't actually have that support.

Saklad: How do you approach tonality, resonance, and vocal qualities?

Carey: Once again we focus on release. We are opening up the resonating chambers, which can be difficult for people to become aware of kinesthetically—that there is space in the throat, in the back of the mouth, and within the mouth. I like to demonstrate different kinds of vocal qualities through the sorts of things that vocal artists do in creating different characters for cartoons or muppets or things like that. Simply raising one's larynx can make you sound like Kermit the frog, or lowering the larynx can make you sound like something altogether different. Resonance work can be entertaining, and students start to realize that those voices are created by muscular action, by changing the tonality of a voice, by changing the resonance space, or by changing the position of the tongue.

Saklad: How might you help your students connect the imagery and the text?

Carey: Imagery and text is about the imagination and relating it to character. Images come out of deep experience, and so I work a lot with poetry and Shakespeare to enable students to realize that heightened imagistic language exists because it relates to that deep experience.

Saklad: How would you describe the relationship between emotion and voice and speech work?

Carey: Emotion is a primary element of voice and speech work. It's part of an impulse connection to speak. Emotion is a physical response to a stimulus that affects us deeply and causes us to breathe in a new way. Emotion causes us to want to express something that if we hold onto, we're blocking. I made this connection when I was on a rollercoaster, because it took me a long time to pluck up the courage to do it. I was an adult before I went on a rollercoaster, and my kids were actually the ones who got me to try it. This adventure happened at an awfully useful time of my life, because I was able to recognize the fear and the excitement and to put that together with the realization that I didn't have to hold on to the fear and excitement; I could express it and could then actually enjoy the experience. Part of the rollercoaster experience is the anticipation of fear and then the release of it. The release of the fear is what allows you to enjoy the experience. If you hold on to it then you're in agony, because you are blocking the energy. If you release it then you reach a heightened experience. You release into something that has energy, which has perhaps an element of excitement and of joy.

Saklad: What strategies or exercises have you found to be helpful when working with heightened text?

Carey: I want to get heightened text into the body and into the imagination. This goes back to the earlier question about imagery and the text. I want the students to experience the text as something that comes from inside them rather than is laid on top. Heightened text, again, expresses experience that is bigger than our everyday level of conversation. It can be useful for the actor to connect to heightened text by physicalizing the language, finding a whole body experience with it, or singing it or using an extended pitch range. Other strategies I like to use involve exploring the particular images or looking at the texture of the individual sounds in the language exploding, as it were, everything that's in the experience of speaking that language.

Saklad: How do you see scientific and/or technological advances influencing your work or the work at large?

Carey: One of the most influential benefits of the scientific study of the voice is the ability to see what's happening on the inside. To actually understand more fully how the muscles function—which muscles are involved in vocal production and speech—to see the larynx at work, and to see the different tension-effort levels that different vocal qualities employ has been most valuable to me. I've found this information to be valuable in a training situation, as well as to show young students a voice that is functioning healthily and efficiently and one that is not. I show them the voice of a fifty-year-old smoker and then one of a fifty-year-old trained singer who's a very vocally healthy person too. The fact that all of that could be valuable impacts the training in different ways. For me, it has enhanced my commitment to the healthy voice. Science teaches us what damage to the voice can do and informs us about the healthy voice. Voice science and technology reinforce the importance of informing our students about vocal health and encourage them to establish a healthy lifestyle and healthy habits.

Moving into the Future

Saklad: What advice would you give to voice and speech teachers at the beginning of their professional careers?

Carey: One piece of advice is to keep working on their instrument. They are a model for their students. Another important thing is to recognize that different learners need different techniques and different tools to embrace what we have to teach them. We have the responsibility to enable the learner to learn. As we know, people learn in different ways, but to recognize that means that we have a responsibility to be able to teach to the needs of the students.

Saklad: What voice and speech advice would you give to performance students on the brink of their professional careers?

Carey: I've kind of hinted at that, which is to recognize that the training doesn't stop at the end of three years or however long it's taken you to get there.

Saklad: In your lifetime have you witnessed an evolution in any aspects of voice and speech training?

Carey: Yes, the connection to body work has grown and grown. This is important in a number of ways: one way recognizes that the voice is not separate from the body. I believe when I came in to teaching voice, that concept was already in place, but we've opened up so much to different kinds of body work in the last forty years that in a way, we've discovered a whole set of new potential connections that can serve voice work. Then, also in the last thirty or forty years, we've explored the area of culturally opening ourselves up to the work of "developing the human being." This has been an important aspect of what has informed the development of voice work, and an area that voice work can also reciprocate and inform the life skills.

Saklad: What do you think the future holds for voice and speech training?

Carey: I hope that we do not lose touch with where we've come from. I hope that we keep renewing the wellspring of voice, which is the breath and which is our pedagogical heritage. One final thing... how wonderful to see in a politician like Barak Obama someone who loves and embraces language. He's not ashamed of language and uses it well to express ideals, as well as practical, hopefully potential, solutions to problems. That, I hope, is something that we as a human race can learn to re-embrace and not be afraid of.

Saklad: What impact do you hope your work will have on vocal training at large?

Carey: For me, it's about the question "Why are any of us artists?" It's because we have deep experiences that we know the potential of sharing them with the world will help inform and change other people. We want to have an effect on other people's lives in a way that we hope will enable them to be better human beings. As pedagogues we have an understanding of the voice, and each time we meet an individual, we have the capacity to change that person's experience of the world, either through enabling them to discover something different about how they use their voices and their bodies, or by opening them up to language in a new way, through different choices of experiencing the world, of imagining the world, of being in the world. That is what I try to do as a voice teacher, and hopefully that is what I'll pass on, in some way or another, through my work.

Louis Colaianni

Louis Colainni is a voice and speech innovator and coach for Broadway, regional theatre, film, and television. He was Will Ferrell's vocal coach for HBO and Broadway productions of *You're Welcome, America*, and dialect coach for the upcoming film *Little Red Wagon*, starring Anna Gunn. He was voice and text director for productions at Oregon Shakespeare Festival, Seattle Rep., Milwaukee Rep., Arizona Theatre Company, Shakespeare Festival of St. Louis, Shakespeare and Company, Trinity Rep., and Kansas City Rep. (fifteen seasons). He teaches workshops in Europe and the US and has taught at NYU, Vassar, Columbia, and many other theatre programs. He currently teaches Acting Classics at the Actors Studio MFA program at Pace University. His books include *The Joy of Phonetics and Accents, Bringing Speech to Life, How to Speak Shakespeare*, and *Shakespeare's Names: a New Pronouncing Dictionary*.

Background

Nancy Saklad: Who were your mentors, Louis?

Louis Colaianni: Well, my way into becoming a voice teacher and my role model for that is Kristin Linklater. I studied voice with her for a number of years and then trained with her to teach voice. In 1987 I became a designated Linklater voice teacher. I acted in her company, Shakespeare and Company, for a couple of years, where she was director of training. I saw her in action a lot. I was first drawn into the process because I felt it gave me access to a further depth in what I was already interested in: language and breath, action, sound, and bringing words to life.

Saklad: What other influences have inspired your work?

Colaianni: I've spent time teaching foreign students to speak English. I think the whole subject of English as a Second Language is a strong thread of my background, a strong influence in several ways. One is it's always challenging to help someone step into the unknown second language, and to find some confidence and comfort and individuality there, and certainly just to form sounds in a way that people in that second language will understand. There were a few ESL teachers that I looked up to and learned from at a certain point in my younger days of teaching when I couldn't always count on the theatre jobs; that would be my other teaching job. It taught me a lot. I also became interested in early learning because I was interested in how new sounds and new words are acquired—back to this theme—how a human being makes language his or her own. So I spent some time reading Maria Montessori and Rudolph Steiner and observing early learning and looking at the difference between the whole-language approach and the phonics approach, which I think is really germane to our processes as voice and speech teachers. So there's a strong influence there as I thought about, "How did I first acquire language, and how do I ask adults to step into a kind of learning that they may have references to from twenty, thirty years ago. How do you step back into that?"

The Voice and Speech World of Today

Saklad: In a snapshot, would you discuss the features or describe the features that distinguish your work in the field?

Colaianni: I guess I'd call this more of a sound bite than a snapshot, but I'd say, at the crux of it for me is: "verbal action from an organic source." There's my sound bite on the matter.

Saklad: Does voice and speech training play a unique role in performance training?

Colaianni: Well you know, that is a tricky question. I think it does, and I think in a way it should. On the other hand, it's also part of the problem that we would say voice and speech plays a unique role. I hate to overemphasize the uniqueness of voice and speech in actor training, because it ought to permeate every class. I suppose voice and speech teachers of other types might disagree, but the unique aspect of voice and speech might be that it continues to place the individual at the center of the process and to expand outward into character and the demands of production.

Saklad: Where does vocal presence come from, and is it teachable?

Colaianni: To be really present vocally, the surrounding environment must be let in. So one key to vocal presence is to be a good listener and to be inquisitive. Without those two things, the voice may be forceful or powerful. But vocal presence is more than that. It is giving back to the environment you're drawing from, so it is in dialogue.

Saklad: This is a fill-in-the-blank question. I'm looking for an image, a metaphor, or something conceptual. The actor's voice is the _____?

Colaianni: "The voice is the expresser of senses, the delineator of thought, the embracer of other people."

Saklad: Do you think students benefit from studying multiple approaches to the work?

Colaianni: My opinion is that it wouldn't do much good to study them at the same time. Perhaps I'm speaking as a purist in a limiting sense, but my sense of it is it might be better to study one approach, or we could put it in a different way, to study with one teacher. Get all that can be gotten out of that, including the passing of time, to see what assimilates and digests, and then perhaps years later study another approach.

Practical Considerations

Saklad: What does the body need to produce optimal vocal work, and do you use any particular type of body work?

Colaianni: Well I have noticed that when I was able to have an Alexander teacher in the room, it was helpful, and they didn't really have to say anything, but just touch bodies and help the actors along.

Saklad: How do you help your students connect to imagery in the text?

Colaianni: That's a basic part of the work, and it involves breath, deep relaxation, being able to think imagistically. Letting words evoke strong images, which the actor can internalize. To be able to turn the whole body into an inner landscape and to be able to see images internally, and let them mingle with and be nurtured by the breath, and in turn, let images emerge as words. Rather than letting imagery form in the head, guided strictly by the eyes, I try to get students to locate images in body parts, such as in the area where you feel your breath, in the area where you register emotion, in the area where you feel sensations that want to turn to language.

Saklad: How would you describe the relationship between emotion and voice and speech work?

Colaianni: Well again, it's integral. One of the first things to be taught is to free the breathing process from tension and control. As soon as someone relaxes muscular defense mechanisms and allows for the abdominal release, visceral shift, and movement in the diaphragm—causing expansion in the lungs for the breath to relax in deeply—inevitably, the plexuses of nerves that relate to emotional receiving and transmitting are going to become directly involved in the incoming and outgoing breath. And feeling can be accessed and expressed through breath and sound. So right from the word go how one feels is integral to the process, and to be able to recognize an emotional impulse and be able to follow it is the recipe for not manufacturing emotions artificially.

Saklad: You've published several books on Shakespeare. What strategies or exercises have you found to be useful working with poetic language?

Colaianni: The first step in it is to make the words your own. That's got to happen. Then you've got to take on epic circumstance. Then you've got to have an instrument open enough to accommodate and express that, and a mental agility that is accurately reflected in your articulators. Then you have to use very strong imagery to elicit strong response, or very particular imagery to elicit very particular response. Then the words have to spark action that affects change. And then it's got to be clear to someone watching.

Saklad: Why do you think some students are more adept at dialect acquisition than others?

Colaianni: Well some of that may be just conditioning, that they've been exposed to that kind of critical thinking with the ear from a young age.

There are students that simply have a good ear. However, it doesn't mean that the student who's not adept has a bad ear. That can be harmful to start making those comparisons in class, because the student might have a very good ear but not very well developed, and that's really the work of the accent class. I've noticed that everyone can improve. Usually the student who has some facility with accents is missing some of the richness of accents. They've gotten more of a general feel of the lilt of the accent, but they may not actually have found every viable sound change, so they can always learn to fill in the details. Then often students need ear training—it actually goes much deeper than the ear, it seems to me—perception training that enables them to identify an accent and be able to, even at first, mimic it. Then they can start to feel it as a causal impulse that they could actually respond to, more or less, from the primal source with the new accent. That's actually the work of the class, and it may take some time. It may take more time than is generally given to that part of speech in a curriculum, but then it plants the seeds. Along the same lines, I've noticed there's always a student who's just not confident about accents. "Can I do it? Can I pull it off? Will anyone believe me? Will it sound real?" Well, there's another student or maybe sometimes the same student who will say, "I'm tone deaf." They will sort of warn me or inform me that they have this problem with feeling pitches, hearing them and matching them, and almost every time that was a matter of conditioning. It went back to a time when in school or somewhere in the chorus they were told to mouth it or whisper it or that they didn't have the ability for music, and they often took it quite hard. So I find, actually, so far anyway, I've never met a student who couldn't match a pitch. It's just how we approach listening and how we approach expressing. Matching an accent actually comes from a similar impulse to matching a pitch.

Saklad: How would you describe the differences between General American Speech and Standard American Speech?

Colaianni: I can give you the details of the pronunciation of the two. But I'll start with more of the political side of it. General American Speech is a majority accent; Standard American Speech is a minority accent. When you analyze the features of General American Speech and you count up the number of Americans who speak that way, it actually encompasses a lot of different accents. So, it's all of the rhotic accents and the accents with less lip rounding in the vowels. Then you get to Standard American Speech and there's more lip rounding and it's less rhotic. So that represents a minority of speakers. Then when you get to a lot of the particular details of Standard American Speech, it represents an elite minority. So it can be traced back to the Ivy League accent in a way or to pockets of New England and to the upper class of the Northeast. The historical moment in time for Standard American Speech as far as I know is in a Barry play like *The Philadelphia Story*, which was written for that culture and that era. But a lot of plays from many cultures have been commandeered by the proponents of Standard American Speech, and we are told that it would be the appropriate accent for those plays. But the criterion for doing that is that Standard American Speech is spoken by a small minority of elite and so the reasoning is a bit thin. Dictionaries used to say it was spoken by cultivated people, you know. Now that's absolutely malarkey. And then dictionaries said it was spoken by educated people. Well, we know that's not true. It's not true that you'll only hear educated people speak that way. Educated people can speak in a rural accent, any sort of Southern accent, or General American Accent or foreign accent. So at one time we were buying this bill of goods that was being sold by people that were promulgating Standard American Speech. The result in the American theatre was that for many years, classical actors rejected our common national accent and deferred to an exclusionary elite accent, which strongly echoed British speech, and our theatre's national identity really suffered for it. Mid–twentieth century American speech teachers were absolutely promulgating Standard American Speech. You can look at Dudley Knight's work and how he traces Standard American Speech to William Tilly and Margaret Prendergast McLean and Edith Skinner, and you can just see this was really an active promulgation.

Saklad: So when does gender come into play?

Colaianni: Well no accent was documented and named in this sociolinguistic way until about 1916, when Daniel Jones wrote a pronouncing dictionary of the English language that documented an upper-class London accent, which he termed Received Pronunciation. This was the British precursor to Standard American Speech. At that time, that meant it was the accent of men. It was the boys who went to public boarding schools, which would be the equivalent of private boarding schools in the

US, and went on to the prestigious universities, and they would speak as their professors spoke, and it would just absorb. Then they would come home in a way having bought an accent. And women only learned it by being the wives and mothers and sisters of the men with this particular education. So this was an elite, high-status accent spoken by a privileged minority. And being passed from male to male, it was a patriarchal accent. Standard American Speech, being the American version of this speaking pattern, has similar connotations. Today, many Americans, particularly Easterners, have certain pronunciations in common with Standard American Speech. But very few actually speak a pure version of this speech pattern. If you take the idiosyncrasies away from William Buckley, Gore Vidal, or George Plimpton, perhaps they speak a pure form of Standard American. Many film actors of the 1930s and '40s spoke this, and TV characters like Fraser and Niles Crane speak this way. Again, it's an elite minority accent. But a lot of us can claim to speak with a General American accent—millions of us.

Saklad: You've created marvelous speech work that involves pillows in the shapes of the International Phonetic Alphabet symbols. Will you talk a little about that?

Colaianni: Over the last eighteen years since I invented phonetic pillows, others have used them as well. Some teachers have really redone their curriculum to accommodate them. Others might use them for a few classes in a semester. I can count about sixty actor-training programs that have used phonetic pillows—in a way, out of my hands. Whatever I would describe to you probably has very little to do with what is going on. I do train and certify teachers in the use of phonetic pillows and what is now called "Colaianni Speech." But out in the larger world, I've sort of let people run with this.

Saklad: Where did the inspiration to create phonetic pillows come from?

Colaianni: Well it does come from a few sources, and first and foremost, it is an extension of Kristin's work. Kristin has a piece of advanced work called "Sound and Movement." I know sound and movement as a term that is used also by acting teachers for certain kinds of theatre games, but this is more of a pedagogy. It's a step-by-step process, and it's specifically designed to enhance the speaking of classical texts, so it's rather advanced work. It requires a free voice, or you're going to probably lose your voice, strong imagery leading to very open sound, leading to the body being moved by the power of sound. That's Sound and Movement sort of in a nutshell, oversimplified. What I appreciated when I learned Sound and Movement as her student was that it linked me to the work I had done in the two years of college when I had studied phonetics. I had learned in college how to break words down into discrete sounds, into their smaller elements, and Sound and Movement was doing the same thing in a very embodied way that our college class had not done, so I thought there really wouldn't be any harm to bring the symbols into this. I didn't feel it was going to, in any way, rob from the experience, so I had that in the back of my mind, and then I was very privileged at a certain point, when I began teaching workshops with Shakespeare and Company, which I did for about ten years. I taught every one of their winter and summer one-month intensives for a period of ten years. Kristin started imparting to me how to teach Sound and Movement, because inevitably you need another Sound and Movement teacher. Once I felt some authority with the Sound and Movement work, I considered asking Kristin what her opinion would be of bringing the symbols in, if they could be brought in sort of as flesh, 3D, touchable, malleable, throw-able, etc. And because Kristin had said in a kind of casual reference something I think she was fond of saying, but one day I caught her saying it in just this way in a lecture she was giving on her opinion of phonetics, and what she said was: "Phonetics was invented [she said with great disdain]...Phonetics was invented by two Boston spinsters who decided to murder language and close the book on it once and for all." At once I knew she was a little bit tongue and cheek—that whoever these people were, they weren't exactly Boston spinsters committing murder, but that sort of summed up the ethos, and so I didn't know if she would have the same militant attitude toward my idea, but I told her about it and all she said was, "What a great idea!" So then, having her blessing, I could really think of it and launch it, not as some subversive thing but as a continuation of Kristin's work. And I did look at it that way, and I actually continue to look at it that way, and I really can't start a phonetic pillows workshop or semester without doing some Sound and Movement first because it really does come out of that.

Saklad: Would you talk a little bit about what the actor might do with the pillows?

Colaianni: Well there are forty-eight phonetic pillows, representing the prevalent vowel and consonant sounds of American and British English. Each is about a foot square, or if it's a double symbol like a diphthong or a consonant diagraph or an affricate, then it's going to be twice that length. They're used in many ways: for various games, for exploring sound personally, for getting a further reach of communicating sound into the room, for maneuvering from the elements of language into words and text, and it's a physical approach. I think I can illuminate a little what I said earlier about Rudolph Steiner and Maria Montessori. A big chunk of our problem when we get to phonetics is sound-symbol identification, and Maria Montessori innovated the early learning process for that identification. Before Maria Montessori, there were blocks with alphabet letters on every side of them, and kids stacked them and played with them. Maria Montessori's innovation—which hardly sounds innovative today, because it's so common—is that she cut the symbols out into cardboard so the exact shape of them could be handled, and then she made a stack of ABCs so you could spell many things with what she called the moveable alphabet. Not stuck on a block or stuck on a page—moveable alphabet. She was working with the poverty-level population in Rome, and a student at the age of four or five, who didn't have possessions, could possess the alphabet, move it around. And she made a very, very stunning and important observation, which is that sometimes when the students *saw* the symbol, they didn't yet remember it, but when they *touched* it, they remembered it. This part of learning is lost on speech and phonetics as an academic subject. It doesn't exist in that realm. So it's not that we have to do the exercises in a juvenile way, but it's that there is something about acquiring symbols that you associate with sounds, that the sense of touch can really enhance. So I learned that bit from Montessori—a very, very keen, insightful teacher. The other person that I learned something about phonetic pillows from, after I had been using them for a little while, was Rudolph Steiner, who created the process he called *eurhythmy*, as visible speech. So it's different than the eurhythmy exercises that some movement teachers use in theatre. It's actually having a different movement associated with each sound so that children dance the alphabet and dance poems, phonetically dance them, before they ever learn to read. So it's in that spirit that I offer phonetic pillows as the tangibility of language in the room to be part of the experience of learning the new symbols and having that code and building the structure of language—that we do it in three dimensions and with sensuality. I think from there you have to read the book. My work has reached a wide audience in our field, not always by me being there. Certainly I've given workshops. Certainly I've trained or aided in the training of many teachers. My work lives out in our field, mostly in North America, mostly in the US, a little in Canada, a little bit in the UK, and even in South Africa, so it's sort of making a ripple into our very narrow discipline within the English-speaking world. It has for some time.

Saklad: What is the single most important truth or guiding principle to you about voice and speech work?

Colaianni: What really inspires me the most is when language is revived, when it comes back to life. So if it is an old play and suddenly the actors are not just saying the words but the words are experiencing their life again, that will keep me inspired. Shakespeare called it a miracle. I agree with that. It's like witnessing a miracle, that what we're doing could potentially revive the words, bring them back to life.

Moving into the Future

Saklad: What advice would you give to voice and speech teachers at the beginning of their teaching careers?

Colaianni: I think to start, to certainly ride the wave of enthusiasm, because people respond to that, but not to depend on it, because enthusiasm may actually give us a false read of how the actors are responding to us, or to our work, to what we're teaching and to find that sometimes less is more. I don't always have to see the fruits of the work in the moment. It may take time. Be patient. Take your time. Listen well and keep the class active on the students' part so they don't become complacent. Involve the students with each other so they're not rehearsing to be virtuoso soloists and to keep going back to text, to test the power of the work at every step.

Saklad: What advice would you give to students on the brink of their professional careers regarding their voice and speech work?

Colaianni: Well, once they've graduated, not to think they've arrived at being trained. To stay open to coaching and challenges that require them to stretch, to continue working on their voices on a daily basis if possible, and to keep seeking so that it isn't that they once sought training, got the commodity, and can now go to the marketplace. I think the best actors out there are always going to be students, always not knowing how they're going to do something and finding out.

Saklad: How has your work evolved since your own training?

Colaianni: One thing that has evolved is that I teach than I did when I began, and I'm less insistent on the change happening in the moment. I'm much more in a frame of mind of planting the seeds, reveling in the change happening in the moment when it does, nudging for it sometimes, and at other times, I hope—I hope it is the way I think it is, appropriately knowing when to step away and in a gardening metaphor, not to overwater, overfertilize.

Saklad: Louis, what impact do you hope your work will have on vocal training at large?

Colaianni: It's hard to know what I would want that impact to be. I'm quite, in a way, satisfied with what the impact is. So—I think language has a momentum. Ideas have momentum. Focused passion has a momentum. So with those elements in play, I'm willing to be happily surprised by what comes next. I've had some quite nice rewards in the professional field, in being able to contribute to productions I've believed in and working with people who seem quite grateful for the work and thrive on it, where it's helping, where I can witness the work I do help the theatre tick. So that's a lovely thing to be a part of as well.

Rocco Dal Vera

Rocco Dal Vera coauthored *Voice: Onstage and Off* with Robert Barton. He also wrote *Acting in Musical Theatre: a Comprehensive Course* with Joe Deer. He is a certified Alba Emoting trainer with an interest in voice and emotional extremes. Rocco was the founding editor of the *Voice and Speech Review* for the Voice and Speech Trainer's Association. He is a professor at the University of Cincinnati's College-Conservatory of Music and faculty at the Xavier University Leadership Center. He is also the resident voice, dialect, and text coach, artistic associate for Cincinnati Shakespeare Company, Cincinnati Playhouse in the Park, Ensemble Theatre of Cincinnati, and Human Race Theatre.

Photo by Taren Frazier

Background

Nancy Saklad: Who were your mentors, Rocco?

Rocco Dal Vera: My voice and speech training in college came primarily from a man named Dennis Turner—not Clifford Turner, another Englishman, probably about his age though. Dennis Turner was a wonderful teacher. His specialty was speech, International Phonetic Alphabet (IPA), and dialects. Then, there was another named Ron Arden who was South African. His focus was on integrating voice and speech into text and acting. I also have to credit Bill and Irene Chapman as singing teachers and as exceptional people. They were instrumental in helping me understand voice science, anatomy, and kinesiology as it relates to singing and speaking. They combined a beautiful mix of artistry and critical thinking about how the voice works. I had a lot of singing training as a child (professional child, boy soprano), but this was my first encounter with a science-based approach to voice production, and it revolutionized my thinking. When I got to Los Angeles and settled in, I made it my business to seek out some more teachers. I worked with Rowena Balos, who was one of Kristin Linklater's master teachers. I also sought out Catherine Fitzmaurice and took a series of workshops with her long before her system was as evolved as it is now. She was teaching incredible stuff, and I found her to be a phenomenal inspiration. I don't claim to be teaching any of their methods, because that seems presumptuous, but their wisdom strongly shaped and continues to influence my ideas, goals, and classroom strategies.

The Voice and Speech World of Today

Saklad: What features would you say distinguish your work in the field?

Dal Vera: I think I've attempted to unify various threads that have come from different sources. I've been influenced by what I believe to be the great teachers, but I haven't subscribed to any of them. If you look carefully at what I've written and what I do in the classroom, you'd probably notice a particular comment is coming straight out of Arthur Lessac, and an exercise we're doing on the floor is probably borrowed straight out of Kristin Linklater. If there is something I'm contributing, it's an operating synthesis of influences.

Saklad: Rocco, your work in the field is as varied as your teaching methodologies. What is your current passion with voice and speech?

Dal Vera: I'm finding inspiring challenges in two broad areas. First, I'm fascinated with the voice in situations of extreme emotion, which I'll discuss later. Second, I just came out of a really interesting meeting for an organization with whom I often consult. They do corporate leadership training. They were interested in picking my brain about whether some of the things we do in voice and speech could be taught through e-learning. Could we translate what we usually think of as a studio activity to learning objects delivered electronically in live and prepackaged formats? It might be hybrid courses where you see somebody live or from a remote location, get direct coaching, and integrate that kind of training with various types of interactive electronic learning objects. Some of what we do can be constructed as an interactive electronic game that would give you feedback to improve your voice. I realize this isn't a new concept, but I did find that the conversation challenged my preconceptions about what I do at a deep level. It is happening in studio-music teaching already. Technology is developing exponentially, and the demands of the market are driving this as well. Professionals want to access information and training in ways they're not able to get it right now—instantly, conveniently, and cheaply. I think this development is coming no matter what, and those who embrace it willingly will discover entirely new ways to train actors and speakers. This will be where we're going to be doing a lot of new work as opposed to the traditional studio and classroom work.

Saklad: How would you describe the current state of affairs of actor training in voice and speech?

Dal Vera: It's never been better, especially if you take only a very short view and look back only twenty-five years or so—about as long as the Voice and Speech Trainers Association (VASTA) has been around. Back in the day, we weren't a profession, and now there are a number of high-quality programs where you can get a degree in the field, and that's exciting!

Saklad: Do you find trends in the layperson's voice and speech that become obstacles in the training of today's student actors?

Dal Vera: Every period has its cultural norms. It's hard to perceive the cultural markers of one's own time, but when we look back we can certainly see them. Every wave of students that comes through has its own particular social and cultural context and behaviors that are approved of or disapproved of. Some that I notice in this particular wave are associated with a studied lack of passion. I teach in a BFA program. I see actors that are straight out of high school, so I get a feel for the social environment and approved behaviors that are present in high school students. Nowadays being cool about things, and so not moved by them, seems to be very approved. This can evidence itself in lots of ways, like low-intensity, narrow or flat/falling pitch intonation, glottal fry, etc. It isn't all bad. I see fewer women behaving in what I would call "girly" ways than I used to ten years ago. Women speak with a bit more confidence and authority than they did in some years past. Let's just say this: cultural speech fashions are always going to be a limitation for an actor because actors need to have transformational skills, and regardless of what cultural fashion you're living in right at the moment, it's going to be a limitation when playing certain characters in certain contexts. So you won't hear me despairing. We'll always have to take students from where they are to the many places they can be. I don't tend to focus on "fixing" actors' problems. The starting point is less significant than the need to maintain a vision of the possible.

Saklad: Where does vocal presence come from, and is it teachable?

Dal Vera: You have vocal presence, no matter what. Everybody has a vocal presence. A person with a tiny voice has a vocal presence. If by presence you mean the ability to command a theatre, that's a kind of presence. In my worldview, there is no voice that, to an actor, doesn't have some utility. Even if it's a little, tiny, squeaky voice you might not find attractive, that voice might make an interesting cartoon character. So there's just no bad here. You can find examples all around of atypical or nonideal voices that have been that person's ticket to stardom. Is it possible to teach somebody to have a voice that commands a room? Can we help actors develop a voice that when people hear them, they feel as though they are living inside a sound that has astonishing authority and amazing musicality? Well yes, that's trainable, and that's oftentimes what people mean by vocal presence, the ability to command a room. I would assert that the real magic comes from an expansion of self, spirit, and identity as much as from development of the voice alone.

Saklad: Do you think performance students should study multiple approaches to the work?

Dal Vera: Let me reach for a metaphor. Let's look, for example, at theological, religious, or spiritual studies. Many people find their fulfillment when they study world religions and world philosophies broadly and diversely. They internalize them and personalize them, and their spiritual journey is one of self-guided eclecticism. That is their path to enlightenment, if you will. There are lots of other people who find their journey toward fulfillment comes from devotion and study to one particular way. These reflect the person as much as anything else. One could say this is true of artists as well. Art is the person. I'm ecumenical. My personal approach is to rip off everybody. I don't want to pretend this is a better approach than training formulations that are highly focused, deep, systematic, methodological, and almost, if you will, devout. It's up to students to shop wisely and get good mentoring so they understand themselves, the nature of the training they are receiving, or the program they are planning to enter, and what's suited best for them.

Saklad: What does the body need to produce optimal vocal work, and what types of body work do you use?

Dal Vera: My own journey started when I was quite young. I was one of those people who knew early on what I wanted to do. I was a boy soprano and got a lot of attention for it when I was little. Along the way I got sidetracked into a dance career briefly. I was with some ballet companies, if you can believe that. So I have a dance background and that informs a lot of my relationship to the body. Then I had a meaningful encounter with yoga, and that also changed my feelings about body work. So those elements filtered together. But this is going to sound very strange, because it seems like it may be off topic, but I promise to pull it through. Alba Emoting has attracted me very much in recent years, because it's a body-centered behavior for entering strong emotional states. Studying it has taught me so much about releasing my former judgments about having perfect alignment and complete coordination—which I recognize as values, but I am now much more interested in how physical states relate to emotional states. We are the emotional warriors of our time. We're the ones that have to go to emotional places audiences don't want to go. They're hoping we will go for them and pull them through the journey and push them out the other side. So we have to be willing to really enter into these places where nobody wants to go, and it's a physical journey. What I'm most interested in, in terms of how the body works to produce optimal voice, is partly to redefine what we mean by optimal voice. I am less interested in beautiful sound than I am in truthful sound. I want the voice to be emotionally connected and to display all the problems of emotional connection in a way that doesn't hurt the actor. This is sort of a roundabout way of saying that one more subject I'm stealing from is Alba Emoting. It is a body-training discipline because it works on the principle that emotions are physiological states. That's really informing a lot of what I do, and it has also changed my aesthetic in terms of what sounds I find attractive or interesting or tolerable.

Saklad: Would you describe Alba Emoting?

Dal Vera: Alba Emoting is a discipline for entering strong emotional states. It is drawn from scientific studies. These studies have arrived at the perspective that an emotion is a physiological state, not a psychological one. While an emotional state can be stimulated by psychological or even chemical circumstance, the state itself is physical. The reason you know you feel angry, for example, is because your body is doing things that constitute a pattern of behavior we call anger. The most critical component of this state, interestingly, is the pattern of breathing. Alba Emoting trains actors to enter these states with a great deal of freedom, intensity, and reliability and then to live inside them in an open way. So you can go into fear or tenderness or eroticism or sadness or joy or anger—any of these strong emotional states at incredible levels of intensity—while still maintaining psychological clarity, because you don't involve the brain in the process; you do what the body does in those states. The danger to the actor is if you enter a strong emotional state from a psychological place, all the psychological chaos of the state tends to come with you, and so you are less able to control your actions, and it's possible to harm your voice and body. If you are deeply in the state, you could be dangerous to yourself. If, as in Alba Emoting, you don't have the psychological component and you enter into a strong physiological state, you can get as angry as you ever could be, but you maintain a certain amount of mental clarity. Then the chaos of those feelings is not intruding on your ability to shout, scream, or lament in a way that doesn't hurt your voice, because you know what you're doing. This work is a fundamental part of the program I teach in, and it is an area that is endlessly fascinating to me.

Saklad: Do you think an understanding of anatomy deepens the relationship that a student has to his or her voice?

Dal Vera: In terms of actor information about this, the best kind of anatomical information an actor can have is experiential. I spend a lot of time talking about anatomy and physiology in fairly small detail, but there's a little voice in the back of my head saying, "Is this really going to help them? Is this news they can use? Is this practical and applied? Is this training or is it schooling, and if it's schooling, is it really what we need to be doing?" I'm rather fascinated by how the body and voice work, and I'll admit I have to have this auditing conversation with myself a lot to be sure my personal interests don't take precedence over the practical needs of my students.

Saklad: Do you find imagery useful in the work as well?

Dal Vera: I try to be extraordinarily careful when talking about the body through metaphor and image. Using metaphors or instructions or descriptions of behaviors that don't contain an accurate sense of how the body operates can be counterproductive. Having said that, I've found the artful use of image and metaphor can be a potent tool. I'm always in search of the most effective ways to connect body and voice, and I'm alert to the possibility that students can be misled if I'm not careful to get it right.

Saklad: How do you approach tonality, resonance, and vocal qualities?

Dal Vera: What I try to teach is transformational facility. "Can you make a really nasal sound? Can you make a really hollow sound? Can you make a really twangy sound? Can you give me a kind of dull quality? Can you make it sharper? Can you increase the breathiness on that? Let's take it to the opposite extreme. Can you give me hyperfunction? Can you give me a really pressed sound? Can you give me degrees of those? What's the effect of that on the listener? Can you do it in a healthy way?" This is where I sort of feel like a football trainer saying, "Can you throw across the field? Can you throw a long bomb? What else can you do?" I'm much more interested in a voice that is really flexible, without the need to have a sense of an ideal. I would really hate it if all the people graduating from my program sounded like merely beautiful voices. I would feel like I failed.

Saklad: How would you describe the role of listening in voice and speech work?

Dal Vera: Listening I think of as trying to sensitively relate to subtext. When you're listening you're really keyed in, in a responsive way, to the full message that's coming at you. That's listening. When I think of hearing skills I think of things like pitch acuity and discerning refined distinctions between subtle sound variations. An enormous amount of what we do is training hearing as well as training listening, and maybe that's a critical distinction.

Saklad: Do you teach the IPA?

Dal Vera: Yes. It's such a fundamental tool for an actor. I teach dialect via the IPA, so I teach transcription skills in their freshman year, and then we apply it pretty thoroughly all the way through. But I have to say it's a tool for me; it's not an end in itself. Even if I never taught dialects I would still want the students to know the IPA, because as a hearing skill students discern things they never did before, in much the way Lessac's consonant orchestra works—which is so wonderfully inspiring as an activity—or Louis Colaianni's phonetic pillow work that he talks about in *The Joy of Phonetics and Accents*. These are such great ways to climb inside the potential of the sound.

Saklad: How do you help your students connect imagery in the text?

Dal Vera: I was in Los Angeles in the late 1970s through the mid to late '80s. I got Neuro-Linguistic Programming (NLP) training early on in my teaching career. When I talk about imagery with my actors, I almost always teach it through the NLP concept of anchoring. When somebody has an experience, they have that experience in every sense of their body, right? They see it. They feel it. They smell it. They taste it. It happens to them on every level, and one of the ways we know somebody is telling the truth is their body, and their behavior is congruent on every level with that truth. So if I say, for example, "I walked out of a bar at three in the morning and saw two guys fighting on the sidewalk," and I'm just making this up—If that actually happened to me all of the experience would be embedded in me in such a rich way that I would be expressing highly detailed and congruent truths through how I told you that statement. This is how I teach imagery. Imagery needs to live at that level. We need to get it in on all the senses. It has to be an experience we had so it's complete when we operate from it.

Saklad: You've talked a little about Alba Emoting. How would you describe the relationship between emotion and voice?

Dal Vera: That's why I use Alba Emoting in our program in a voice and speech class. We have acting teachers, and one of their jobs is to sensitize students to their emotional lives. The reason I am trolling in this pond is I have to teach students to do violent behaviors with their voice in a healthy way, and also a truthful way. The problem was I could do one or the other but not both. I could get them to scream safely and I could get them to act with commitment, but not at the same time. A focus on either one undid the other. I have to be able to get the students into an emotional state with a clear head. I can teach someone to scream, but if I can't teach actors to scream while being completely in the emotion, their ability to scream in a healthy way will disappear in the psychological chaos of feeling. They'll lose all technique, or if their only access to the emotion is psychological, then when they are clearheaded and technically alert they won't be engaged. I have to have both. I have to get people to do these challenging behaviors, but I have to get them into truthful intense acting as well; otherwise, I haven't done the job. So I teach stressful vocal behavior independently; then I teach how to enter these strong emotional states, and then I put the two together and ask them to do both at the same time. I also find working on powerful emotions sensitizes them to a fuller expression of subtle, fleeting affect. The tiny moment-to-moment truths become less masked and more expressive.

Saklad: How do you see scientific and/or technological advances influencing your work or the work at large?

Dal Vera: There's a lot we don't know about the voice, but there are a lot of really cool things people are doing in the area of voice science. When I put the *VASTA Journal* together, when we were founding the journal, it was a high priority that we have a voice-science section for this very reason. I don't know whether we've completely fulfilled the potential for it, but one of my intentions in making sure we had a department devoted to voice science was we needed to drive research as it pertains to our work, and it wasn't happening, really. I felt that if I gave scientists a place to publish and an audience to pay attention, more research would start to happen that was directly applicable to the kind of work we were doing and the practical and theoretical questions we were encountering.

Moving into the Future

Saklad: What advice would you give to voice and speech teachers at the beginning of their teaching careers?

Dal Vera: I think it's a smart idea to look at this as a life journey, that really this is only the beginning. I would encourage them to attend a graduate program specifically in the area of voice and speech pedagogy, then go out and get certified as a Lessac trainer, fully certified as a Linklater trainer, certified as a Fitzmaurice trainer, learn Alba Emoting and get certified to teach it, become an active member of advancing the field, join the Voice and Speech Trainers Association, and become a participant in shaping the future of the field. It's a profession, not a job. I would encourage them to embrace it with the passion of a profession.

Saklad: What voice and speech advice would you give to performance students on the brink of their professional careers?

Dal Vera: Regardless of where their careers take them, it's important they have a voice support team they can access. They need resources for training, care, and coaching. They need to know, for example, wherever they go who the best voice doctors are. It's a smart idea to discover who the savvy trainers and teachers are, too. They need access to the people who specialize in professional voice. I counsel them to make sure they have their support group, and I encourage them to maintain the discipline of their practice.

Saklad: Have you, over the course of your professional career, witnessed an evolution in how voice and speech is taught?

Dal Vera: Yes. Voice and speech training used to be highly prescriptive. There were ideals one matched and a notion of perfection one should shoot for. I perceive the training of voice and speech has moved away from this and continues to do so. In my conversations with trainers and coaches, I notice a more conscious intention to question our ideas and techniques and to challenge ourselves to rely less on tradition and more on evidence that something works. I think also there's a lot more genuine knowledge of the field that trainers and teachers are contributing today than in the past.

Saklad: What do you think the future holds for voice and speech training?

Dal Vera: Well, I think we're going to see a continual professionalization of the field. VASTA has had a huge hand in the professionalizing of what we do. There are lots of voice and speech organizations around the world, but I think few of them have had the enlightened dedication of the core group that founded VASTA.

Saklad: Rocco, what impact do you hope your work will have on vocal training at large?

Dal Vera: It feels disingenuous for me to say, "Well, I really don't think I'm going to have an effect on the field at large." But an intent to influence isn't what motivates me. When I wrote *Voice, Onstage and Off* with Robert Barton, *Acting in Musical Theatre* with Joe Deer; when I started the *Voice and Speech Review* and wrote three years of monthly articles for *Dramatics Magazine*; or when I make conference presentations or give workshops, those are all activities I hope will have an influence beyond the day I do them. But I don't really have lofty personal goals in this regard. I teach because I want to understand. I have written to share, but more to grasp the subject myself. I'm really just a teacher who takes pleasure in my students' progress. Class is the high point of my day. I think if I do a good job, there is a potential to change a person's life forever. Any profession pursued passionately can be meaningful. This one moves me. I think acting is one of those professions with a great potential for transcendence of the individual. Selfishly and candidly, I'm doing what I do because I'm in search of it for myself, and my students are phenomenal teachers.

Catherine Fitzmaurice

While Catherine Fitzmaurice was attending the Central School of Speech and Drama in London on a three-year full scholarship, she won the prestigious national competition the English Festival of Spoken Poetry, sponsored by Edith Sitwell and T. S. Eliot. In 1965 she returned to the Central School to teach voice, verse speaking, and prose reading. Today Catherine has taught all over the world and has held teaching and consulting appointments at Juilliard School's drama division, Yale School of Drama, New York University, Harvard University, the Moscow Art Theatre, the Stratford Shakespearean Festival, the Guthrie Theatre, Lincoln Center, and many others. Catherine has also presented her work internationally at major theatre and medical conferences.

Photo by Terry O'Connell

Background

Nancy Saklad: Catherine, you were a student of Barbara Bunch and Cicely Berry. How did their work affect your own?

Catherine Fitzmaurice: Their work completely inspired mine. I was a child when I started with Barbara, who directed the plays and taught acting and verse speaking at my high school, and not much more than a child when I studied with Cicely Berry at the Central School of Speech and Drama—I was just seventeen. And Cis was a student of Barbara Bunch's when she was a child, too, so we're very interconnected. I learned rib swing and abdominal support from both of them—they called it diaphragmatic support—and poetry reading. With Barbara it was all strictly text-based work, but she was very creative inside of that. And Cis primarily taught voice and verse speaking at Central, which is what I taught at Central a few years after graduating.

Saklad: So from poetry reading to work in some of the most notable theatres in the United States and internationally: the Goodman, Arena Stage, the Moscow Art Theatre, the Guthrie, and the list goes on. What impact has working with the actors and directors at these esteemed institutions had on your own work?

Fitzmaurice: Working with such people is tremendously demanding, in the best sense. The questions they ask are stunningly probing, and what they expect of you is nothing short of brilliant text analysis and focused attentiveness to the physical/vocal needs of the actors and to the project of the play as a whole. The generosity, specificity, and creativity of the directors I worked with was exciting, and all of them impacted my voice, speech, and text work. I did five Shakespeares with Des McAnuff, and several others with Mark Lamos, Frank Galati, and Joanne Akalaitis. These directors gave me an opportunity to contribute to the production. After he listed me on the title page of the programs—then an innovation for voice coaches—Des McAnuff at La Jolla Playhouse told me a wonderful story. His audiences used to say, "Oh, we understand your plays so much better" than those at the big theatre nearby, where Shakespeare was very formally spoken. "What translation do you use?" He indicated that the "translation" he used was my text coaching. In fact, I had changed not a single word of Shakespeare's text, only had helped the actors use conversational inflections, not the "musicality" of, say, Gielgud's readings. And when Mark Lamos introduced me to artistic director Emily Mann at the McCarter Theatre, he said, "This is my secret weapon." So I felt like I was able to contribute, especially in Shakespeare productions at these theatres, and at the Stratford Shakespeare Festival in Canada, and elsewhere. I encouraged the actors to listen actively to each other and to phrase for meaning, allowing the complex rhythms of thought to override formal verse structure. I do not believe in requiring actors to breathe at the end of every line when speaking Shakespeare, for instance. That disturbs thought/language processes, and makes the text more difficult to understand.

Saklad: You've also presented at medical conferences for voice professionals. What topics have you offered?

Fitzmaurice: Primarily, I've talked about my interest in breathing as foundational to vocal health. That has been my mission all along. I've presented at medical conferences in Australia, Chile, and Germany, and in America at the Voice Foundation in Philadelphia, where I've offered my observations on how the central nervous system and the autonomic nervous system have different functions in respiration when speaking and not speaking, and why it's important to understand the difference, and where the effort could most efficiently be focused when speaking. A lot of work on the medical side of voice—for rehabilitation, etc.—is centered on the larynx. But the larynx can make no sound at all without breath.

The Voice and Speech World of Today

Saklad: You are frequently described as a pioneer in the fields of voice and breath work. What features would you say distinguish your work in the field?

Fitzmaurice: I would say that one distinction is the depth of my interest in breath. Breathing is my passion, both intentional breathing in speaking and survival breathing while not speaking. Because of my students' perceived difficulties with breathing, I explored all kinds of somatic work and brought it into my voice classes in America in the early '70s, before anyone else was doing that. We explore the Tremorwork® I teach, and also yoga, which is now commonplace, but my adaptations for voice are different from straight yoga. I've also quite extensively explored energy work as it impacts breathing and vocalization. And I've adapted the breath support I was taught. Nowadays there is a surge of interest in breathing—some of it not so useful for voice—but many voice teachers still prefer to work with other aspects of speaking, because for most people the interesting thing about the voice is what you *do* with it, how you interpret the text, and how you place yourself in interaction with other actors and with audiences. But in order for any of that to happen optimally, the breath has to be free to be spontaneous and responsive to the moment while being healthily and skillfully managed. That's what I've primarily explored—free *and* focused breath work, for purposes of health, efficiency, and creative range, and how one can use the energy of breath as creative inspiration. As a result, I'm more interested in what the speaker is *doing* vocally than in how he or she *sounds*. While the sound has to be *loud* enough, and it has to be *clear*—intellectually, I mean—I do not aim for "good," "beautiful," or "correct" sound. There is no particular sound that is "right."

Saklad: What aspects of the work most inspire you?

Fitzmaurice: Well again, it is breath that inspires me—and the opportunity when the breath is free to allow brilliant, immediate, white-hot thinking to emerge—whether one is offering one's own feelings and ideas or is interpreting text. With such freedom, text can still be fresh and newly minted every time. Amazing, it's an amazing process, languaging—exciting. Language inspires me too.

Saklad: How would you describe the current state of affairs in American actor training in voice and speech?

Fitzmaurice: My concern is that too much voice training is about *sounding* right or good or interesting. But I think there's a growing sophistication in voice training, and as a result, this is beginning to shift. Voice training has come out of the shadows and become a respected field of study, the benefits of which have begun to be recognized in a wide variety of other fields.

Saklad: What are the greatest voice and speech obstacles that the student actor faces?

Fitzmaurice: We are all such a construct of our specific upbringing: our cultural environment, our parents, our peers, our life events. So much pressure is put on many of us to conform, to be like others, to be part of the main group. That conforming process can unconsciously continue in class. Our challenge as teachers is to ask the actor to think for himself and to become more truthful, to live and explore something deeper than those familiar cultural layers. I believe that's why many seek out actor training—as part of a process of self-discovery, and ultimately to understand and be understood by others, often beyond their original cultural milieu. Without an element of self-discovery, a student actor could experience voice and speech class as a negation of his or her identity rather than an opportunity for growth.

Saklad: Do you think voice and speech training plays a unique role in performance training?

Fitzmaurice: I think its role is unique in that it can be so personal and the growth it promotes so individual. A mutually respectful intimacy often occurs when you're working with somebody else's breath and body as it's opening itself up to an awareness of its own humanity. It's impossible to fake release and freedom—one of the primary goals of my Voicework. There are no skills to flaunt or hide behind, as one might be able to do in acting class. Voice work brings the student/actor face to face with him or herself.

Saklad: Where does vocal presence come from, and is it teachable?

Fitzmaurice: Presence very often correlates with one's breathing patterns, held or free. I do think presence is teachable, and I think it begins with a literal listening in to one's own autonomic nervous system. I don't think it's mystical at all. I want to make the idea of presence for an actor completely practical. As one explores one's own reflexive behavior in my Destructuring work, letting go of habits or chronic physical holds or controls, or the often ego-laden or identity-crusted personality, simple—and complex—*presence* is what is revealed. For everyone. When one is willing to live in that self-trusting center, other people feel you to be present. When one is struggling to be "right" and struggling to make up for insecurities and struggling to appear as other than what one experiences oneself as, one can't be present: One can't hear, one can't listen, one can't notice others, and one can't feel present to oneself or to others. One can't interact.

Practical Considerations

Saklad: Do you think students benefit from studying multiple approaches to the work?

Fitzmaurice: Yes. I think that exposure to multiple approaches is a good idea. In a way, my Voicework in itself *is* multiple approaches. As I suggested in my article "Breathing is Meaning," Fitzmaurice Voicework® is not a closed "system" but an agglomeration of techniques that I've drawn from a wide spectrum of fields. I looked everywhere to find things that would help my students, and adapted these to voice work. Many of my teachers have studied with other teachers. When my son Saul Kotzubei started to teach voice, I told him to go study with all of the great teachers, and he is doing that. And he has now developed his own voice as a teacher. I love working together with him and with many of my teachers, because our principle of inclusiveness allows them to bring their own specific skills and interests to a group. I bring mine, they bring theirs, and we collaborate. It's sometimes volatile, and it's mostly huge fun. It's different every time. Dudley Knight knows much more about speech than I do, for example, and I work together with singing and movement specialists too.

Saklad: Your work fully engages the body. What does the body need to produce optimal vocal work?

Fitzmaurice: Freedom and focus. The opposite happens to muscles when one doesn't allow oneself to breathe enough or when one is trying to limit one's activity in order to please other people. The muscles themselves get rigid, and when muscles get rigid they can't organically interact with one another. Because of the voice's dependence on breathing—which is what we do to survive, *and* what helps to inhibit our feelings and our behaviors when we hold or restrict or limit breath in certain ways—the voice is one of the first parts of us to show the stress of constraint. My Destructuring work offers a measure of freedom that helps to ease such constriction. That's the primary thing. Secondarily, in the Restructuring phase, my work teaches healthier habits of vocalizing and communicating with minimal but focused effort.

Saklad: Do you think an understanding of anatomy deepens a student's understanding of his or her voice?

Fitzmaurice: I do. It's not essential, but I think understanding how the bits work and how they contribute can be valuable. Anatomy gives one an objective understanding of what one may be experiencing internally, and acts as a reference point that can then be developed into a subjective experience.

Saklad: Do you find an imagistic understanding of the voice to be helpful?

Fitzmaurice: It can be helpful, though I think that *only* thinking of the voice imagistically is insufficient; you've also got to be able to honor the anatomy and physiology and be accurate in any instruction when that's helpful.

Saklad: Your work involves something called "tremoring." Would you speak a little about it?

Fitzmaurice: Tremoring is hard to speak about because it's like talking about what salt tastes like. You have to experience it. The fact is that every single body has experienced tremoring—though the idea of inducing it, and the idea that it is healing to the body, are new for most people. Tremoring happens spontaneously in the body when it is cold, because it warms the body. It happens in the body when it's fatigued, because it increases circulation and thereby brings nutrition to the muscles. It happens in the body when you're scared, because it offers flexibility and alertness. It keeps the body and mind open. It relaxes the brain, as in deep meditation. It is the opposite of "freezing," as in cramping or becoming petrified. It's a natural way of healing from trauma. So when you're not in crisis and you induce this tremor, you're giving yourself all the health-giving benefits that I've just mentioned, as well as others, including oxygenating every cell in the body. It's like charging yourself, like plugging yourself in to an outlet and giving yourself a dose of energy. It's a wonderfully freeing tool and a way of coming back to your own reflexes, your autonomic self, your authentic self. For some people it's also very important to experience how they can be charged and relaxed at the same time. There are many ways that one could tremor. The involuntary tremor that I use is induced by angling the joint of the knee or the joint of the elbow only. I'm not looking for a tremor created by muscle tension. Nor is it an intentional shaking. It's the way that the body begins to reflexively tremor when it's a little unclear about what you want it to do. That angle of uncertainty is the crevasse that one's need for control can slip into, and that can open up and offer one an experience of newness, chaos, freedom, creativity. This state is, I think, what a clown is looking for when he allows himself to become unbalanced, resulting in spontaneous movement and spontaneous thinking and speaking. It makes available the kind of reflexive responses that are gold—that people pay to see in movies. I think our Tremorwork® is a marvelous tool. Obviously. I advocate teaching it to everyone, not just actors. But it requires a sensitive, experienced teacher.

Saklad: What does it mean to you to support the voice, and is it true that Restructuring borrows from the *bel canto* school of singing?

Fitzmaurice: Breath support is essential to vocalization. There is no sound without airflow, and to articulate and phrase meaningfully, we need to sustain the exhalation, and often take the next inhalation before we actually need oxygen for survival. No one ever talked to me about *bel canto* when I was a student at Central, but I did hear that Elsie Fogerty had talked to Italian singing masters and had come back to London to offer some of their techniques to the world of theatre. She founded the Central School of Speech and Drama in 1906. Elsie Fogerty directly trained Gwyneth Thurburn, who directly trained Barbara Bunch, Cis Berry, me, and then Patsy Rodenburg. So *bel canto* was an integral part of the classic Central experience. The physical actions of using the external intercostals to widen the ribcage for the inhalation as a thought occurs, and then specifically the *transversus abdominis* muscle for the exhalation as one expresses that thought, are what I teach as Restructuring. It is an adaptation of the technique I was taught at Central, based on what I observed occurring naturally in a healthy body when one is speaking. It's not the same as simple survival breathing, nor does it involve abdominal pushing or "squeezing." And I do not teach "rib reserve." Restructuring is much more flowing and always involves the act of communication. I usually only teach Restructuring after I've worked with a student to open up the body with my Destructuring, using hands-on work, Tremorwork®, and release work similar to yoga or Feldenkrais. The isolation of the transverse for breath support, as opposed to the use of the whole abdomen together with the rectus and the obliques, is very specific, and very learnable, very doable, and way less effortful and much easier than people imagine. Some voice trainers say, "Oh no, no, you must never engage the abdominal area," but what I teach is not what they may assume I'm teaching—rib reserve. It's very different. Again, Restructuring is what a healthy body naturally does when speaking. But not all of us have healthy bodies. Most of us have habits that limit our vocal expressiveness, and practice is required to instill new habits that are functionally effective. Athletes, dancers, and musicians understand this learning process of training the body. Acquiring muscle memory for skill in speaking is no different.

Saklad: What role does listening play in voice and speech work?

Fitzmaurice: It plays a huge role. If one doesn't listen, there's no point in talking. It's crazy to talk without having listened, because how could one have an appropriate response? One wants to always respond to what's going on—a mixture of what's going on externally and what's going on internally. One needs to listen to sound values, rhythm, melody, inflection, emphasis, intention, humor, and even silence, to understand meaning and the whole complex reality of another human being. And one needs to be able to listen to one's own impulses. And then there might be value in what we choose to speak. It's very hard to learn to listen fully. I think it takes a lifetime. I'm still learning to listen.

Saklad: What is the relationship between the actor's emotional expressiveness and the breath work that you do?

Fitzmaurice: This relationship is absolutely prime. Free, spontaneous breathing, in subtle combination with breath management, together allow emotional expressiveness as well as clear expression of ideas. This is fundamental to what I teach. However, I do not push for emotion. Emotion is a byproduct of experiencing and relating. Pushing for emotion can create vocal problems.

Saklad: Do you devote time to teaching vocal characterization?

Fitzmaurice: Yes, I do. Again, all my character voice work depends on Restructuring—supporting the voice in a healthy way—so that one doesn't attempt to manipulate the voice solely from the larynx. Certainly in creating a character voice the pharynx is manipulated, but the sound doesn't come *from* that manipulation. The sound still has to come from the abdominal support and move *through* any manipulation, so it's like changing the shape of the instrument to create change in the sound, but not changing the way you play it. And I am interested in exploring how people find truthfulness even through that kind of work.

Saklad: How do you see scientific and/or technological advances within or without the field influencing your work or the work at large?

Fitzmaurice: I'm interested in understanding more of the neurology of breathing and speaking. One of the speech pathologists that has trained with me has been working with brain-damaged people, and other associates are also very interested in neurology. I hope these people will make a huge contribution in the future to our knowledge about what's going on when we use our voices. And other teachers I have trained are exploring relationships between technology and voice. Joan Melton has been involved in sonogram research into the use of the *transverse abdominis* with speaking and singing. I would welcome more scientific studies of our Tremorwork® and of Restructuring while we speak and sing. I believe they can be very useful in working with some voice disorders. It would be good to be able to evaluate how my work affects the brain as well as the body. However, my personal interest is in keeping the holistic concepts we work with in human and present artistic vocal expression alive, even while other more analytic minds probe, measure, and experiment.

Saklad: What belief do you hold most dear about voice and speech training?

Fitzmaurice: That it's applicable to anybody, not just actors. That it's a— it seems a little presumptuous to say—a spiritual path—but I do think it is a way to self-development that is useful for anybody in any field. Humankind depends on communication.

Moving Into the Future

Saklad: Have you witnessed much of an evolution in voice and speech training over the course of your career?

Fitzmaurice: Yes, I think it has changed enormously. I think there's a lot more information available, and many more people are interested in the field. Voice training for actors in America used to be confined to professional conservatories like Juilliard or Yale School of Drama. Now there's at least some kind of voice work offered in almost every theatre department, even if only for one semester. One of my associates, Rebekah Maggor, developed a program for teaching speaking skills to nonactor faculty and students throughout Harvard University. And the world at large is getting a little more interested in sound and voice and noise. VASTA is an organization that has been hugely responsible for spreading interest in voice training. And I'm hoping all of the different approaches—these so-called methodologies—will one day seem less isolated and less like separate disciplines. I think information needs to be explored and shared.

Saklad: What voice and speech advice would you give to performance students on the brink of their professional careers?

Fitzmaurice: Stay healthy! Make sure voice work isn't something you leave behind after you've finished your in-school training. You don't go to a gym during your student years and then say, "Oh good, now I'm fit for life; now I never have to exercise again," and the same thing is true of the voice. You have to continue to take care of it. You've got to keep hydrated. You've got to keep the breathing free and active. You've got to warm the voice up and warm it down. You've got to be conscious of it in the way you're conscious of diet or exercising or conscious of maintaining your relationships. It is a relationship. Remember, and take the time, to keep your relationship with your own voice healthy.

Saklad: Catherine, what impact do you hope your work will have on vocal training at large?

Fitzmaurice: I hope that the importance of organicity, of reflexivity, will spread into the analytic fields of vocal science, and into the lay world, and be thoroughly, healthfully maintained in the artistic world. I also hope that the specificity of breath support with the *transversus abdominis* is understood and used properly, because it is *bel canto*; it is "beautiful" in the sense of healthy, harmonious, effortless, and coordinated behavior that keeps the voice healthy into old age in all circumstances. It is not about beautiful sound—though that may be a result. I think these two aspects—reflexive freedom and accurate support—are essential. I'm certainly not claiming them. I didn't "invent" them. I didn't invent tremoring. I just collected a lot of information from many diverse fields that touched on these concepts—what I called *"Destructuring"* of limiting habits and *"Restructuring"* of organically healthy habits—and applied them to breathing and voice. Destructuring and Restructuring are a pair of concepts that I think go way beyond voice work for performance and can contribute significantly to vocal rehabilitation and self-expression in general, as well as to movement training of all kinds. I hope these concepts will be understood thoroughly, explored further, and become widely useful. Everybody breathes. Everybody speaks.

Jan Gist

Jan Gist is currently the voice, speech, and dialect coach for the Old Globe Theatre and professor at the University of San Diego Graduate Theatre Program. Previously she was head of voice and speech for the Alabama Shakespeare Festival for nine years and 140 productions. Her regional coaching includes La Jolla Playhouse, Oregon Shakespeare Festival, the Shakespeare Theatre Company (DC), Milwaukee Rep., Arena Stage, and others. Recently she gave workshops at Russia's Moscow Art Theatre and London's Central School of Speech and Drama. She has been published in *The Complete Vocal Workout*, *More Stage Dialects*, and VASTA Journals.

Photo by Alan Decker

Background

Nancy Saklad: What drew you to voice work, Jan?

Jan Gist: I tell the story that when I found out there was such a thing as voice work, I felt like it must feel if you're a tall person finding out there's such a thing as basketball. I felt it was the place I belonged. When I went into theatre, I studied with Jerry Blunt at Los Angeles City College. He had published *The Composite Art of Acting*, which has a lot of voice in it, and had also published dialect books. Then he made me the tutor of dialects in my third and final year there. So Jerry became my mentor, and I demonstrated dialects for him at conferences. I'm on the recording in his *More Stage Dialects* book. (I'm one of the two Yiddish voices.) Then I went to Carnegie Mellon for my BFA, where Edith Skinner taught. I didn't identify with Edith's work, but I learned there was such a thing as the

International Phonetic Alphabet (IPA). I had learned from Jerry that there was IPA, but Edith clarified it and introduced her "narrow transcription." I went to Wayne State's Hillberry Repertory Theatre for my MFA in acting, from 1974 to '76. When I graduated, I was looking for "what to do now," and it seemed like teaching voice was the thing. In 1992 I worked with Cicely Berry, who brought about fifty people from all around the world into what she called "Voice '92," held at the Royal Shakespeare Company in Stratford-upon-Avon. I saw this gathering of international theatre-voice specialists and realized I felt a kinship with people as far away as India, New Zealand, and Australia. There was a similarity of perception and sense of purpose. We are all facilitators of other people. We are listeners. We are lovers of story and culture and humanity and language. All those intersections were places where I could do what I wanted to do. And just as my career began, the Voice and Speech Trainers Association (VASTA) was also beginning. Mary Corrigan, Bonnie Raphael, Dorothy Mennen, Lucille Rubin, and Barbara Acker, all of those dear women who founded the organization, welcomed me into the field and told me if I was going to go into voice work, I'd need to know anatomy and verse and Shakespeare, and they told me where to start looking. So I kind of fell into it.

Saklad: Were there others that you consider your mentors?

Gist: First of all, Jerry Blunt is the main mentor—he and his wife Andy Blunt. (Betty Andrews was her writing name.) She was a television writer in the 1960s and a poet and a playwright. The two of them were sort of my theatre parents. They were absolutely informative to me personally, as well as professionally and artistically. Jerry taught me how to work in theatre. He used to love to invent phrases. He would say, "Go to work hard, early." And he loved coining things like, "Everything on stage should be definite, dynamic, economic, and meaningful." So everything had a kind of coinage of phrase, and he gave me his library of dialect interview tapes when he retired. Then Edith Skinner taught me. I didn't even know how much I was learning from her until I started teaching voice and speech. At the end of my very first class I looked at the blackboard I had been writing on and thought, "That's what Edith's board used to look like." Her approach was more linguistic than Jerry's, more specialized. Another early mentor was Bonnie Raphael. When I got my first coaching job of Shakespeare at the Utah Shakespearean Festival, I called Bonnie and asked, "What do I do?" And Bonnie told me to look up every word, scan every line. "Start there." So that's what I did. Susan Sweeney has also influenced me. I met her when she was vocal coaching at a summer theatre in Milwaukee and I was performing Emily in *Our Town* and Hermia in *A Midsummer Night's Dream.* Susan showed me the journey of thought through Shakespeare's language, sentence structure; how to move through the ideas to move the argument and debate forward; phrasing, emphasis, pitch to lift the words—that sort of thing. That was in 1983.

The Voice and Speech World of Today

Saklad: What features would you say distinguish your work in the field?

Gist: I start with a sense of purpose and the question, "What is the purpose of the work we're walking into?" If I have been given an assignment for a class, I ask, "What is the purpose of this particular class for these specific students?" When I'm coaching a show I now ask, "What is this playwright's purpose in writing a play? What is the purpose of speaking for these characters?" Pinter's characters speak for a different reason than Shaw's characters speak. Then, I suppose influenced by Jerry, I also invent mottos for myself. One that's been long lasting is, "I want to be of service and have fun." So how can I be of service? I often will sit in a vocal coaching session and I look at that actor and think that I have no idea how to help, or even if he or she wants any help. So I sit back, I give them room, and I think to myself, "How can I be of service and have fun?" Then I listen more carefully to them and ask questions like, "how can I support you?" Once the actors see that my goal is to be of service to them, they can relax, drop their defenses, trust me, and we can get down to deeper, more courageous work.

Saklad: You have worked in such an extensive range of prominent theatres. Would you define your role as professional vocal coach?

Gist: I think of myself as the facilitator between the script, the director, the actor, the audience, and the space of the theatre. I try to bring all of those elements together—like what Arthur Lessac said at the 2009 VASTA conference, "there's communion"—so everyone's life is enhanced through this experience.

Saklad: Are there universal elements in voice and speech work that allow you to traverse the boundaries between graduate actor training, professional coaching, and other professional work?

Gist: No matter where I work, there in front of me is a human being. The voice is the same basic anatomy, and there's a soul and an intellect of some kind. We are looking for a relationship of trust. I try to be sensitive to each person's capabilities and possibilities. I often tell them my job is to congratulate them on what they already are doing well, then to see how far I can encourage them to go further. Over the years of working with accents, my strategy was to find real-life human beings who lived through similar circumstances of the story of the play. Then I would interview them for the sound of their accent. But if they were willing, I would ask them to speak of their lives. Usually when human beings feel witnessed with patience and compassion, it is such a rare and delicious event that they respond by opening up to reveal themselves. When I worked at Alabama Shakespeare Festival in the 1990s, we did a lot of plays that took place in many different parts of the American South. I interviewed family members who descended from slave owners, and other members of neighboring families who descended from slaves. Not only did I record the way they spoke, but I asked them to open up with their life experiences and family stories. Then I could take back to the actors the culture and history of these real people, so there was depth to the rehearsal process. So, talk about "invitation," here's an example of my inviting the dialect interviewees to speak from their depths, and their responding invitation to me to enlarge my appreciation of them and bring that into the theatre. All of this is very human and requires tremendous trust. These issues of humanity and trust enter into our work with everyone: interviewees, students, and professional actors.

Saklad: How would you describe the current state of affairs of actor training in voice and speech?

Gist: My understanding of actor training before universities took over was that if you wanted to be an actor, you went to a theatre company and found a willing mentor who would personally work you into that company or that kind of theatre. There was a personal, individual responsibility to develop the next generation one person at a time. When training shifted to universities, some things got mixed up. One example is that in order to have grades and semesters and class hours and credits, skills had to be separated from one another. So we had to have a separate voice class, a movement class, an acting class, and a styles class. Each of which is great, but students get the impression that there is such a thing as acting without voice skill or movement skill. In truth, all of those disciplines must work together. Really they are all one thing. In theatre, there is no such thing as acting without voice or voice without acting. So I've had to learn how to take a nontheatre structure like the university system, and translate it and integrate it to make it work for theatre training for professional employment. Within the university system it is possible to train those skills to work together, and you can train them very well, but only if you recognize that you have to consciously design the fit of theatre into the university schedules and structures. Nowadays there are more jobs for teachers than performers, so there is more theatre going on at universities than in professional theatres. The good side of putting theatre in a university is that there is a community of great intelligence, so students and productions can deepen their understanding of language, history, culture, etc. So I think internships at professional theatres are very important. Young actors need to get onstage with experienced actors. This way we are helping student actors become professionally employable, and helping theatres have more skilled actors.

Saklad: What unique role does voice and speech training play in performance training?

Gist: It teaches actors how to work. A lot of acting in America has moved into internalized psychological space rather than the physical space and time of the theatrical event. That's why Anne Bogart's Viewpoints and Laban movement work have been so helpful, because there's been a diminishing of the idea that a rehearsal is about physically and vocally filling space and time. So since acting has gotten more and more internalized, movement and voice have taken over to say, "How about expressing something so an audience can get it?" It's not about the actor feeling it; it's about the audience feeling it. Voice training is really acting training while you're talking.

Saklad: Some of the obvious benefits of voice and speech are an evolved instrument and an improved use of it. What are the indirect benefits?

Gist: Self-awareness, better communication, improved health, patience, a work ethic, an efficiency of work, a love of language... Good voice work is an awakening of your humanity through your voice.

Saklad: Where does vocal presence come from, and is it teachable?

Gist: Yes, I teach exercises about vocal presence. At an NEH conference I even taught English professors how to stand onstage and have presence—physical/vocal—because I don't think there's such a thing as vocal presence without physical presence.

Practical Considerations

Saklad: Do you think that performance students should study multiple approaches to the work?

Gist: I do. Every master teacher has brilliant gifts, uniquely magical. Let's put it all together; let's draw from all of them.

Saklad: What does the body need to produce optimal vocal work?

Gist: I have certain things I do that include release and alignment and efficiency of effort—release the jaw, release the tongue. When I'm coaching individuals, I look for those releases, but we must pay attention to individual processes. There are some people who are not released but have fine voices even within their tensions. Each actor must be viewed as a distinct individual, not as proof that our beliefs about voices are right. And to truly produce optimal voice work, the speaker must be aware of the theatre acoustics and, as Jerry Blunt coined it, "fill the space with ease."

Saklad: What types of body work do you use?

Gist: I draw from everything: Alexander technique, martial arts, dance, physical therapy, yoga, walking and talking, sports analogies—anything that will connect to anybody. And I turn those things into exercises in the class. I believe in hands-on—you know, my hands on people's ribs and bellies—and I have my students partner with each other, hands-on, to feel the anatomy working.

Saklad: Does an understanding of anatomy deepen the student's relationship to his or her voice?

Gist: Very much so. They need a scientific and a metaphorical understanding of anatomy. Anatomy needs to be poetic because it needs to fuel their imagination and their personal ownership of their body. It must not be only a science that separates the body from the head. For actors, the study of anatomy must engage the imagination and sensual awareness.

Saklad: How do you address breath work?

Gist: I draw from everything. We lie on the floor. We move through the room. We partner holding each other's ribs and bellies. We speak memorized text and we speak spontaneously. We do the ballet bar exercise. It's one of many to enlarge inhalation, expand duration of exhalation, enhance tone placement, and increase pitch range. (You can get this in Janet Rogers's workbook: *The Complete Voice and Speech Workout.*)

Saklad: What does it mean to support the voice?

Gist: Supported breath means you have enough breath to speak the thought clearly with rich resonation that fills the house easily. Breath is the fuel that the voice runs on. Inspiration means both getting the idea and getting the inhale. Both are a simultaneous, at-once impulse. With memorized text, the speaker needs to have the idea occur. Something triggers the idea to speak, and that trigger also causes the inhale, which naturally brings in enough air to fuel the whole length of the idea to the end of the sentence. Or there is the intention to speak to the end, and if the sentence is long, a catch-breath comes in, in between phrases, to support to the very end. The inhale turns into speaking with tone placement to carry that thought, to convert the listener to the speaker's intention. The actor is supporting the vocal instrument and at the same time fueling the character's need to win the argument. As the trigger changes and the idea changes from line to line or beat to beat, the breath automatically changes. And by automatically, I mean that in rehearsals, the actor explores how the breath becomes the character's natural and efficient thought process. And all this happens because the muscles have been trained to respond to the need. Abdominals, intercostals, all the muscles from the floor of the pelvis through the torso are coordinated within a released and spacious physical alignment.

Saklad: How would you describe the role of listening in voice and speech work?

Gist: When you are speaking, you want your voice to not only go to the front of your listeners. You're not speaking to the surface of their face. Your voice is breaking past the obstacle of their contrary debate, past their face bones and into their brains, past their rib bones and into their heart. Likewise, when you are listening, you are not listening at the outer level of your skin and ears. You the listener are taking in what that speaker is saying into the organs of your brain and guts, into the spirit and organ of your heart. (I draw from body/mind centering work here.) From your deep internals you are feel-hearing, which causes deep responses that then trigger you to speak with internal, personalized connection and passion. Also, in complex text you have to hear the specific words that make you know that you are winning or losing your intention toward that speaker.

Saklad: Do you teach the International Phonetic Alphabet (IPA)?

Gist: Yes, I teach Edith Skinner's version. IPA is an important aid for precise articulation. It helps people understand the specific job of the articulators in forming each vowel and consonant sound, and it makes listening more precise when you're hearing other people speak, finding the pronunciation of words and discerning and learning accents.

Saklad: Do you teach Standard Speech?

Gist: I teach an evolved, more current version of Edith Skinner's standard. She called it "Good Speech for American Actors in Classic Plays." I teach a comparison of old Standard American (based on Northeastern **American Received Pronunciation** of about the early 1900s to about 1940s) to General American (or Western Standard) compared to varieties of Standard English, of many eras, styles, and classes. I talk about the history of how Standard American and Standard British have evolved. Then I say, "Here's the standard I learned. Here's what I am hearing the standard transformed into," and then we work on a range of standards. So, you could have a liquid /u/ and not an "ask" list. You could have a blown /hw/ and not a liquid /u/ or vice versa. You could have varying degrees of rounding of the vowels in "all honest fathers." You could have varying degrees of "r-color." So there are options; there are ingredients. It's important to teach that there are reasons to choose different options for different styles of production, for different characters, and even for different moments within one character's storyline. The study of Standard American Speech offers skills to hear and speak a wide range of distinctions.

Saklad: How would you describe the relationship between emotion and voice and speech work?

Gist: Emotion needs to serve the play. It is an actor's job to be emotionally connected and open and available and honest. Emotion is certainly part of the toolbox. I find many times actors put too much value on their own personal emotion and no one can tell what they're saying. That's not of service to the play. There needs to be the question of purpose—you know, what is the purpose of the moment? Technique and feeling need to go hand in hand; one does not work without the other and both must always serve the play and serve the audience's reception of the play.

Moving Into the Future

Saklad: What advice would you give to voice and speech teachers at the beginning of their professional careers?

Gist: You need to know the actor's process personally if you're going to work with actors. You need to study everything the voice might possibly do so that you're well rounded. Go to a lot of theatre. Expose yourself to what voices have done in the past by reading theatre history and reviews of plays from earlier times and by watching old movies, especially movies that show great actors who were trained for the stage. Listen to recordings of actors from the 1920s and onward. Then compare all that to what they're doing now on stage and screen. Learn about vocal health. Have a good voice. I think you should not be a voice teacher unless you yourself have a good voice and good, clear articulation, because I don't think you should be teaching what you can't do. Excel at every skill you teach. Inspire as a good example and model of authenticity and believability.

Saklad: What advice would you give to students on the brink of their careers?

Gist: Learn how to tolerate not knowing. It's a muscle to develop. Learn what you care about so that you are studying what you care about. You need to know what you care about. Go to work hard early. Learn how you learn. Learn how to work. Translate what you're told into something you can do. Read. Speak out loud. Read out loud. Cultivate a sense of humor. Cultivate your wellness. You need to know how to be well—physically, vocally, spiritually, emotionally. You need to become more and more well. Do not put your sickness on others. Be kind to yourself and to everyone around you. Be generous. Be responsible. Learn how to schedule work. Select your teachers. Teachers are going to teach differently, so find teachers that you want to learn from. And keep learning. You never stop learning. Your education is going to be the beginning of your learning career.

Saklad: What do you think the future holds for voice and speech training?

Gist: Well, I fear that we're becoming more splintered into disciples of particular gurus, but I hope we are joining together and that the master teachers are forming a conversation together. So I have a fear and I have a hope. I don't want us to be splintered into combating religions, and I don't want voice teachers to limit themselves. So I hope that we are all learning from each other as voice and speech teachers. That's one of the reasons I'm in VASTA, to continue to learn and teach each other as voice teachers. And I hope that we keep helping people become more literate, more able to embody all sorts of language and speak it with imagination and commitment for an audience to receive it deeply.

Saklad: What impact do you hope your work will have on vocal training at large, Jan?

Gist: I hope I can influence people to come together for the conversation of what voice is, what training is, so that I encourage people not to separate into different religions of voice. I hope I encourage the conversation between us all. Personally, I just hope I'm making my contribution of what I was built to be, so I keep looking for what is the purpose of my life, and that includes speaking and helping other people have a voice, have their voice, have the voice of the play. I hope I can help theatre be better. I think there's a lot of crap. And I'm sad and tired of plays that are bad for people, bad for actors, and bad for audiences. I would like to help intelligence: intellectual intelligence and emotional intelligence and spiritual intelligence, through theatre and voice.

Andrea Haring

A director, actress, and vocal coach, Andrea Haring is the associate director of the Linklater Center for Voice and Language, and the coordinator for Linklater Voice Teacher Training. She is currently on faculty at Columbia Graduate Theatre School, Circle in the Square Theatre School, and Fordham University. She was a founding member of Shakespeare and Company in Lenox, Massachusetts. She has taught at various theatre schools and companies in Spain, Italy, Germany, Iceland, and England. Andrea coaches extensively on and off Broadway and is a member of Labyrinth Theatre Company.

Photo by Alexis Savino

Background

Nancy Saklad: What drew you to voice and speech work, Andrea?

Andrea Haring: Well I began learning the Linklater progression as a singer and theatre student at Smith College where Pat Mullen, an early Linklater teacher, was instructing. Kristin Linklater was head of voice at NYU University Theatre Department at that time. She suggested her friend Tina Packer as a director for a Smith College production I was in of *The Learned Ladies*. During the rehearsal process, Kristin joined us to teach a workshop. It was around that time she and Tina decided to start Shakespeare and Company at Edith Wharton's house in Lenox, Massachusetts. The company was formed by some members of *The Learned Ladies* cast, a number of NYU grads and equity actors who had worked with Kristin and Tina in earlier Shakespeare projects. We all moved to the Berkshires and trained as a company with Kristin for three hours every morning, rehearsed our shows with Tina in the afternoon, and performed at night. All the work was geared towards bringing Shakespeare's language alive. So that experience just got in my bones. So often voice work for outdoor theatre becomes about how loud you are and about making the sound carry to the back row, but Kristin's exercises were as much about awakening the whole person as exercising our voices and bodies. In order to fully meet the demands of Shakespeare's text, we started by opening and deepening the release of breath, connecting the sigh of relief on vibrations of sound to a truth in ourselves and our character's emotions and thoughts, and undoing our habitual tensions in the jaw and tongue. Then we focused on awakening the full three- to four-octave range of our speaking voice so the range of the character's thoughts and feelings could make use of the range of our voices. The last thing we did was to wake up our articulation to encourage clarity and purpose of thought and action on stage. Kristin's vocal progression freed and strengthened us vocally. Her sound and movement exercises explored the roots of language—how language evolved from primitive humans to heightened poetic text. The precision of her text work trained us in the essential elements and structures of language that are the backbone to bringing the richness of Shakespeare's imagery and passion to life, such as onomatopoeia, alliteration, antithesis, and rhetorical devices where one builds or shifts thoughts to prove a point. The creativity, rigor, and fun of this work drew me to want to train to teach it.

Saklad: Besides Kristin, were there other mentors?

Haring: Certainly Tina Packer was an important mentor for me. Her text exercise called "dropping in" allows the actor to explore the words of a play in a vertical sense by dropping the words of a play in one by one; by muttering and tasting each word, while a partner murmurs questions to evoke the actor's imagination and the complexity of associations those words might have for him or her. This process gives actors the chance to arrest the drive for linear meaning, so they can explore the subliminal meaning of the text first. In this way the imagination awakens its ability to connect with the words before an action is pursued. I also had the privilege of teaching at the New Actors Workshop for many years with the great acting teacher George Morrison. George had trained in his early years with both Lee Strasberg and Sanford Meisner. His approach to acting made use of both of those acting philosophies, as well as his own connection to Stanislavsky that he brought to his work. His process helped the actor find authenticity and a spontaneous action and reaction to a moment. It also helped to bring the mental, emotional, psychological, and sensory humanity of the actor into the story of the character. Another person who influenced me was Richard Armstrong. Richard is a terrific Roy Hart singing teacher. The Roy Hart technique encourages singers to explore the farthest reaches of their range. The technique holds the belief that all the facets of one's psyche should be expressed—not just the lovely tones. Then there's Erika Berland who is a Body-Mind Centering teacher. This technique, developed by Bonnie Bainbridge Cohen, addresses how to move and be influenced by the different systems of the body—bones, muscles, organs, fluids etc., and help the systems to interrelate and support each other. This work is a great way to awaken different states of being and movement/voice qualities.

The Voice and Speech World of Today

Saklad: How would you describe the current state of affairs of American actor training in voice and speech?

Haring: I think we are at a very exciting place. There seems to be more dialogue between practitioners of different techniques than in years past. This encourages a broader, less dogmatic point of view on how voice and speech can support the actor. I'm especially interested in the give and take between various movement, voice, and acting techniques. It feels as though there is a greater willingness between teachers to exchange information.

Saklad: What features would you say distinguish your work in the field?

Haring: Ideally my work is an equal exchange between organic connection—imagination, sensation, association, and emotion—and technical exercises. I try to give actors ways to be aware of their tensions and ways to open and free the communication between their mind, body, voice, and feelings. For me this also has to be about the actor contacting his or her inner truth, finding a desire to communicate, and getting energy moving through the body and mouth. I use a range of imagery to wake up the imagination and mind with a physical and vocal progression—to connect all four together with a series of games and improvisatory work to find a sensual, playful experience of language that is linked to the actor's intentions or actions. There's a wealth of neurological information available now so we know that the nervous systems—which relay feelings, sensations, emotions, and associations—are enlivened by images. Images are the building blocks of language. Many of the nerve endings that connect to sensation and feeling are in that area between the diaphragm travelling through the organs down to the pelvic floor. The lower half of the body sends an amazing amount of information up to the language/speech cortex of the brain. So what I'm trying to do is to get actors' intelligence out of their heads and into their organic, feeling brains in their middle.

Saklad: What unique role do you think voice and speech work has in performance training?

Haring: Voice and speech work is crucial in acting training, especially for live theatre. So much of the nuance of the actor's inner world is conveyed through the free human voice. Conversely, a voice trapped in habits of tension will suppress that nuance instead of expressing it. A good vocal and physical warm-up helps the actors bring themselves to a state of readiness. Voice and speech work extends beyond the actor being heard or understood—although that is certainly useful. Its purpose is to develop voices that are emotionally expressive and alive to the depth of feeling the play demands, and also energized and flexible enough to follow the complex thoughts and actions of the play. Voice and speech work limbers up the speaker's ability to be alive to heightened language. It develops skills that are very necessary for Shakespeare and classical text.

Saklad: Where does vocal presence come from?

Haring: Well I suppose it begins with the human spirit and the authentic sense of one's self. It is not necessarily about beautiful sound. I had the great pleasure of vocal coaching several plays that the great actor George C. Scott acted and directed towards the end of his life. His voice at that point was pretty ragged from a lifetime of "active" living, but I have to say he had one of the most expressive voices I have heard. His vocal presence was undeniable because his voice was so aligned with his thoughts and feelings in the moment, and his purpose. His voice had incredible nuance and inflection, because it could travel wherever his thoughts and acting intentions went.

Saklad: Do you think students should study multiple approaches to the work?

Haring: You know, this is a matter of timing. I really enjoy taking classes in other techniques now. The thing that worries me is that if young actors get a "smorgasbord" approach to training they may not get trained with enough specificity and depth to experience a shift. I had heard it takes three years to organically shift a voice so that the new good habits are organically there. So the question for the young actor is: will that voice and body "shift" if it is training in constantly changing techniques? For right now, I'm of the philosophy that actors should stay with one technique until they know it well. Then, when that training is really assimilated, branch out and do other disciplines. It is good to discover other approaches and learn from them.

Saklad: What does the body need to produce optimal vocal work?

Haring: I enjoy several techniques: Alexander technique, first and foremost; then Feldenkrais work; and Body-Mind Centering work, which is wonderful to develop sensitivity. But I was also trained in the work of the great British movement teacher Trish Arnold, which you can learn about on the website www.teawithtrish.com. I love her progression of work with swings—arm swings, leg swings, and full-body swings. She taught at Shakespeare and Company, and Merry Conway teaches it periodically now in New York City in private classes and sometimes at The Linklater Center for Voice. Swings charge the battery of the body. We swing our arms when we walk; so often we feel looser after walking two miles than we did before we started. Swings encourage a release of energy through the whole body.

Saklad: Do you think an understanding of anatomy deepens a student's understanding of his or her voice?

Haring: I do, but I'm concerned that a clinical approach to anatomy with a lot of pictures can be introduced too soon. I like to have my students play with their imaginations and the sensations in their bodies first to see what responses they evoke through a kind of experiential anatomy, and then bring in my anatomy charts later. If I bring the charts in too soon, my students might feel restricted by the actual pictures, and their imaginations could get squashed. Anatomy work is very useful once the students have really investigated the imagistic work. Their ability is developed to translate the image on the page into an internal sensation, such as seeing the shape of the jawbone and then being able to feel the weight and shape in space of that thicker back part.

Practical Considerations

Saklad: Would you talk about breath work and what it means to support the voice?

Haring: There are many different points of view about this. I suppose it depends on what I'm doing. If I were singing opera, I might need to use my breath differently than when speaking. With the work I do, I loosen and stimulate the breath mechanisms. The exercises I do are for waking up the interaction of the nervous system to the involuntary responses of breath to impulses of thought and feeling. When I was a singer many years ago I had a teacher who encouraged me to do a lot of sit-ups and abdominal strengthening for support. I found myself getting very tight in my tongue and larynx. Recently there have been some interesting articles from sports clinics around the world stating that the traditional approach to "core support" by tightening the outer abdominal walls does not actually give support. In fact it is detrimental to finding release through the body. It has been proven scientifically that the outer conscious musculature is not able to respond as immediately or efficiently as the proprioceptive muscles near the nerves. Therefore, any breath work that brings effort will be less effective, and the larynx, tongue, and jaw are much more likely to get involved. I prefer to focus on the freedom of the diaphragm to respond to the demands of larger and larger thought and emotional impulses, and to help accommodate that, to stretch the intercostal muscles as well as the musculature down through to the pelvic floor. In the Linklater work, we have a series of exercises to increase breath capacity. Then we work on panting and sighing on arpeggios to increase the voice's ability to respond to greater demands. For me, breath support comes from a connection between what I'm talking about and *why* I'm saying it. This involves intention, action, the desire to communicate; as well as the breath, the body, and the voice being responsive to that. The acting impulse will find what it needs from the body and voice if they are alive and energized.

Saklad: How do you approach tonality and vocal qualities?

Haring: I like to think of pitch as a frequency of thought/feeling/sound energy. After loosening the breath and sighing with relief on vibrations, we will vocalize on pitches to encourage clarity in the connection of the vocal folds. Often people who speak with an excess of breath or with too much pressure in the throat and back of the tongue can find a vocal clarity and ease on different pitches. I begin in an easy midrange and then travel down and up on various pitches with open sounds and hums. We want to bring the feeling of release to the whole range so we can be comfortable not only in one part of our range but in the entire range. We will add physical release work such as dropping down and undulating the spine, releasing the lower back and hip sockets, and rolling the neck to stay free as the voice gets more exercise. Then the Linklater progression activates the resonating ladder—chest, mouth, teeth, sinus, nasal, upper sinus, and skull—to activate access to the whole three- to four-octave range of speaking voice. We will sigh through octaves on arpeggios while releasing the body through arm swings, leg swings, or lower back stretches. Also, with her sound and movement exercises that connect sounds to all kinds of images, Kristin has developed her own vowel-ladder exercise that taps into the resonating frequencies of the vowels and connects them in the body. Much of the improvisational play that we teach connects to images and sensory information that is designed to express a variety of vocal qualities.

Saklad: How would you describe the role of listening in voice and speech work?

Haring: As an actor, if I can imagine that my listening antennae live in my breath center somewhere in the middle of my body, between my diaphragm and my pelvic floor, then I can breathe in what someone is saying to me and receive it all the way down to that deep, experiential-processing center in my organs and the nervous systems of my lower body. Neurologists, such as Antonio Damsio, author of *The Feeling of*

What Happens, and Michael Gershon, author of *The Second Brain*, have written about the amazing ability of our "gut center" to receive, process, and transmit all kinds of messages to our brain and the rest of our body. Ideally then, what I've heard has the ability to evoke a response that could affect and change me in some way. Listening is about receptivity and allowing an exchange between my inner experience and the world outside me that informs what I need to say and do in that moment. So for the students doing exercises in dialogue with a teacher or a piano, it might be useful for them to ask themselves, "Can I let that sound enter into me and evoke a thought or feeling?" "Am I willing to be activated and engaged?" Listening is about being present. As a teacher I also try to listen with my body/mind awareness so I can channel it through my own physical awareness to get a kinesthetic sense of what my students are experiencing.

Saklad: Do you teach the IPA?

Haring: Yes, I have been working with Louis Colaianni. I have had a great time learning to teach his IPA pillow work. The pillows are a playful, kinesthetic way to learn IPA. I appreciate how his work does not prescribe a certain way to speak, but gives actors the skills to recognize different sounds, know their own personal pronunciation patterns, and make choices as to how they want to speak for a particular situation, whether it is with a dialect or accent, or to adapt to the formality or informality of a moment. When you wake up your ability to shift gears in your speech, you wake up your mind.

Saklad: How do you help your students connect to imagery and the text?

Haring: When actors are connecting to imagery, the first thing I like to do is to engage their imagination. The ability to use one's imagination is like exercising a muscle; it needs to be done regularly for it to work. Techniques that encourage daydreaming and bring in sensory and associative information are useful. (In the back of the revised version of *Freeing the Natural Voice*, Kristin Linklater suggests approaches to text that engage the actor on a more subliminal level.) After picturing the images, I do exercises to physically express the images in order to embody them. The Michael Chekhov technique is great for this as well. The Linklater sound and movement work is designed to help the actor discover the primitive impulses from which language was born, and evolve those impulses into language structures that we use today, such as alliteration, assonance, sound symbolism (where certain sounds are linked to particular actions), and onomatopoeia. Louis Colaianni talks about this in *Bringing Speech to Life*, and other good related reads are *The Language Instinct* by Steven Pinker and *The Mother Tongue* by Bill Bryson.

Saklad: How would you describe the relation between emotion and voice work?

Haring: Intrinsic, but there must be equal measures of emotion and action. If the actor is completely purpose oriented when speaking, he or she runs the risk of only engaging the head, and the work will be rather dry and heartless. The humanity won't be there. Conversely, if the actor speaks with emotion but without purpose, he or she is likely to be quite self-indulgent. Our voices should express the breadth and depth of our emotions, but also the clarity and intentions of our thoughts.

Saklad: How do you approach the teaching of range?

Haring: The second half of the Linklater progression deals primarily with opening vocal range and restoring the breath power necessary to support it. We go through the resonating ladder, which awakens the three to four octaves of speaking range. The different parts of the range help each other. The chest or lower resonances keep the actor grounded, open, and relaxed; the midrange can be very useful for speaking directly and with authority; and the upper range can often find an openness, a transparency, as well as extroverting the lower resonances. So to blend them and strengthen them, we sigh through arpeggios while going through a physical system of release: loosening hip sockets, rolling the pelvis, undulating the spine, and swings to keep the body free while the upper range is activated. Kristin Linklater's vowel-ladder (found in *Freeing Shakespeare's Voice*) encourages the different vowels to find their own place of resonance and to live in various parts of the body. The low vowels live in the bottom parts of the body, and midvowels live in the middle, and upper vowels travel up through the face and to the top of the head. This may seem arbitrary but it's not. You can hear the pitch difference between /o/, /ah/, and /ee/ when you whisper them, keeping the tongue relaxed.

Moving into the Future

Saklad: What advice would you give to voice and speech teachers at the beginning of their careers?

Haring: Keep taking classes. I've been teaching since 1981, and I always seek out new techniques, workshops, classes, and different teachers with whom to work. Take acting classes. Our job is to support the actors and directors and the creative work that's happening in rehearsal and onstage. The more we exercise the application of the work with ourselves, the more insight we will bring to our teaching.

Saklad: Andrea, what impact do you hope your work will have on vocal training at large?

Haring: Since 1990 I've been involved in supporting Kristin Linklater in the Linklater teacher training of over 100 teacher trainees around the world who have become, or are in the process of becoming, designated Linklater teachers. I am currently the associate director of the Linklater Center for Voice. I would hope that the teacher training work I do helps to create voice teachers who are compassionate, inventive, playful, clear, purposeful, and rigorous in their use of the Linklater progression. The designation process takes about three to four years and is very detailed. My job is to give actors tools to find their authentic self that communicates freely and with ease, with a wide range of expressive choices at hand. I would hope also that my work is joyful and pleasurable, while simultaneously tapping into deeper, richer parts of the human expression. I want the profound and playful to coexist, and more than a "lovely sound," I want to hear the human being behind the voice.

Nancy Houfek

Nancy Houfek, head of voice and speech, American Repertory Theatre/ Institute for Advanced Theatre Training at Harvard University, teaches voice, speech, dialects, and text to the MFA acting candidates; coaches the actors of the professional theatre company; and administers the MFA in voice-training pedagogy. With a BA from Stanford University, Nancy received her MFA from the American Conservatory Theatre. She has coached hundreds of productions at ART, the Guthrie Theater, and ACT, among others; acted and directed in regional theatres nationwide; and consulted to professional speakers throughout the United States since 1978. Nancy is a master teacher of Fitzmaurice Voicework®.

Photo by Kati Mitchell

Background

Nancy Saklad: What drew you to voice work initially, Nancy?

Nancy Houfek: I was an acting student at the American Conservatory Theater in San Francisco in the mid '70s. Catherine Fitzmaurice was my voice teacher. I also had an extraordinary scope of training in other aspects of voice and speech during that time. I studied with Edith Skinner, Tim Monich, Deb Sussell, Bill Ball, and David Hammond. After I completed my acting training, I moved to Seattle. I performed in roughly five shows a year for the three years that I was there. I also taught one voice class after another, culminating in teaching dialects for the University of Washington Professional Actor Training Program. It was a natural progression. For twenty years my performing career and my teaching career paralleled each other. Only when I came here to the ART in 1997 did I decide to let go of acting and focus simply on teaching. And it's been great.

Saklad: You've talked a little bit about some of your mentors. How have they influenced your work?

Houfek: Well Catherine is the major influence. I've been teaching her Destructuring/Restructuring breath and voice work since 1978. So that's a very clear through-line. A wonderful movement teacher named Peggy Hackney was also really influential. When I was living in Seattle, I took Peggy's classes in Laban Movement Analysis and Bartenieff Movement Fundamentals. This work made me reexamine how the body is organized. By experiencing the psoas as the center of the body around which axes of movement occur, a dancer learns to bring spine and limbs into an integrated whole. At the time I was thinking: "How does this experience interface with what I already know about breathing and voice?" Working with Peggy really deepened my understanding of how the body functions and is now a basis for my teaching of physical awareness in relation to vocal production. Another influential movement person was Bonita Bradley at ACT. She expanded my understanding of breath in yoga practice, as well as how best to work with the basic yoga positions that are fundamental to the Fitzmaurice Voicework® tremors. I also was privileged to study with Frank Ottiwell, who was one of the great Alexander teachers; and Bill Ball, who founded the American Conservatory Theatre. There was Edith Skinner, of course—a woman of absolute rigorous detail; and David Hammond—text analysis and Shakespeare; and Colleen Carpenter-Simmons, a singing teacher whom I studied with in Seattle. She really clarified vocal support for me. Currently, I would say Scott Zigler, director of the ART Institute, has had a huge influence on my work. He teaches a discipline called Practical Aesthetics, which is a combination of Meisner technique and action-based acting theory. The work we do in voice class goes hand in glove with what he's teaching; voice is the expression of action, moving outward and, as it lands, affects change in the scene partner. I must also mention Marcus Stern, associate director of the institute, who is our other acting teacher. He has a wonderful way of talking about actor-to-actor work. I use his vocabulary all the time.

The Voice and Speech World of Today

Saklad: You head up the vocal pedagogy program for the MFA students at Harvard ART. What makes your program unique?

Houfek: What's really great about our program is the amazing array of artists our students get to work with; plus they get to travel to Moscow to teach and study. We take one student a year. During the first year of training, the voice student takes both the first- and second-year voice curriculum of the MFA acting program: voice, speech, text, and dialects. The focus is on learning the content. The second-year voice student repeats the first- and second-year voice curriculum, experiencing it in a different way the second time, focusing on learning and practicing new pedagogical tools. Each voice student also gets a lot of hands-on experience coaching, because every production in the institute and on the ART mainstage gets assigned a vocal coach.

Saklad: What a wonderful opportunity.

Houfek: Yes. There are at least six institute productions every year, as well as a varied mainstage season. As a result, the voice students get lots of coaching experience, either as my assistant or with shows of their own mentored by me. They get to work with world-renowned directors, actors, and designers. The voice students also attend a number of acting classes. Scott Zigler, director of the institute, genuinely respects voice as an integral part of the training process. He often says that any acting problem can be solved if you solve the voice or the movement problem. I make sure the voice students attend Scott's acting class because he will use them as a voice coach. On the spot, they have to start thinking like the voice person, integrating voice with acting work, learning how a voice note can help the actor with more than just voice. The voice student also starts a practicum in the second year, teaching a speech-drill course called voice lab to the first-year MFA students. And all of our students study Russian. The voice students travel to Moscow in the spring of their second year to teach an expanded voice lab to the first-year students, adding voice and text to the basic speech work.

Saklad: Would you describe the features that distinguish your work in the field?

Houfek: I teach voice. I teach speech. I teach dialects. I teach text. I do it all. I don't view these elements as separate disciplines. When I'm working on speech with a student, it's as much about breathing, opening up the resonance, using support, and finding the space that allows you to have forward placement. When I'm working on text, it's as much about speech, breath, and alignment. When I'm working on dialects, it's as much about placement and melody as well as all the other aspects of vocal production. It's possible to be rigorous in each area as well as understanding how they weave together. And they're also not separate from acting.

Saklad: Where does vocal presence come from, and is it teachable?

Houfek: When I think of vocal presence, I think of a voice that is balanced in resonance, a voice that is bright and has depth simultaneously. We have a particularly difficult theatre space for the nonamplified voice here at the Loeb Drama Center. The actor's voice really needs to have a ping to it to be heard. A voice that is only deeply resonant might not actually have presence in that space. It's not going to penetrate. Conversely, a voice that's just bright isn't going to have the depth that moves people. So that's my litmus test for teaching our students. I think about it like a stereo; I want to teach them to balance the treble and the bass, to adjust the resonance so their voices are like three-dimensional surround sound. It's also about the deep pleasure of making consonants and open vowels and the desire to contact others. If there's no desire to actually connect, the voice is going to be fake and very "beautiful"—you know, distancing. And yes, I believe vocal presence is teachable. That's what I'm trying to do!

Practical Considerations

Saklad: Do you think students should study multiple approaches to the work?

Houfek: Absolutely. I think it's a mistake to become too wedded to one way of working. It limits your style of acting and limits the way you use your voice. You become identified as that particular kind of actor or speaker, rather than being open to a range of experiences.

Saklad: What does the body need to produce optimal vocal work?

Houfek: It needs to be free, flexible, aligned, and strong, but not bound. The actor needs to have the ability to isolate muscles, to feel what their muscles are experiencing—a really strong mind/body connection. I use elements from Bartenieff Movement Fundamentals, yoga, Alexander technique, and Feldenkrais—as well as elements from modern dance—to teach use of center, energy flow, alignment, and breath. Fortunately, I'm not alone in this at the ART. We have a wonderful combination of Alexander training, yoga, and dance to bring our students to a deeper awareness of self and movement. And one of the great strengths of our Russian collaboration is the rigorous movement training they undergo while in Moscow.

Saklad: Does an understanding of anatomy deepen the student's relationship to his or her voice?

Houfek: Yes, within limits. Sometimes, when acting students are required to learn too much anatomy, they get stuck in their left brains and stop experiencing their bodies. Their learning must be linked to physical experience. I want my students to understand their bodies on a nonlanguage level.

Saklad: Do you find an imagistic understanding of the voice to be helpful as well?

Houfek: Yes. I use lots of images in my teaching. One of my favorites is the idea of lines of energy. Catherine Fitzmaurice refers to a related line of energy called "the focus line." I use a slightly different image—six lines like a starburst streaming out the limbs and spine from center. When these lines are activated with breath and vibration, they expand the body and become the connective energy from actor to actor. Other images that I use are wearing a crown—which helps the actor feel the spaces between the cervical vertebrae—feeling the head as a helium balloon floating upwards with its string hanging downwards as the spine, or imagining the body as a Plexiglas vessel filling with liquid vibration. Those are just a few of the images I use. Images or metaphors are absolutely necessary to make abstract language become a crystal-clear physical experience for the student.

Saklad: How do you address breath work?

Houfek: To begin, I teach the Fitzmaurice Destructuring sequence to help students find out how to naturally breathe more fully. Then I spend a lot of time on alignment. I do a crawling and walking exercise I learned from

Frank Ottiwell, the Alexander teacher I trained with at ACT. When we are moving on our hands and knees, the body gets quite organized. The ribs expand and contract like an accordion as we reach forward, and the belly naturally releases. Breathing becomes a part of movement, not a separate activity that we have to think about. The idea is to transition to an upright position and still retain the ease of breath that we feel crawling. Then we start in on the mechanics of Restructuring. I do a lot of exercises to stretch the intercostals, the upper chest, and the back. Students can really feel how it's possible to change how our muscles are being used. I do a lot of exercises to release the belly. I like to use the image of the body as a beach ball for inhalation. This creates the sense of the three dimensionality of the inhalation. It has width, and it expands front and back, bottom and top. Then we begin to investigate support.

Saklad: What does it mean to support the voice?

Houfek: For me, and I understand there are various perspectives on this, to support the voice means to activate the lower abdominal muscles. This action feels like an upward motion of the pelvic floor. And what that means is that we're not using the exterior intercostals or latissimus dorsa to hold the ribs open. What the lower abdominal activation does is allow the ribs to float down gently, letting a managed, not controlled, steady stream of air to flow past the vocal cords. If we use the upper abdominal muscles in front of the diaphragm to press the air out, the back of the mouth drops and the space inside gets really small. So by keeping the support coming up from the pelvic floor, you're keeping the soft palate raised. And when there's no support? Number one, without support, typically actors will squeeze the ribs to push the breath out, and immediately they get throat tension. Or if the ribs just collapse, they may get a super breathy voice.

Saklad: How would you describe the role of listening?

Houfek: My listening as a teacher and a coach is a diagnostic tool. I'm not listening with my ears only; I'm listening with my eyes soft and with my intuition heightened. In my classes, I'm also intent on the students listening to each other, soliciting responses from them about what is working and why. I want them to be actively engaged in listening with the whole self. This holistic kind of listening helps them learn experientially, even when others students are working. When actors listen to their own voices, it is not productive. One can notice that the vibration remains contained in the body, seeming somewhat trapped, not moving forward spontaneously, affecting a scene partner or audience member. What this means in teaching voice, speech, or dialects is that I focus on the physical experience of expression rather than suggesting that actors check their voices by hearing themselves.

Saklad: Do you teach the IPA?

Houfek: Yes! It's a great tool for the actor. It can make speech and dialect work incredibly detailed and precise. It's also a shortcut to learning languages. I was coaching a production of *Oedipus* at the ART with many sections of the text to be spoken in ancient Greek. After phonetically learning the Greek myself, I had to teach it to the actors. One actor knew the IPA, and so he learned the Greek very quickly and accurately. Another actor didn't know the IPA, so I transposed his text into a phonemic system that, by its nature, could not be as precise as the IPA. For example, if I were to write "ay," you could pronounce it either /ei/ or /ai/, unlike IPA where each symbol has only one pronunciation. As a result, this actor's learning of the Greek text was slippery and constantly needed correction.

Saklad: Do you teach a Standard Speech or General American?

Houfek: I teach what I call "nonregional American speech."

Saklad: Is this your own coinage?

Houfek: Yes. The only regions that it is spoken are on the American stage and television news broadcast. I don't call it a standard; I call it a dialect of English that is useful for the stage. I think that every American actor has to have a nonregional dialect (or something close) so that they can audition for any role in any play. Otherwise they're only going to be cast by how they sound regionally or culturally. The dialect I teach has some of the same qualities as Edith Skinner's usage, but without her more formal, slightly British-sounding aspects. I want my students to actually sound American.

Saklad: How would you describe the relationship between emotion and voice and speech work?

Houfek: Having a deep, available, present emotional life is a gift. Not everybody has this. Where actors get in trouble is when the emotion overrides the action. If the language is overtaken by the emotion, we won't actually understand the action. Emotion is great fuel, but it's not the be-all and end-all of acting. The playing of action is primary; emotion arises out of getting or not getting what you want—if you're open to it. What happens frequently with young actors is that they invest time and energy in generating emotion. This may make the body squeeze and the voice tighten. A false feeling of tension substitutes for the essence of true moment-to-moment experience. There are two more parts to this. One of the many great things about tremoring is that by freeing the breath, the inner emotional life that may be trapped in the body gets churned up and starts to release. Consequently, the actor becomes much more present with the inner life, which starts flowing outward rather than remaining pent up. When an actor speaks the text while tremoring, the emotional experience may be quite overwhelming, but the goal is to keep the text moving and the action going. If an actor can sustain forward motion— actively pursuing an objective while all the inner life is coming up—the give and take between the two can be extremely exciting. That kind of edgy performance is what we are longing for: deeply connected emotional life fueling high-stakes pursuit of objective. That said, sometimes the actor has to technically produce a heightened emotional state. This is why I teach extreme voice. If the actor can create the form of an extreme emotion in a physically truthful way, and if the given circumstances of the play support the action, a truthful emotional life is going to be experienced by the audience, which is all that matters in the end.

Saklad: How do you see scientific and/or technological advances within or without the field influencing your work or the work at large?

Houfek: One of the biggest changes is in the current use of electronic amplification in shows. It alters what's necessary vocally. The actor still needs to have a very focused voice and really crisp, clean consonants, but not necessarily a lot of volume or projection capability. There's also a huge increase in online resources. You can find everything online: dialect samples, Shakespeare text-analysis, the IPA, and so forth. For example, Paul Meiers's IDEA (International Dialects of the English Archives) site on accents is an unbelievable online resource.

Moving into the Future

Saklad: What advice would you give to voice and speech teachers at the beginning of their teaching careers?

Houfek: Find a great mentor. Teach and coach as much as you can. Find private students. Experience is the only way to get better as a teacher or coach. And always stay focused on the purpose of the task, which is not just to teach well, but for your students to learn well.

Saklad: What voice and speech advice would you give to performance students on the brink of their professional careers?

Houfek: Make a voice workout or warm-up an essential part of your daily life. Be sure to warm up physically and vocally prior to every audition. You'll be more present, calm, and available. Be sure to warm up physically and vocally prior to every reading or performance also. Keep your text skills sharp. Read Shakespeare out loud. Keep your IPA and dialect skills sharp. Keep learning new things. Take workshops. The only thing that acting school can do is set you on a path. Continue on that path. And don't smoke.

Saklad: Have you witnessed much of an evolution in any aspects of voice and speech training over the course of your career?

Houfek: Definitely. One thing that's happened is there's no longer a demand for classical stage speech. Strict Standard Speech is gone, which is a really nice shift. Unfortunately, on the flip side, not everybody is teaching the IPA anymore. Some people associate the IPA with Edith Skinner alone and think that learning the IPA is going to make their speech sound fake. That's not true. Phoneticians and dialecticians and linguists use the IPA to describe oral expression by assigning a symbol to each spoken sound, not to limit how the sounds are spoken. As I mentioned earlier, it's an important and useful tool for the actor, just like reading music might be important for the singer. Another change is an increase in the need to study dialects, particularly for actors wanting to go into film. That's primarily due to the phenomenal work of Tim Monich, who is the dialect coach on so many films today. It used to be that only British or Australian actors were considered to be good in dialects. Now people are accepting that American actors can perform well in dialect. Therefore, there's more need for actors to be trained to hear the nuances of a variety of sounds and pick them up quickly. I find it's more challenging to teach heightened text now. This has to do with the lowered standards of American primary and secondary education. Many students don't get the grammar, language structure, and poetic conventions that perhaps you or I got in our educational system and certainly still exists in England. And perhaps this is the best shift: there is, among the generation of voice teachers now emerging, a wonderful cross-referencing between various vocal-training systems and pedagogical techniques. We're no longer feeling strictly bound to one single way of teaching.

Saklad: What do you think the future holds for voice and speech training?

Houfek: I'm finding more and more that the spoken word in the United States is diminishing. So I would say, in my idealistic world, there is a strong tangible need and calling for vocal expression to continue to be celebrated.

Saklad: Nancy, what impact do you hope your work will have on vocal training at large?

Houfek: Well, I hope that my students in the theatre will speak with spontaneity and specificity and power. I hope that they will be really rigorous in their research of a role, not just to perform from habit, but from choice. I also want to inspire a new generation of voice teachers. I hope they will not be committed only to the material or the content, but committed to this idea of teaching—what it means to be a teacher—to really listen, to really understand the culture the student is coming from. And then to be willing to change tactics, change style, and change what they're bringing based on the individual's needs, based on each student's culture and learning style. So this notion of teaching, the art form of teaching, is what's most important to me now, and that's what I'm actually trying to impart to my voice students.

Deb Kinghorn

Deb Kinghorn is a master teacher of Lessac Kinesensic Training. She currently serves on the board of directors of the Lessac Training and Research Institute and regularly teaches and conducts research at the Lessac Summer Intensive Workshop. She has been the voice, dialects, and text coach for over 100 shows in many theatres including the Alley Theatre in Houston, Texas; the Dallas Theatre Center; the Houston Shakespeare Festival; and Fordham University in NYC. She received the University of Houston Teaching Excellence Award in 1995 and the Lessac Institute Leadership Award in 2009. Presently Deb serves as chair of the department of theatre and dance at the University of New Hampshire.

Background

Nancy Saklad: Who were your mentors, Deb?

Deb Kinghorn: I consider Arthur Lessac to be my primary mentor and Sue Ann Park to be the next person from whom I've learned the most in my life. I studied with other people, but those are the people who have had the most significant influence on me.

Saklad: What aspects of the work most inspire you?

Kinghorn: What inspires me most is how quickly and easily the students hook into the Lessac training. I am also inspired by the basis of musicality in the work. I've always believed that people's voices are inherently musical and that the musicality is healthful. Neuroscience and other scientific research is finally beginning to confirm this. Research states that music can have a positive effect on our psyche, our emotional state, and certainly our physical state. If we know that music is good for us—in fact, promotes health and wellness in the body—then why not explore and expand the inherent musicality of our voices? I would say the most inspiring aspect of the work for me is its broad applications. When I first started teaching this work, I focused solely on the training of the actor. Over time, I've seen that this work also offers a variety of applications for life outside of the actor's realm. For example, we can connect with speech therapy or voice therapy. Those are pretty obvious connections, but for the Lessac work, which also involves movement, there is dance and the therapeutic movement of the body, and when you are working with the body you are simultaneously working with the voice. Arthur has used the work with the profoundly deaf and with stutterers with very positive results. In other words, voice and speech and body work are not just a matter of speaking clearly or creating good tone; they have the potential to create a solid foundation for health and wellness. So there are many possible applications, and I find this exciting and intriguing.

The Voice and Speech World of Today

Saklad: Would you describe the features that distinguish your work in the field?

Kinghorn: I think the work is distinguished by learning through your own physical sensation rather than by imitation of someone else. This seems so simple, yet you will often find that people teach voice by demonstrating it first and then asking the student to copy them. So we learn through feeling—the feeling process—meaning we become aware of and pay attention to the wisdom that the body already possesses, and learn from it. This happens by discovering familiar events, actions we perform easily and spontaneously, which lead to organic instructions for all areas of voice and body work. The result is an integrated approach to training that results in instinctive, believable behavior in any acting situation. In my own research I am passionate about transferring this base of knowledge beyond the theatre world, because I believe that there are many health benefits for everyone, not just actors.

Saklad: You are currently working on a book with Arthur Lessac. Would you talk a little bit about the book?

Kinghorn: The book is an exploration of how to function in everyday life through the feeling process—as opposed to the thinking process. From the time we are children, we are trained to favor the intellectual process. In school we are tested and rewarded for how we think. Throughout our lives, the intellect is given great value. In other words, reason—logic, proof—trumps instinct—hunches, feelings, being in the moment. Quantum physics has changed that, but that's a longer story. In short, artists have not been given credit for functioning primarily through what we call "the feeling process." Yet people do function that way, including doctors and scientists and mathematicians. In fact, everyone begins learning through the feeling process as a baby. It is just that it is overshadowed so utterly by our reliance on intellect that it gets pushed to the background. So the focus of this book is to give viability to people who operate primarily from a feeling sense and also to explain how we all can learn through the feeling process.

Saklad: How would you describe the current state of affairs of American actor training in voice and speech?

Kinghorn: I see it as mostly positive. The fact that we have voice and speech classes in schools large and small is positive. That it is felt to be an essential part of actor training programs is also positive, since only recently it wasn't. On the negative side, I feel that there's still too little intentional crossover and integration in voice, movement, and acting. You still hear stories about teachers protecting their turf, or asking students "not to do their voice and speech work in acting class." And from a personal gripe, I think there is a lot of misplaced emphasis on breath work. I ruffle a lot of feathers when I start talking about this, because the general consensus is that the Lessac person doesn't deal with the breath, which of course isn't true. But often it seems that all solutions are related to the breath, which I do not find to be true. I do think that voice begins with breath, but I don't think that every solution comes back to the breath.

Saklad: What are the greatest voice and speech obstacles that the student actor faces?

Kinghorn: Self-judgment and then their habits. If they can release their self-judgment, then they will be able to tackle those things that are habitual and can eventually be diffused and altered.

Saklad: Do you think voice and speech training plays a unique role in performance training?

Kinghorn: I believe it all has to be integrated—voice, body, imagination—and should be taught in an integrated manner. Voice is a part of the whole.

Saklad: Where does vocal presence come from, and is it teachable?

Kinghorn: Vocal presence comes from the individuals and their ability to play their instrument like an artist with joy, with artistry. Is that teachable? Yes, absolutely.

Practical Considerations

Saklad: Do you think students benefit from studying multiple approaches to the work?

Kinghorn: I stand firmly in the camp that when a student is first training, he or she should study one approach and not mix and match because that can be very confusing. Beyond that, once students come to an understanding of their voices—and by that I mean a "feeling" understanding—they feel free, they feel lack of tension, they feel a free flow, they feel variety, they're expressive—all the things that we would look for—then yes, they should go explore everything, because they will only add to that solid base that they have.

Saklad: What does the body need to produce optimal vocal work?

Kinghorn: Good health, rest and relaxation, and the recognition that relaxation is not indulgent, but a vital and invigorating part of life. You have to do your best to move away from anything that's an anesthetic—that deadens your sensation—such as exhaustion or stress.

Saklad: Do you think an understanding of anatomy deepens the student's relationship to his or her voice?

Kinghorn: No, I don't think so. From my experience, knowing how to produce a good vocal tone has little to no relationship to knowing anatomy. Even if you can name every part of the laryngeal structure, it does not help you understand how to produce the voice. That is something that only occurs when you let go of thinking and focus on feeling—feeling vibration, feeling musicality, feeling your posture, feeling your facial muscles, etc. Now, when students discover they can feel these things, then you might choose to name them if that is important. The teacher, on the other hand, definitely ought to know the anatomy. Knowing the placement and function of the zygomatic and levator muscles will help me as I watch for their telltale movement in forward facial posture, for example.

Saklad: Do you find an imagistic understanding of the voice to be helpful?

Kinghorn: Imagery that is generated by the teacher is not productive as a teaching device, in my opinion. I train people to become sensitive to the physical sensation of their voice. The instructions are concrete and simple. I want the students to feel vibration—a sensation that is concrete—and to be able to feel the movement of the vibration throughout the body. This movement is called energy. The coursing of energy through the body creates unlimited responses, or harmonics, and one of these harmonics is imagery. Last summer at the Lessac Summer Intensive, we had a student who had undergone facial surgery as a result of a serious accident, and had lost all sensation in several areas of his face, including his hard palate. So the work was quite a challenge for him. But once he began to feel sensation in a few places, he was able to focus on that feeling, and a wonderful thing happened; the sensation spread. So he awakened sensation in places where it had been completely deadened, and that vibration gave him something concrete to focus on. When this person began training, his voice was entirely in his throat. There was no quality vibration in the head bones at all, because he could not feel it. But by the end of the workshop, he had regained all of that sensation and was doing remarkable work. He understood, and more importantly felt, the difference between a tone that was in his throat and one that was what I might call "fronted" as they say in music—one that was in the bone. But more than that, as he learned to feel more sensation, his imagination also blossomed; his imagery became more and more vivid, as he described what he was feeling, physically and emotionally. So returning to this question of imagery, I give students something concrete in training, something that can be perceived sensorially. Once a student has the feeling or sensation, once they experience the harmonics, then they will come up with their own imagery. Any image that I might suggest will never be as valuable as the image the students discover themselves.

Saklad: How do you address breath work?

Kinghorn: As I mentioned earlier, one of the misconceptions about Lessac work is that people seem to think we don't address breathing, which of course is not true. The breath work is never separate from the voice and body work. First, we address it by exploring the body's natural way of breathing, and the best way to discover that is to smell something with a lovely aroma, such as a flower. This experience teaches you that the movement of the breath is not restricted to the abdomen or the front of the body but that in fact, a great deal of the expansion of the torso occurs in the back, which is a place many people don't feel when they breathe. It also demonstrates how incredibly easy it is to get a full breath quickly. Secondly, we address the breath through all of our physical work, which has the dual effect of releasing tension in the body while developing good upright posture, and which together results in full, natural breathing. I read an interesting study a few years ago, which stated that telling someone to inhale and then to exhale is antithetical to the natural functioning of the body. The body does not perceive this as "natural" breathing. But when we smell a flower, or any fragrance that is pleasurable, we also experience the energy of the natural breath—and with that we experience the harmonics of that energy, such as enjoyment of the fragrance or even love of the fragrance. And with this comes a gentle feeling of muscular "yawning" inside of the body, which steadies you and gives you a sense of calm strength. So teaching breathing through smelling a flower seems a perfectly reasonable way of approaching the natural breath. Finally, and perhaps most importantly, we always know that when we feel tone and *don't* feel breath, then the breath is being used optimally.

Saklad: What does it mean to support the voice?

Kinghorn: I think the very word *support* gives the impression that somehow we've got to push the words up and out. Support is really the engagement of the diaphragm. This engagement occurs fully and completely when you are producing good tone. The diaphragm does what it's supposed to do because the vocal folds have come fully together and are vibrating and allowing very little breath to puff through. Too much breath coming through will give you a breathy tone. That is why we stay away from imagery that suggests that the voice and the breath are one and the same.

In fact, the breath has an important function. It instigates and perpetuates the vibration of the vocal folds. The less breath that is used to do that, the cleaner the tone and the more we feel like we are using no breath at all, even though we are. That is support at work. It's impossible to support by forcing some sort of abdominal engagement. By this I mean that we have to create the conditions under which the diaphragm can engage naturally, and if you focus on tightening or squeezing or pumping the abdominal muscles, then you are adding a tension to the body, which is defeating your purpose. There is also a tendency to think about support as happening in the front of the body, when in fact the diaphragm connects all the way around the torso and must be engaged equally all the way around. If you work with breathing from only a frontal perspective, you will never get the full support that you need.

Saklad: How do you approach tonality, resonance, and vocal qualities?

Kinghorn: I like the word *tonality*. If we take the definition as used in music, it means "the sum of relations, melodic and harmonic, existing between the tones of a scale or musical system." In terms of the human voice—a wonderful "musical system"—this means feeling a fundamental tone and also feeling the harmonics that result from it. Harmonics manifest themselves as sensations that can include such things as pulsations, rhythms, temperature changes, inner sounds, moving colors, shapes, and images. In more concrete terms, it is feeling vibration in the bones and seeking out the sensation of more vibration wherever it occurs in the body, as well as the resulting emotions or images. There are many specific explorations that we do to develop the awareness of vibration, but in the end, the idea is for you to feel your voice as pure motion or energy within your body. This leads me to resonance. Resonance is best achieved by feeling vibration within yourself and coupling that with creating and nurturing the optimal housing for good wave-reflection. Resonance is what people really want from you when they tell you to project—which I think is a poor word-choice because it indicates that you have to "throw" your voice, which is impossible. The more you fill up the "theatre in your head" with vibration, the more resonance you will have. Tonality and resonance together create voice quality.

Saklad: What role does listening play in voice and speech work?

Kinghorn: There are two roles to listening. Listening to oneself has no place. We really cannot gauge what we sound like, because we hear ourselves both through air and bone conduction—literally, inside our heads. When we listen to ourselves on a recording, we are only hearing through air conduction, and so our voices sound very different to us. This difference is why we cannot trust the ear to give us good feedback on our quality of tone. So listening to oneself is not an accurate device for teaching yourself. Listening to others, however, is essential.

Saklad: How do you help your students connect imagery and the text?

Kinghorn: We do what we call "explorations" of the text using the various energy qualities that the student has learned. For the voice these energies— often referred to as NRG's—are: Consonant, Tonal, and Structural energies, and for the body: Buoyancy, Radiancy, and Potency energies. Say they're doing Ophelia's "O what a noble mind is here o'er thrown," and they're not connecting with the terror or the woe or perhaps the wonder or whatever might be there. That suggests to me that they are in a pattern or a habit that is deadening their ability to respond to their own inner imagery. But as I said before, I can't give them imagery, because then they are only working with my imagery, not their own. But by asking them to simply explore the text, leading with an energy quality—for example, structural energy, vowels in this case—they will unconsciously diffuse the pattern or habit they have acquired, and so open themselves up again to inner response and behavior, and imagery will follow quite naturally.

Saklad: How would you describe the relationship between emotion and voice and speech work?

Kinghorn: They're very intimate. I don't find them frightening, though I think many people do. Sometimes there's a fear attached to the release of the voice and the subsequent release of emotion. There are many reasons for that fear, which I won't go into here. But any work that you do with voice and speech will stir up emotion, because you are dealing with physical sensations in the body that shake it up and trigger more sensations to be felt. We call them "harmonics." Every emotion has its unique feel. I think one great thing about voice and speech work is that vocal control, in particular tonal energy, gives you breath control, which gives you an automatic emotional experiencing control. I don't mean that you squash your emotions, far from it. I mean that good voice and speech training provides you with an avenue to feel all emotion fully without fearing that you will lose control.

Saklad: How do you see scientific and/or technological advances within or without the field influencing your work or the work at large?

Kinghorn: I spoke about this a little earlier regarding the sciences confirming things we formerly thought were true. We now understand that laughter is beneficial for the human body, and one of the ways we can maintain wellness and facilitate recovery is to engage in laughter medicine. We now understand that singing has amazing properties for healing the human body, from helping stutterers overcome their stutters, to firing up all four quadrants of the brain to peak performance. The research that is happening in medicine and in science is having a tremendous effect on our work, partly because it is validating many things that we have known on an instinctive level to be true. As far as technological advances, I'm going to invest in a very simple new computer program. It's called "Sing and See." You sing or speak and the computer shows you a spectrograph of what's going on with the voice. I find it to be really interesting for research, because I would like to be able to capture the difference between the placement of a Y-buzz and an /ee/ vowel, for example. I'd like to capture the difference between a Call and a dilute tone on the same pitch. This program can help a visual learner see when the voice is in the throat, for example. This is not a replacement for feeling, and should only be used after the student has had time to engage his or her own feeling process, but as a tool I think it could be a good support.

Moving into the Future

Saklad: What advice would you give to voice and speech teachers at the beginning of their professional careers?

Kinghorn: Don't be afraid to say you don't know. The best thing you can do is tell your students you don't know, and you'll find out and get back to them. This is the way you continue to grow.

Saklad: What advice would you give to performance students on the brink of their professional careers?

Kinghorn: You only have one chance to study voice in the depth that you get in a training program, so use it wisely. And learn to incorporate your voice training into your daily life. If you do so, you will always be ready for the next job when it comes along.

Saklad: Have you witnessed much of an evolution in voice and speech training over the course of your career?

Kinghorn: Oh yes. The changes that have occurred have been astonishing. First of all, the sound of American English has changed significantly from what we heard in the 1940s and even the 1950s. In particular, when I was in college in the early 1970s, we were still studying speech standards that were used in the 1940s and 1950s. There was a sense at that time of being taught to speak one specific way. That has totally changed. Another thing I've noticed is greater authenticity in dialect work, which I think is very good. I also think today we truly recognize the necessity for voice and speech training.

Saklad: What do you think the future holds for voice and speech training, Deb?

Kinghorn: I can talk about where I see myself going. I would like to see our work—and by that I mean not just mine, but all voice and speech work—reach out to empower everyone with a voice. There are many, many people today who are voiceless, meaning powerless. The work we do empowers people by giving them ownership of their voices, and recognizing that we have a right to be heard, that we have a right to speak, as Patsy Rodenburg said so brilliantly. The right to speak is desperately needed in the world. Voice and speech training has the potential to go far beyond the limitations of the theatre or of the entertainment world.

Saklad: Where is the next place where you'd like to make an impact, Deb?

Kinghorn: Well right now I'm doing that, as a matter of fact. At my university I'm taking what I do for actors out into the university community at large. I'm teaching the body NRG's, the vocal NRG's, and how those can have a positive effect on every individual's wellness. I'm making the connection between what I teach and wellness and I'm doing that for a larger community.

Dudley Knight

Professor emeritus of drama at the University of California, Irvine, where he was head of acting for eight years and vice-chair of drama for ten, Dudley Knight's forty-five year teaching career has included teaching engagements at many major theatre training programs throughout America. He is certified as a master teacher of Fitzmaurice Voicework®. His influential articles on his own approach to speech training for actors have appeared in journals and in the books *The Vocal Vision* and *Standard Speech*, both published by Applause Theatre Books. He regularly conducts workshops and lectures on voice and speech for actors and voice teachers nationwide and abroad. A founding member of the Long Wharf Theatre in New Haven, Connecticut, his extensive stage career includes major roles in regional theatres along with hundreds of roles in film, television, radio drama, and voiceover.

Background

Nancy Saklad: What drew you to voice work?

Dudley Knight: I became interested in voice at a very early age for several reasons. One was that my house when I was a child was filled with music. My mother was an amateur musician, and my father had spent much of his childhood in India and learned to play Indian instruments. My mother played the piano and flute. We also had an enormous number of classical music recordings in the old 78 rpm albums, and we used to listen to those all the time. The second thing was that my parents took both my brother and me to theatre and opera when we were at a very early age. I recall being at operas when I was four years old, and also at productions of plays. So we gained a very early and very avid interest in theatre. But the most important thing was that our parents and our grandmother read to us all the time. Even before I had learned to read I had memorized a number of children's stories from having heard them read to me repeatedly. I became interested in singing at a very early age and participated in that in amateur ways with a great deal of commitment since I was in my early teens. So by the time I finished my training at the Yale School of Drama, I was very interested in continuing as an actor, but also continuing with a kind of an emphasis in voice work.

Saklad: Who were your mentors, Dudley?

Knight: My most profound mentor for voice training has been and continues to be Catherine Fitzmaurice. I met Catherine in the late 1970s in Los Angeles. When I started working with her, I perceived that her work provided some things that I found lacking in my own voice teaching, in my own voice training, and in my work as an actor. Catherine's Destructuring/ Restructuring work had a very powerful effect on my ability to connect with impulse as an actor and then to support vocally the acting choices that I was making. She also totally reshaped the way that I was able to work with classical text. Her work, for me, achieved a fusion between the impulsive and the deliberative sides of the acting process that was unique. The second mentor I would say is actually an earlier one, and if Catherine was—and continues to be—the most profound of my mentors, I would name Kristin Linklater as being the more radically transformative for me at a very early stage of my voice study. I worked with Kristin in a small group that was selected from around the country on a Rockefeller grant back in 1965. This was actually the first group of teachers that she worked with. Even though I left her program before its completion, her work created a huge change in my thinking about voice. Prior to that time my voice training had been very, very traditional, and my voice work as an actor and as a singer was very traditional as well, so I came into Kristin's work with a lot of really bad habits. Her work changed much of that, and even more significantly, made me painfully aware of just how much I needed to change. I still employ some of Kristin's work in my teaching, although my teaching has primarily become based on Fitzmaurice Voice-work® in the area of voice production.

Saklad: Have there been other influences that have inspired your work?

Knight: One of the things that has really changed my work a lot has been the tremendous development of voice science in the last twenty-five years. This has always been an interest of mine, and it is something that in my work—primarily in developing speech pedagogy—has enabled me to test a lot of hypotheses that were essentially untestable before. For instance, there has been a lot of controversy about the issue of use of abdominal muscles and opposing theories about breathing in terms of the singing training. You had the "stomach out" advocates and the "stomach in" advocates and the "hold your ribs out and keep them there"; the "rib reserve" advocates and the "rib swing" advocates and so on. There has been such interesting scientific work on this, and especially work that points toward establishing the dominance of the transversus muscle in both involuntary and controlled, deliberate breathing action. That's meant that all those things have started to become sorted out in terms of voice science, and therefore voice teachers have had to take that concrete information into strong consideration in developing, and in some cases, radically modifying their teaching.

The Voice and Speech World of Today

Saklad: What features distinguish your work in the field?

Knight: The work that distinguishes me from some other teachers in the field is my development of pedagogy in speech training. This really takes two parts: one is my critique of traditional methods of speech training for actors, and the second and more important part is my development of a new approach to pedagogy in speech training and accent work for actors. The accent training leads out of the physical skills in articulation that actors can develop in the speech training, so that that arc of exploration is very much of a piece.

Saklad: How would you describe the current state of affairs of actor training in terms of voice and speech?

Knight: I've been fortunate enough to see acting training change quite a bit over the past forty years, and certainly to see voice and speech training essentially come into existence as a field in that time. When I did my work with Kristin Linklater back in the mid '60s, there were very few voice teachers for actors in the United States, and prior to the growth of the regional theatre movement, there was really little demand for such teachers. It was only after regional theatres emerged that people started building a demand for voice teachers. Actors started to locate in individual artistic centers in communities around the United States, where they started to emphasize the classical repertoire more, and where actors were together for a long enough period of time that they could engage in ongoing training. It was also the case that as regional theatres started up, they discovered that an excellent way to keep their heads above water financially was to create adjunct fee-paying theatre schools that were connected to these regional theatres, so a lot of regional drama training programs began. Similarly, to feed the appetite for classically trained actors in this growing regional theatre movement, we started to see the development of MFA programs. When I was at the Yale School of Drama—I naively applied only to Yale because frankly, I didn't have a lot of choice—there were two or three MFA programs around. I could be wrong about this, but certainly less than ten MFA programs existed in the US in the 1960s. Today, for better or worse, there are hundreds of them—probably too many. Nonetheless, it's offered a lot more opportunities for people to make a livelihood as a voice and speech teacher, so the employment possibilities increased tremendously during this period. From that standpoint, the state of affairs of voice training has gotten a lot better. I think that in general, the quality of voice training has improved tremendously too. There's also a lot more material available in terms of voice science and literature on the subject and varied ways of working, the incorporation of a lot of cultural voice techniques and so on, most of which simply wasn't available when I started teaching.

Saklad: Do you think voice and speech training plays a unique role in performance training?

Knight: I acknowledge myself to be highly biased in this area. I think voice and speech training is perhaps the most important part of actor training, certainly the most important skills area of performance training, and it is the area in which students today need the most training as we move from the primacy of direct person-to-person conversation to the cell phone, the iPod, the email, and the texting. And who knows what the latest technology of vocal isolation will be by the time this book is published?

Saklad: Where does vocal presence come from, and is it teachable?

Knight: Well, the process of sounding fully interesting as an actor is the process of sounding fully interesting as a human being, and again, it's not a separable skill. It's something fully integrated in the acting process and the process of becoming a total person. I've always felt very strongly that the goal of vocal training and speech training and accent training is finding the unique voice of the character. You don't want to call attention to a voice for its own sake.

Practical Considerations

Saklad: Do you think performance students benefit from studying multiple approaches to the work?

Knight: I think that all the major approaches—deriving from a few master teachers or from the people in the field who've been innovative in some way—all of that is very useful. Following along in any given approach in a reasonable amount of depth will reap benefits. Once one has done that, it's often useful to explore other avenues. I understand the argument that focusing on a single way of working can be limiting, and I support the view that teachers should have a broad knowledge of varied methodologies. But the danger of that breadth is that people can end up with a cafeteria approach to voice work—a little from this and a little from that. It's really important to have a depth of understanding. Otherwise you just end up teaching a random group of voice exercises with no coherence to them.

Saklad: Do you find an understanding of anatomy deepens a student's relation to his or her voice?

Knight: Absolutely. I'm a big believer in that. I established at UC Irvine's drama department a quarter's work on anatomy right at the beginning of the training process for our MFA students. When I started working with Kristin Linklater many years ago, the work was almost entirely imagistic. I support that, but I realized fairly early on that work with image-based approaches needs to be combined with a really strong nuts-and-bolts sense of vocal anatomy and physiology. When an actor gets both the images and the anatomy, he or she gains authority over the images rather than submitting to them passively. It also allows actors to find the links between approaches to voice work, because the actor can interpret, and maybe resolve, the apparent differences between the images of different approaches.

Saklad: How do you address breath work?

Knight: I really embrace both the Fitzmaurice Destructuring and Restructuring. Catherine's teaching is centered on breath and the connection of breath to total vocal process, right through to text. Catherine's approach has the wonderful quality of being—on the one hand—radical and transformative, and on the other hand inclusive of older approaches that truly have value. It's a good example of how reexamination does not always mean rejection. Some things really do bear up under scrutiny.

Saklad: How do you address tonality, resonance, and vocal qualities?

Knight: I still do some of Kristin's work with resonance, because I think she focuses in a quite interesting and tactile way with the basic resonating areas. Obviously what both Catherine and Kristin share is the value of releasing unneeded tension from all of the skeletal muscles, so that you allow all of that nice vibration to flower. For the speaking voice and for actors generally, variety and responsiveness are the prime priorities.

Saklad: How would you describe the role of listening in voice and speech work?

Knight: In my book, which has the working title *Speaking With Skill*, the first thing I talk about in shaping vocal sound into speech is silence. Part of the process of releasing residual tension is the process of resensitizing the body. Actors need to be able to perceive a lot of things that most of us in daily life—including the actors—need to shut out. We need to be able to resensitize ourselves to those things, so the process of listening becomes extremely important.

Saklad: You have been instrumental in the development of a unique, non-Skinnerian approach to speech work that is described in your book *Speaking with Skill*. Would you describe some facets of the work?

Knight: Well I feel that this is the area where I've made some contribution to the field. For a long time, initially, I didn't teach speech because I had worked with Kristin. and she was very opposed to speech training at the time. Then I found myself in the situation where I needed to teach speech. Originally, my exposure to the field was via the Skinner work, because that was essentially the only thing being taught other than Lessac work, which was similar to Skinner's work, but adopted a different and somewhat idiosyncratic approach to vowels and consonants, because it didn't use the IPA. Skinner used the IPA, but in a rather old-fashioned and limited version. What I ended up doing was starting to teach Skinner work, and I taught out of Edith Skinner's book *Speak with Distinction* for several years. I saw the advantages of it, but I also began to see that there were serious impracticalities about it. I started, over a period of years, to reexamine the basis of what speech training might be. All during this time I was working actively as an actor, frequently using dialects, and I was beginning to see that the need for a variety of expression was a real priority. I also was aware—because I was teaching on the West coast—that a lot of my actors were going into film and television, and the idea of them being drilled over a long period of time in Good American Speech was not going to serve them terribly well in film and television. Even though it certainly improved their skills in certain respects, it also ignored a lot of the things they really did need to be able to do in terms of speech work. For me it was a long period of assessment, reassessment, and reexamination of the field. My opinions about it went sort of hand in hand with my exploring ways of redefining the teaching of speech. I came out, initially, with a presentation at one of the ATA conferences and did a huge amount of research into the history of speech training in America as it led toward the then-current practices in the theatre, which turned into a longer presentation at an ATHE conference, which turned into a short article for the VASTA newsletter, which turned into a reprinting of that article in Louis Colaianni's book *The Joy of Phonetics and Accents* which turned into an invitation to write a longer and more exhaustive piece on the subject for the book *The Vocal Vision*. I did even more research for that article, which, when published, turned out to be quite controversial. As I was working on that, I was constantly redefining for myself what the curriculum of a speech training program would be. At that point I was teaching at the University of California, Irvine. I had been at UCI since the early 1980s, so

I had the experience working with my students in these various reformu-
lations of the speech training program. As I did that, the reconsideration
of it became more and more radical. I didn't have a sudden break and—
boom—I came out with this new approach; it was a constant reexamination.
That's something that I have to say is really important for voice and
speech teachers to do—especially because we exist within something of an
apprenticeship model—that is, to reexamine what we're doing. To take a look
at it, see if it really works, and more than that, to see if the assumptions
on which it's based are valid. What I was able to do, I think, with speech
training was really to think about the assumptions, the criteria, the goals
of that speech training to understand the long history of what was called
Skinner training—or Good American Speech, or a Mid-Atlantic Accent,
or Standard Speech—and to rethink it. Also, on the other side of the
issue, to reexamine my assumptions I'd gotten from Kristin Linklater who
had, when I worked with her, rejected all speech training. (I believe she's
revised this opinion since.) In my case, I came to the understanding that
speech and articulation training is actually a necessity within a curriculum,
and that it needs to be presented quite differently from the way it had
been presented in America before I started looking at it critically. Over
this period I kept revising what I did, and I found in each case that the
more I looked at my teaching the more different parts of it needed a radical
change. It wasn't change for its own sake. It was change that was based on
a close consideration of what a professional actor really needs. It's also the
reason why my book has taken so long to write. Here's a good example:
For years I taught a formulation of the skills training that I called a "detail
model." It was based on the premise—which I still hold—that the only
immutable standard that we can have for absolutely all verbal actions on
stage is intelligibility. But I have very recently completely reformulated my
practice away from a "model" of anything, because I realized that some
teachers were tying these separate skills together to form a new kind of
speech pattern, which is just what I want to avoid. So the "detail model"
had to go.

Saklad: Would you talk a little about your approach to speech work?

Knight: These days I treat all speech actions as totally separable articulation skills; all of them are unified only by the actor's need to be easily
understood by the audience. We may have other situational standards

about the way things should sound onstage, but in terms of an overall standard that would guide speech, the only consistent standard we can have is intelligibility. It's generally agreed in the language-acquisition field that intelligibility increases across diverse accent groups when more linguistic information is provided for the listener by the speaker; more detailed linguistic information in its simplest form means that you put in more sounds that define the word or the connected phrase more specifically. It's a crucial thing to know how to do, so I have explored what speech actions would provide this detail. Some of these things are tried and true things that you would find in Skinner or anyone else teaching speech. Some of them aren't. The difference from Good American Speech is that the criterion is simply detail—not that these elements sound better or that they're more euphonious or that they sound more cultured or cultivated or any of those socially imposed things, but simply that they have more linguistic information. There is a continuum from formal to informal speech. It's hugely useful for an actor to feel what is going on with the articulators along this continuum. We don't want to be frozen into a relentlessly formal way of speaking, and we don't want to be frozen into informality either. What we do want is to be able to let our impulses constantly renegotiate the mix, in order to meet the communicative needs of the character and his or her interaction with the audience, and also the acoustic demands of the physical space. My work is based on the recognition that in theatre, and in life too, this is a constantly renegotiated moment-to-moment set of events that defines the way the character actually speaks. That's the challenge, and having these flexible skills is what's really useful to an actor. These same methods assist the actor in finding the variety that allows her or him to explore all sorts of accents through the development of skills in sound-shaping that take the speaker into any accent very quickly and easily.

Saklad: How do you use the IPA?

Knight: Phil Thompson and I, at UCI and now in our workshops, teach all of the International Phonetic Alphabet—all the sounds that you make in language. We've found it an extraordinarily valuable tool for working with actors, because actors are incredibly curious about sound change. They may not like to learn phonetic symbols, but they're incredibly curious about doing interesting things with the way that they shape sound. So rather than simply working on immediately drilling actors in a "good" speech pattern, one that purportedly is better than their own "bad" speech pattern, what you're getting in our approach is something where actors are beginning to open up to a vast array of speech-sound possibilities, which again creates a wealth of skills in shaping sound, which allows them to work fruitfully in any sort of environment. It also allows them to own those skills, so that when they're no longer sitting in our classes, they've got something they can take out into the real world of theatre—if that isn't a contradiction in terms. They know how to research an accent. They know how to listen to an accent, listen to a native speaker. They know how to notate what the native speaker is doing. They know how to shape the articulators in a way that allows them to communicate the accent very easily in a full physical characterization—specifically as a physicality of the vocal tract, which is why we explore the vocal-tract posture as a way of learning accents. Most important, they have the ability to find what linguists call the "idiolect" of a character, the precise way in which a character talks. All of that is material that hadn't really been done before in speech training, and all of that happened because we kept looking again and again at our own assumptions and saying, "Maybe we can go a little deeper in this work."

Saklad: How do you see scientific and/or technological advances affecting your work or the work at large?

Knight: Voice science technology has changed radically. Over the last twenty-five years, the technology of voice analysis has become incredibly sophisticated, and that has all worked to the benefit of voice teachers, as voice teachers become more aware and more adept in the use of technology. In terms of voice analysis, it's been amazing, and the use of voice analysis equipment has permeated the voice-teaching field. What's more, voice teachers have understood the uses of the utility of voice science as a way of testing their own assumptions or of corroborating their own perceptions or their own intuitions. A lot of times those intuitions are very accurate and lead the science, so that voice teachers are actually educating voice scientists at the same time as voice scientists are educating voice teachers. It's not just a one-way street on this; really both things are happening.

Moving into the Future

Saklad: What advice would you give to voice and speech teachers at the beginning of their teaching careers?

Knight: Run away! Run like the wind! But perhaps I simplify. Other than that... There's really a wealth of possibility. I think that the golden age of easy job-availability for voice teachers in academic settings is nearing an end because of the fact that so many people have entered the field in the last thirty years. But there will always be places for really good voice and speech teachers. The big area of growth today is in private practice, coaching people out there in the real nontheatrical world. I still encourage people to go into the field, and a lot of my students have done so successfully out of UC Irvine.

Saklad: What impact do you hope your work will have on voice and speech training at large?

Knight: I think that a lot of what I'm doing has radically challenged the way that speech training is taught. I obviously hope that the attitude toward that work—not just the specific methods that I use, mine and Phil Thompson's—will continue, and that means an attitude of constantly exploring what really works for actors, what's really useful for actors, in order to facilitate the actors' communication with their audiences in the richest, most varied, and most exciting ways possible. It's simply about that process of expansion and of constantly challenging one's own assumptions to permit new ideas and practices to evolve.

Saul Kotzubei

Saul Kotzubei teaches voice in workshops, in ongoing classes, and to private clients in Los Angeles. He is a lead trainer for the Fitzmaurice Voicework® Teacher Certification Program. Saul has taught Fitzmaurice Voicework® at NYU's CAP 21 Studio, New York's Actors Center, and in workshops throughout the US and the world. A performer with an MA in Buddhist studies from Columbia University, Saul has studied a variety of acting approaches, including a year of clown with Philippe Gaulier. In addition to teaching voice, Saul also teaches public speaking in Los Angeles.

Photo by Conroe Brooks

Background

Nancy Saklad: What drew you to voice and speech work, Saul?

Saul Kotzubei: My mother, Catherine Fitzmaurice, it turns out, is a gifted voice teacher, and so there is a strong gravitational force there. I avoided her work for thirty years, and when I finally decided to try it, I realized it could help me. It didn't take me long to realize that many other people—actors and nonactors, really—need to learn how to find and then effectively use their voices too.

Saklad: Besides Catherine, who are your mentors, and how have they influenced your work?

Kotzubei: My most important teachers are my students in Los Angeles and the people I've worked with who've gone through the Fitzmaurice certification program. There are also a couple of voice teachers outside of the Fitzmaurice tradition, wonderful teachers who have taught me and have deeply influenced me—Patsy Rodenburg and Richard Armstrong. They are true voice teachers, each very different than the other. Then there's my therapist. I know that's personal, and that he's not a voice teacher, but for me he's been a necessary part of my learning about my voice. I've also had a few mentors who never explicitly addressed voice, who nevertheless profoundly influenced my teaching. For many years I did conflict resolution with a man named Peter Chipmann. In the '70s, Peter was a leader in the computer industry. He had 20,000 employees working under him, and he travelled all over the world opening new factories. Then one day in Puerto Rico, touring his factory and seeing the nice cars and the golf course the workers now had, he also noticed that the workers had lost a vitality in their eyes that they had had before the factory was built. And at that moment, he saw clearly that his work wasn't meaningful to him anymore. So he left and found his way into doing conflict resolution with corporations, nonprofits, and what we would probably now call terrorists—a wide range. When he hired me, late in his career, he sat next to me under a big oak tree and said, "Saul, there are a few reasons why I'll fire you, and I want you to know what they are right now." I was immediately apprehensive. Then he said, "First, if you don't learn something every day that we're working together I will fire you. Second, if you don't contribute something every day I'll fire you. Third, if we don't have fun together I'll fire you. And finally, if you don't fail often I'll fire you because it means you're not taking risks." Wow. I felt whole new parts of myself begin to breathe that day. Then there are two acting teachers in Los Angeles who taught me something that really affected my teaching: Richard Seyd and Stuart Rogers. Richard really knows something about acting, but what made him so special to me was witnessing how he helped his students access and reveal their humanity without ever beating them up, dominating them, or puffing them up with false praise. The other teacher is Stuart Rogers. He taught me how to bring myself into a part while still staying true to the part. An important aspect of that was learning to enter the subjectivity of a character, to become a character. A lot of teachers talk about this, but Stuart showed me how to do it. Before working with him, I only played the *idea* of a character. When I played the idea of a character, I created a lot of distance from myself that in turn led to a lot of distance from others. There's a corollary in voice work. A lot of actors come to a voice class thinking that they are going to learn how to sound "good." The nonperformers I work with often start by asking if I can teach them to sound "confident" or "correct." But focusing on getting the voice to sound good or correct actually distances students from themselves and others. Here's a personal example. When I was just starting out as a voice teacher, I had a telephone answering machine. My outgoing message started with something like, "Hello my name is Saul Kotzubei... If you're calling about voice coaching—" I spoke the words with my best resonant voice. I had a notion—created out of my own unacknowledged fear—that I was supposed to sound like a "good" voice teacher. That was not a voice teacher I would want to study with. That was somebody who was, albeit unconsciously, putting on the *idea* of a voice that sounds good. It took me a year to recognize what I had done. Once I recognized it, I decided not to change the voice message. I left it on for another year as a reminder to myself of the limitations of going in that direction. When we get stuck in some rigid idea of good, correct, confident, even resonant— *that* is using the voice to hide more expertly. Ultimately voice work should open up the voice so one can fluidly reveal to others what is important in any given context.

The Voice and Speech World of Today

Saklad: How would you describe the features that distinguish your work in the field?

Kotzubei: First, my work is rooted in Fitzmaurice Voicework®. That work is aimed at helping people develop freedom and flexibility in their breathing and voice and in their ability to communicate effectively with others. Based on Catherine's own search of how to accomplish this, she has drawn together various areas that were not originally developed for voice training, and modified them to make them relevant. She has, for instance, modified Reichian body work, shiatsu, yoga, and many other modalities, so they would be relevant to freeing the breathing and the voice. This work is mixed with voice training that Catherine studied at the Central School of Speech and Drama. She calls her work "Destructuring" and "Restructuring." Destructuring releases habitual holding patterns in the muscles involved in breathing and voice, and then Restructuring is about focusing the resultant freedom of breath, energy, musculature, awareness, feeling, imagination, and melding it with thought into effective communication. In terms of my particular body of work, I use the principles that my mother taught me and mix them with many others. My mother encouraged this from the beginning by saying, "I want you to learn from everyone to be the best teacher you can be. My work is not a fixed thing but a living, growing body of principles, exercises, and ways of knowing to be applied uniquely and specifically in different circumstances." Another element that distinguishes my work with actors—probably because I teach in LA—is that it is intimately connected to the performance and audition process. I'm interested in how students build a bridge from their voice work to their acting. How do students reveal their humanity through the voice and body—fluidly, moment to moment—within the highly specific needs and language of the story? One big way I approach that is through encouraging presence and focus—becoming aware of what one is actually experiencing internally and externally—and then leaning into what is important for the character. Another area I'm very excited about is in helping students use, rather than reject, the challenges they face in the moment of performance. I'll elaborate on one aspect of this. Many actors habitually *split*, by which I mean they reveal something in performance while unconsciously hiding more challenging parts of their experience. When this happens, wonderful nuances of the story become muted, students' voices become flat, and the performances fail to sizzle, to reveal. For example, an actress who is nervous does a scene in an acting class. It doesn't go so well. The acting teacher points out that she's missing something really important in the scene, tells her what it is, and asks her to investigate it further. That teacher might be spot on, but from my perspective, it's also true that the actress probably did a fantastic job during the scene of communicating how important it was to her not to be afraid. In this example, that's the *split*; the actress believes she's working on communicating as her character, while she's really doing a tremendous amount of largely unconscious work to try not to experience or be perceived as experiencing fear. We could say she's doing a poor performance of what the writer intended, but an accurate, perhaps brilliant expression of what the actress is really putting her energy into. That split often begins in preparation for a part. When she's preparing, and she feels anxiety about getting something "right" instead of splitting away from her anxiety, she could begin to acknowledge it and learn how to let it be, so she doesn't have to do so much work to push it away. Having acknowledged her anxiety, she can then focus on what's important to the character. As part of that process, she may very well need to do more work to get to know what she's saying and the context that she's in. But once she's performing, if she's afraid, there's a different need—to incorporate what *is* into the story. Once she has become aware of her fear and accepted it, she can focus on what's important for the character, or she can incorporate her fear as a part of her character's experience in whatever way makes sense for the story, or she can wield the energy of the fear and transform it through the subjectivity of the character. When she has some facility with those options, her performance will be become more vivid, fluid, and appropriate for the piece. Of course, actors can learn to work this way with all manner of challenges and experiences, not just fear. In developing this part of my work, I have drawn from many teachers, but it is rooted in my mother's work on opening to the self as a basis for revelatory voice work.

Saklad: So in performance you're incorporating all of the given circumstances—and that includes the actor and all of his or her *stuff*—fear, breathing, yearning, openness, etc.?

Kotzubei: Yes. It's so valuable to learn to expand the flexibility of your imagination and the fluidity of your sense of self enough to be able to include almost anything you experience in the moment as a part of the character's experience. Some of what you experience will be important and some not so important, just like in life. Whether and to what degree the experience is relevant depends on your character. The idea isn't to rewrite the story in order to include what is, but to allow "what is" to integrate into the story to help reveal the rich humanity of the story as opposed to just a one-dimensional idea of the story. One can begin to see almost every problem that is encountered in the moment of performing as an opportunity to experience something as the character rather than something to suppress in order to "act well." That process is, of course, different with every actor.

Saklad: When I see and hear somebody like Ben Kingsley or Mark Rylance, I would guess that they do that.

Kotzubei: Great actors do this, and they often do it intuitively, and sometimes they've been taught. They do it, and we see and hear nuances that simply can't be manufactured in advance. They're too complex, too spontaneous, too human, too reflective of what is being received in the moment from the other actors. That is the integration of voice work with acting. Moving beyond just having an open, flexible voice and clear understanding of the text, to revealing one's moment-to-moment humanity through the voice, all within the needs of the story, the realities of what the character needs to communicate. This integration emerges in the moment, often through relating with other characters. When it happens, something inside an audience wakes up.

Saklad: Do you think voice and speech training play a unique role within actor training?

Kotzubei: Yes. But we get into trouble when they become an overly isolated part of the training, and actors don't learn how to integrate the work with their acting training.

Saklad: Some of the obvious benefits of voice and speech training are an evolved instrument and improved use of it. What are some of the indirect benefits?

Kotzubei: One benefit is helping students experience what it is to be present, or at least aspects of what it is to be present with oneself and with others, in a space. The possibility of presence or lack of presence emerges a lot in voice and speech work.

Saklad: What is vocal presence, and is it teachable?

Kotzubei: Vocal presence is being present to what is happening and, with a sufficiently available voice, communicating what is important in the moment. Being able to communicate implies not only that the other characters get what you say, but that the audience also gets to share in it. If you can do that, and do it in a way that is vividly accurate for the character and healthy for you, you've found pretty damn great vocal presence. What vocal presence *isn't* is important too. Generally speaking, it's not "sounding good." My mother used to say that after she coached a show, if the reviews mentioned anything good or bad about the voices, she hadn't done her job. The voice is a vehicle for communicating something. It's not the thing we want an audience to pay attention to unless the character is supposed to have an especially noticeable voice.

Practical Considerations

Saklad: Do you think students should study multiple approaches?

Kotzubei: Yes, with this caveat. It can take many years in a particular kind of work, or with a particular teacher, to really learn something deeply. That said, the danger of not studying other approaches is that one develops too narrow an experience of the voice or thinks one has access to "The Only Truth." If you get to study with two great voice teachers with different approaches in your lifetime, you've done really well.

Saklad: What does the body need to produce optimal vocal work?

Kotzubei: It needs to be able to respond to the needs of the moment in a flexible, efficient way.

Saklad: Would you talk about the breath work you use, "Destructuring" and "Restructuring?"

Kotzubei: Destructuring helps the body/mind become flexible, less rigid. It is the work that Catherine developed, and is still developing, to help people access release. Release can mean a lot of different things to different people. By release, I mean several things: release into gravity, release of unnecessary tension, acceptance of and release into what one is experiencing—I often think of release as vibrant release, not dead release—and finally, letting the breathing go as an expression of being with what is. Let me talk a little more about this last point. When I first ask people to let me witness their experience of released breathing, most people do some kind of graceful, very slow breathing. But that's not release; it's management. Discovering the experience of release is a crucially important process. Release needs to be experienced, not just on the ground, but also standing up, as a kind of vibrancy. But release isn't enough. You've got to focus the freedom found in Destructuring into healthy, efficient, and effective voice use. That's where Restructuring comes in. I think of Restructuring as a technical process for waking up the support and natural resonance that are needed when you genuinely communicate with someone. There are a few key elements here. One is how breath pressure is being initiated and changed in order to power the voice. Catherine has found that many highly gifted speakers organically accomplish this, often unconsciously, through the deepest muscle of the abdominal wall, the transversus abdominis. That muscle works in tandem with the diaphragm and the external intercostals of the ribcage, with only limited engagement of other muscles. Next there's relating breath to the vibration of the vocal folds in an efficient and healthy way. Eventually there's doing that while being able to find natural resonance, while actually relating to somebody else and communicating what you want to communicate. The practice of Restructuring is meant to wake up the key elements of what someone with a free body/voice does organically when he or she wants to communicate. Once you've woken up the necessary connections through the technical work, there is a crucially important final stage: trust. You let go of the technical in favor of communicating with someone. It's like a pianist practicing scales. The point isn't for him or her to get good at practicing scales. The point is to practice scales so he or she can eventually let them go and play stunning music.

Saklad: How do you approach resonance, tonality, and vocal qualities?

Kotzubei: I address them as naturally needed aspects of the voice that arise in vivid communication in specific contexts. I address them technically in exercises, but always with an eye to communication. For resonance specifically, I address it differently from Catherine because of influences from other teachers. But I take seriously her warning to avoid getting stuck in resonant patterns that we associate with a "good" voice.

Saklad: How would you describe the role of listening in voice and speech work?

Kotzubei: I am inspired to speak by a combination of what is inside of me and what and who is external to me. When I stop listening, what's the point of speaking?

Saklad: How would you describe the relationship between emotion and voice and speech work?

Kotzubei: We shouldn't try to make students be emotional. Instead, we want to slowly and gently encourage them to allow themselves to be available and emotionally responsive. Some actors fall into the trap in voice work of seeking emotion—as if that's the goal. If part of what actors do is reveal the human condition, the fact that we have to acknowledge is that much of the time in daily life, people try to avoid being emotional or are private with their emotions—which is completely different from trying to avoid being emotional. When appropriate, actors need to be able to contain or even repress emotions while they are speaking. That said, some people fall into the opposite trap and believe that actors shouldn't ever be extremely emotional when they speak. Sometimes there may be very little obvious emotion; sometimes there may be a lot, depending on the context. Someone who has learned to be available and to manage that availability can respond to the needs of the moment without manufacturing or unconsciously repressing emotion. I want to say one more thing here. It's very personal work for each actor to discover how to open in voice class, and other acting contexts, and then learn to integrate those experiences in healthy, meaningful ways outside of class. For many students, as well as teachers, that work is very, very challenging. Partly for that reason, teachers should not try to force students to be open.

Saklad: How do you approach the teaching of range?

Kotzubei: I'm assuming you mean pitch range, though I also think about range in terms of the range of our humanity that we can experience and communicate, which is of course broader than pitch range. Early on as a student I really misunderstood the notion of exploring pitch. I thought of it as purely technical, and so I had strong resistance to it. Now I understand that doing pitch-related exercises is a way to help actors open to the richness of the possibilities of revealing the self. So, what I do is teach exercises while finding ways to encourage the exercises to be human. That is, I ask people to engage their imaginations, their minds, their bodies, and sometimes simply their awareness of what is inside and outside, while exploring pitch.

Moving Into the Future

Saklad: How has your work evolved over time?

Kotzubei: After doing whatever specific preparation I do for teaching on a given day, I'm now more willing "not to know." By "not knowing" I mean being willing to enter a situation without deciding in advance exactly how it should be. That helps me discover a "knowing" that lives only in the moment of interacting with an actor, which for me is very similar to what I'm asking actors to do onstage.

Saklad: What advice would you give to voice and speech teachers at the beginning of their teaching careers?

Kotzubei: Spend time with this question: when you teach are you unintentionally helping some of your students hide behind "good" voice or speech? That sounds harsh perhaps, but it's so important. I continue to be curious about my motivations for teaching. We're talking about teaching voice here, and voice is so huge and so personal that it behooves us as teachers to continue to explore our own humanity and communication so there really is something to teach. Finally I would say that perhaps even more than through the specific approach that you teach, your students will learn by being with you.

Saklad: What advice would you give to performance students on the brink of their professional careers?

Kotzubei: Be porous to others but don't abandon yourself. Keep learning, and learning to trust yourself. Continue to seek out genuine, excellent teachers, and trust your instincts about whether they are empowering you to find and use your voice to communicate effectively with others.

Saklad: What do you think the future holds for voice and speech training?

Kotzubei: I will tell you once we get to the future. That's not me being glib. I don't know what I will be teaching in ten years. How could I know? I hope it won't be the same as what I'm doing now. That would mean that I haven't kept growing. So how could I know what the future holds for all of voice and speech training? I'll tell you when we get there.

Saklad: Saul, what impact do you hope your work will have on vocal training at large?

Kotzubei: I realize that I hold a unique position in the context of Fitzmaurice Voicework®. I am, as it were, a lineage holder. My hope is that I'm internalizing the richness of my mother's work and making it my work. It's complex—learning the principles of a body of work, and specific processes for teaching it, and internalizing them in such a way that the body of work has continuity and also changes as its practitioners grow and change. At the same time, I'm a voice teacher, not just a teacher of an approach to the voice. I hope my own work and curiosity will help a lot of other teachers and students discover what is helpful for them.

Nancy Krebs

Nancy Krebs has been teaching the Lessac Kinesensic Training for close to thirty years, and attained master teacher status in 2002, trained by Arthur Lessac himself and senior master teacher Sue Ann Park. She has been a theatre department faculty member at the Baltimore School for the Arts since 1981 teaching voice production; has operated her own private studio, *The Voiceworks*, since 1994; taught at the Lessac Intensive Summer Workshop from 1995–1999; and later became associate director from 2000–2004 with Arthur Lessac and Sue Ann Park. Since 2006, she has been the codirector of the summer intensive with master teacher Deb Kinghorn, and developed both a one-week introduction to the Lessac Training at the University of Mary Washington and the Teacher Training Workshop with fellow master teacher Barry Kur, hosted by DePauw University. She was one of three master teachers of different voice pedagogies featured at William and Mary College for the Voice Methods Workshop in June of 2005 and July of 2008 in New York City at Marymount Manhattan College. She is a much sought-after dialect/vocal coach, singer and musician in the Baltimore/Washington region.

Background

Nancy Saklad: Would it be true to say that your work is intimately connected with Arthur's, and how did you come to work with him?

Nancy Krebs: My work is completely connected to the training that Arthur Lessac created and developed. I only teach his Kinesensic Voice and Body Training. I first became introduced to his work while at graduate school at the Dallas Theater Center in 1972–73. I immediately fell in love with this sensory-based training, and told myself that from this point onward I would never be without this training in my personal and professional life. I never dreamed I would someday teach it myself—but at the time only thought I would use it for myself as a performer. Eventually I was invited to teach voice production at the Baltimore School for the Arts, where I began the arduous journey of learning how to share this training with high school–aged acting students. I met Arthur through David Simon, the first director of the BSA. David had been the illustrator for Arthur's original version of his voice text *The Use and Training of the Human Voice*. What are the odds? So I asked David if there was any possibility of Professor Lessac coming to the BSA to teach some master classes for my students. David told me he'd work on that. And that year Arthur did come, did teach, changed my life—and thus began my long association with him. I decided that year (1991) to attend the Lessac Summer Intensive Workshop so I could learn more about the body work, and experience the voice work from the master himself. Then in 1993, after being certified in the training, I was invited by Arthur to teach at the summer intensive, and I continued my training, learning, teaching, and growing in this work, and still do so to this day! Arthur himself is a wonderful instructor, as you might imagine—as is Sue Ann Park, the senior master teacher and director of training for the Lessac Training and Research Institute. So both have been very important models for me as a teacher of voice and body myself. Their voices still ring in my ears as I hear their words often coming into my mind while teaching my own students. My instruction has been fueled and fed by their example, and their influence will always be with me.

Saklad: What it is about the work that most inspires you, Nancy?

Krebs: This training is not based on imitation, ear training, inspiration, rote drill, or outside imagery. It is based solely upon the *awareness* of sensation, and using that awareness and physical sense-memory of the various sensations to be our guide to reproducing the desired result once again. This is what I find most inspiring—the fact that we are teaching our students through what Arthur coined as Kinesensics. I always tell my students, "My job is to make myself obsolete." I want them to learn how to be their own guides for continued monitoring and developing healthy voice and body use.

The Voice and Speech World of Today

Saklad: Would you describe the features that distinguish your work in the field?

Krebs: I am a Lessac master teacher who shares the unique Lessac Kinesensic sensory-based voice and body work with students of all ages and backgrounds who want richer, more resonant, clear healthy voices and more flexible, user-friendly bodies.

Saklad: What are the greatest voice and speech obstacles that the student actor faces?

Krebs: Student actors need to become aware that there are many kinds and stages of "reality" that require certain skills. Not every stage play, teleplay, screenplay, radio play, or any other kind of play, contains the same vocal requirements; so the best training will result in the actor knowing how and when to use the skills necessary for each situation. I think every actor—every human being—needs a "vocal toolbox." In my toolbox I want power without pain, strength without strain, music, variety, ability to express heightened emotion without hurting myself; as well as meaningful consonant awareness, focus and proper placement for my voice, a dynamic range, and more. Another problem facing student actors today is that they are constantly being bombarded by a steady stream of poor role models for vocal production—friends, colleagues, family members—even instructors as well as the performance models—who rely upon personality instead of skill.

Saklad: Are there trends in the lay person's voice and speech that affect the training of today's student actors?

Krebs: Oh, yes. It seems to be a trend among younger people to place their voices so far back into their throat that there is that raspy quality and loss of vibration that has become the new "natural." This coupled with the total lack of energy or movement in the lips and other articulators creates slushy articulation and no depth of tone because the oral cavity itself is completely closed when speaking, so almost anesthetized. This is carried over into what student actors perceive as natural speech, so they resist any instruction that asks them to become more energized, even though they recognize that when they do become more energized, positive results occur.

Saklad: Do you think voice and speech training plays a unique role in performance training?

Krebs: It certainly plays a vital role in performance training. If the eyes are the window to the soul, the voice must be the door! We express our deepest emotions, our passionate views, all the nuances of communication through the voice. Henry Wadsworth Longfellow once wrote, "How wonderful is the human voice! It is indeed the organ of the soul! The intellect of man sits enthroned visibly upon his forehead and in his eye; and the heart of man is written upon his countenance. But the soul reveals itself in the voice only." So this aspect of communication, the voice, has to be developed in order for the speaking or the singing performers to be truly whole. In Lessac training, the voice is trained through the body work. A healthy voice resides in a healthy body. A high-quality performance program wouldn't be complete without sound (pardon my pun) voice and body training.

Saklad: Where does vocal presence come from, and is it teachable?

Krebs: "Vocal presence" is not a term that we use in Lessac's training, but to me it could mean the quality, richness, focus, clarity, and musicality in the voice, essentially—vocal life. It could also be the synergy of physical, spiritual, emotional, intellectual, and vocal energies creating a wholeness, a totality, a completeness in the performer. Is it something that can be learned? Well, of course. It is also partly a gift. But it can be taught through the gift of awareness.

Practical Considerations

Saklad: Do you think then that students can benefit by studying multiple approaches to the work?

Krebs: If you mean approaches to voice training, then I believe that students can experience some benefit or perhaps more benefit *after* they have been trained in one approach with good results. I think young students can easily become confused by differing terminology and other information that seems contradictory even when it's not, when they're exposed to multiple approaches at the same time. This confusion can sometimes cause damage to young voices. Staying with one approach, one pedagogy, will create a grounding for these students and a basic understanding of how the voice wants to function, optimally, for that student. Then after that individual understands his or her voice better on a very basic level and has more confidence, he or she can absorb different approaches more easily without suffering any potential damage to the instrument.

Saklad: You do very engaging body work. Would you talk a little bit about it?

Krebs: Well I teach Arthur's body training, you know, the Kinesensics training, based on his book *Body Wisdom*, which is the use and training of the human body. In this book he states that barring injury, birth defect, or illness, we all possess an amazing, perfect instrument, a physical instrument, like a Stradivarius violin. And we are born capable of unlimited physical, mental, spiritual, and vocal achievements, but through time we lose our ability to communicate with our bodies, and our potential is never fully realized as a result. We become disconnected, like talking heads. But all the cells of the body actually communicate with one other. There is an innate wisdom in the body. Our role is to learn to reconnect, to relearn how to communicate with ourselves, so that we can reteach ourselves to function optimally the way the body was designed to operate. We do this by a self-teaching through the sensory process of feeling sensations, recognizing and identifying those sensations, and then responding to those sensations with awareness so we can use them as guides to produce healthy functioning in the body.

Saklad: What does the body need to produce optimal vocal work?

Krebs: Simple answer? If we have good, salutary posture this will give us ample, healthy breathing, which in turn will help to produce quality tone in the voice, which can create effective communication. Effective communication can eventually lead to world peace. (Arthur always wants to get that in.) World peace can be the peace within oneself, or the world between two people, which is two worlds: your world—my world. We are among many worlds. When we function optimally as we were meant to, we have a constant monitoring system that recognizes when something positive is present or absent. We call that awareness. Awareness is recognizing when something positive is either present or absent from vocal experience. We can't have an optimal voice functioning in a suboptimally functioning body. So that's why we train both at the same time.

Saklad: Do you think an understanding of anatomy deepens the student's relationship to his or her voice?

Krebs: Basic knowledge of the functions and inner working of the human body is helpful, and certainly understanding how the vocal mechanism operates assists. But we in the Lessac world want our students to focus on what they are *feeling* inside—the actual sensations of breathing, vibrations, music, dynamics, springing away actions—rather than individual parts of the body and the voice. Our training is more holistic, rather than compartmentalized.

Saklad: Do you find an imagistic understanding of the voice to be helpful?

Krebs: In Lessac training, *images* are evoked from within ourselves, rather than imposed from the outside. Arthur has a whole section on imagery in his book *Body Wisdom*. His images spring from the action in which we are engaged in the moment, such as muscle *yawning*, muscle *floating*, and muscle *shaking*, which form the basis for the body energies of Potency, Buoyancy, and Radiancy. Imagery can extend into different variations, such as placing ourselves in a pool of water in order to experience Buoyancy or muscle floating. What does this feel like physically? How would you describe this sensation? Then, once we've memorized that set of physical sensations, we carry our memory of that experience out of the water. We then can use the image-feel of being in the pool to create a feeling of Buoyancy once again, even though we are *not* in the water. That's the kind of imagery you'll find in the Lessac work—the *image-feel* of a familiar event, so we can give ourselves the organic instruction to recall that experience in order to produce the sensation once again.

Saklad: How do you address breath work?

Krebs: Many people unfamiliar with his work felt that Arthur didn't deal with the breath, and that is a misconception. Breathing and posture are crucial aspects of the Lessac training. There is an entire chapter devoted to this duality in *The Use and Training of the Human Voice* and additional chapters in *Body Wisdom*. As he states (and I'm going to give you a page number) on page twenty in the voice text: "Nothing contributes more to optimal body condition and vocal health than proper breathing and posture." If you stand properly, you will breathe well. If you breathe correctly, salutary posture will follow. Our work is geared toward training our students to recognize and develop active and instinctive breathing and a posture that is supportive of that breathing process.

Saklad: How does the work approach tonality, resonance, and vocal qualities?

Krebs: In this training, our attention is directed to feeling the presence of vibration experienced on the hard palate—especially the upper gum ridge—moving upward, and continually being guided by that constant flow of buzzing that keeps my voice forward in a healthy placement. Arthur calls this Tonal Energy—the awareness and development of concentrated and dilute resonance within the bones of the face and head. Tonal Energy builds strength and a full, flexible pitch range. There are three components to this part of the training: the Y-buzz, +Y-buzz and the Call. All three create a rich, vibrant, powerful, and focused voice. The Y-buzz alone protects against throat strain, vocal fatigue, breathiness, and nasality. You'll find a lot more information in chapter 6 of his voice text.

Saklad: What role do you think listening plays in voice and speech work?

Krebs: We actually hear through bone conduction and air conduction. Bone conduction takes place within the body. Air conduction takes place outside and strikes the outer ear. One of the basic premises of the Lessac work is to rely on the inner *feel* rather than the outer *hearing* when in the process of training our voice. When we listen to others, our ears are absolutely necessary, but the ear is an ineffective instrument for changing deeply inbred vocal and verbal patterns in ourselves. It always wants to reinforce the mistake. Instead, we want to learn how to depend upon the bone-conducted vibration that travels inside the face and head to be our guide for training purposes. This is not to deny the natural role of the ear or the value of ear training, which develops sharper and better hearing for external air-conducted sounds. When we listen to our voice on a recording for example, the outer ear is entirely reliable for objective judgment. But when we listen to our voice as we produce it, the outer ear is an unreliable guide.

Saklad: You teach an alternative to IPA training. What is it called and how would you describe it?

Krebs: Well the IPA system is known as *phono-sensory*, meaning it is a set of symbols that are learned through the hearing process. I put a symbol on the board. I say that symbol aloud. Students read the symbol, and through their own auditory processing learn what it sounds like through my voice. Lessac symbols are *tono-sensory*. That is, they are guidelines as to how to produce sound. The Lessac symbols represent the identifiable sensations that create the vowels, the diphthongs, or whatever the vocal sound that we're trying to communicate.

Saklad: Your approach to speech work is fun and inventive. Would you give us an overview of the approach?

Krebs: My approach to teaching this work is based on my general approach to life—have fun. I want my students to enjoy learning because this work is fun, it's enjoyable. It feels good, looks good, sounds good, moves forward, and communicates. This work is a self-teaching modality, so I see my role as facilitating that process in those I instruct, so that they learn to rely upon themselves and their own inner harmonic sensing system. Inventive? Well, I think mainly any inventiveness such as creating scat bands with various consonant orchestra instruments came out of my own musical background, and a desire to reinforce the musical leitmotif that runs throughout the voice text. After all, each chapter is titled "The Music of the Consonants," "The Music of the Vowels," "The Music of the Voice." I just try to find ways to keep the music flowing.

Saklad: How would you describe the relationship between emotion and voice and speech work?

Krebs: When students are introduced to all the Lessac vocal "energies," they discover that by developing their mastery over the sensory process, they learn how to control, yet simultaneously release, strong emotions. The true test of their mastery will be in moments of stress, passion, or extreme intensity, but when guided by tonal energy, which is feeling that vibratory process—feeling the voice well placed, feeling the continuum of that vibration—they become efficient in maintaining their own emotional equilibrium, and they avoid becoming vocally compromised.

Saklad: How do you approach the teaching of range?

Krebs: That comes under the heading of Tonal Energy, which gives us the pathway to building a full, flexible pitch range in the voice. But even with the first vocal energy introduced in the book, which is Consonant Energy, range is explored through humming on various consonants such as the *n*, which is referred to as a violin.

Saklad: If I remember this correctly, each consonant is equated with an instrument of the orchestra.

Krebs: Yes. The consonants are given instrumental identifications because they possess the *feel* of that instrument. Once we establish the sensations that determine what an "n-violin" feels like, for instance, we carry those sensations to higher and lower pitches. This is the progression that we usually follow when teaching any of the elements of this work. Then we would carry all of the sensations and the melodies into words, sentences, poems, and eventually, extemporaneous speech. Once the students are more familiar with dynamic range and the music they can create in their voices, it's an easy journey to continuing the same progression with vowels and diphthongs and concentrated tones voices. That's how we teach range.

Moving Into the Future

Saklad: Have you made any important discoveries about the work over the years?

Krebs: You'd think that teaching it as long as I have, since 1981, I would have made amazing discoveries over the years, but the biggest discovery I've made is how interconnected all of the Lessac training is. One component feeds directly into another, and all the work is synergistic, which means it is more than the sum of its parts. Each part of the work can stand on its own, but all the parts together create a stronger, more holistic experience. It's what Arthur refers to as "vocal life."

Saklad: Arthur's the prime model of that, too.

Krebs: He is. He's been his own guinea pig.

Saklad: What advice would you give to voice and speech teachers at the beginning of their teaching careers?

Krebs: All right. I would ask, "So, you want to be a voice and speech teacher. Why do you want to do this kind of work? What attracts you to it? Why does it excite you?" Answer those questions first. Then find the best training that works for you personally and professionally, one you believe in passionately. Learn to communicate that kind of training by studying how it should be taught. Then go out and teach what you know. You can only teach what you can do yourself. Teaching is an ever-evolving process. We learn to teach more effectively through our students' experiences and questions. They are the best teachers.

Saklad: What voice and speech advice would you give to performance students on the brink of their professional careers?

Krebs: Well this is a huge question, and I'm sure I won't do it justice. If I were starting out today, I would want to be the best trained vocally and physically that I can be—equipped with all the skills necessary to play any role within reason. If you feel you have those skills in place, go out and get to work. We learn best by doing. If you feel that something might be missing, find someone to help you acquire that skill; then go out and get to work! Secondly, never do anything that hurts you. If you find that you are getting hurt vocally or physically because of something you are doing—in rehearsal, in a performance—figure out why, and get assistance in order to perform it without damage. We only get one body, one voice. We need to learn how to be protective of our equipment.

Saklad: In your lifetime, have you witnessed an evolution in any aspects of voice and speech training?

Krebs: Absolutely. I have witnessed a growing understanding and recognition in conservatories, universities, and colleges as to the importance of having voice classes offered as part of the theatre or performance curriculum. You have to understand that thirty years ago there was very little out there to help students develop and maintain their voices. I consider the exponential growth that's been taking place in theatre programs throughout the nation and the world to be very exciting and positive. Also, years ago there were very few voice pedagogies that were accepted and advanced in higher education, and now there are many different varieties and approaches recognized and celebrated.

Saklad: What do you think the future holds for voice and speech training?

Krebs: I'm hoping that we move in the direction of more holistic learning for voice and speech training. That we think of the voice—speaking and singing—as one voice. My hope is that we will become more complete in our understanding of how the voice wants to function, how the body feeds into that equation, and become better teachers of the work—all of us.

Saklad: Nancy, what impact do you hope your work will have on vocal training at large?

Krebs: My wish is that those with whom I have had an opportunity to share this body of work will continue to grow personally and professionally, using the skills that they've learned from this training to their benefit, vocally and physically. I would love to see more of my own students, who love this training, begin to teach it themselves. Many of them would make great Lessac teachers. There has been a tremendous renaissance in recent years for the Lessac work. Our workshops are exponentially gaining momentum, and more and more people are becoming familiar with the benefits and the gentle, healthy way in which it is taught. So my hope is that my ability to share this work, which has been passed down to me by Arthur and Sue Ann Park, and listening to other teachers of the work, will inspire others to appreciate its value and want to share it with people from all disciplines. It has such far-reaching, therapeutic benefits, not just for actor training but for people from all walks of life. That's, hopefully, what my legacy will be.

Gillian Lane-Plescia

Gillian Lane-Plescia received her theatre training at the Royal Academy of Music. She taught for many years at Florida State University, UNC Chapel Hill, and the University of Michigan, and now teaches dialects at the Juilliard School's drama division. Her series of self-instructional dialect CDs is widely used, not only in the US, but in the UK, Canada, Australia, Russia, Italy, and Germany. The CDs are based on the principle that the study of dialects is best based on authentic models, and to this end she has traveled widely, collecting the recordings for her series. She works as a dialect coach on Broadway and in regional theatres all over the US, specializing in British dialects with particular emphasis on classic Standard British.

Photo by Mike Haberman

Background

Nancy Saklad: What drew you to voice work, Gillian, and dialects in particular?

Gillian Lane-Plescia: Dialects is something I've always been interested in. In my family, we used to talk with accents a lot, just for fun. The voice work was really accidental. When I was in graduate school at Florida State University, Mary Corrigan, who is one of the Voice and Speech Trainer Association founders, came to work at the Asolo Theatre, and they discovered that I had been trained by Iris Warren, the famous British voice "magician." They were very excited about this and gave me an assistantship to teach voice based solely on that. It was really accidental. My master's degree was in children's theatre. So I did the assistantship and then after I got my MA, they kept me on to teach voice, and that's how it started. Then they decided that since I was a voice teacher, I should do the accents for *A Streetcar Named Desire*. So, I'm a Brit, and there we were in the South, and I was going to teach them to do Southern accents. So I embarked on my first dialect-coaching journey with the help of Jerry Blunt, and taught the actors to do the Southern accent as he had described in his book. I was hearing Southern all around me, but it was a very different accent than the rather posh Southern accent that is usually used for *Streetcar*. So that was my introduction. Then I set up some dialect courses to be included in the program at Florida State and had a lot of fun with it, so I went on doing it. A lot of my success has been luck and completely haphazard timing. Gradually I moved into doing a lot of dialect coaching. When I finally went freelance in Chicago, I was always coaching people for various accents for different plays, and I thought I'd make these audio tapes for people, and so I made a tape for Standard British because that's the one I was doing the most. Then I thought I'd go over to the local theatre bookstore and see if they might like to carry it there. And that was the beginning of what's now my CD business. That particular bookshop had connections with other bookshops, and I took it upon myself and started approaching different bookshops around the country. It just grew. And that's how I began to morph from being a voice teacher to primarily a dialect coach.

Saklad: You mentioned Iris Warren. How did her teaching affect your work?

Lane-Plescia: Iris Warren was a force of nature. Iris's approach to voice teaching was very different from a lot of what was being taught in England at the time. Hers was a much more organic way of doing it. One can see a very clear through-line from her work to Kristin Linklater, who studied with her very closely.

Saklad: Were there other mentors for you?

Lane-Plescia: Yes, I was also influenced by one of my instructors at the Royal Academy of Music Theatre department. Her name was Greta Colson. She was the one who really woke up my ear. She taught a great phonetics class. It wasn't just the International Phonetic Alphabet that we think of that many students learn. It included all of the phonetic sounds, even beyond what we commonly use. We learned clicks and flaps and all that. I realized that I had a good ear, and it improved amazingly because we had to do phonetics of French. I was quite naïve and hadn't realized that French actually had different sounds than English. So it was a huge revelation to me, and that initial work with Greta in the IPA has been tremendously influential in my approach to dialect. Then, obviously there was Kristin. I took workshops with Kristin. Cicely Berry was an influence through her books and knowing her a little bit, and then Patsy Rodenburg. They've all influenced me, and each introduced some kind of new impulse as each of them came into my life or into my awareness.

Saklad: You've worked as a dialect coach on Broadway and all around the US in regional theatres. Do you find that many people pick up accents with ease?

Lane-Plescia: I had some really interesting things happen in terms of people who thought they couldn't do accents. There was an actor I worked with at the Guthrie Theatre, and he had already informed me via the director that he was hopeless at accents and he just wouldn't be able to do it. He was content to do what he always did, which was simply no accent. Well it was essential that he have a Cockney accent in the play. So I suggested we just meet to see what we could do. To cut a long story short, we found out that he could do a Cockney accent. He could learn a Cockney accent by shouting it at the top of his voice. We were, at that time, at the old Guthrie Theater, and the dressing rooms were three stories below the stage. We would go down into these dressing rooms and he would shout his way through his lines and he was fine. The Cockney accent was perfectly acceptable. Once he got it and felt that it was okay, he was able to speak it at a normal vocal volume. You need to meet actors where they are, and sometimes that's not a very good place, but they must be met at their starting point for the work to be productive.

The Voice and Speech World of Today

Saklad: You are perhaps best known for your dialect resources. Would you describe what they are and any other features that distinguish your work in the dialect field?

Lane-Plescia: The obvious distinction is the use of authentic speakers for each of the dialects, and the fact that I don't demonstrate the accents except when it's my own dialect. I'll demonstrate sound changes, but I don't do my version of accents so much. I believe that's not really how you should teach accents. For one thing, I don't think I'm good enough, consistent enough, and I don't want to set up an inauthentic accent as a model for others. Then it all becomes an imitation of an imitation and you get caricature and stereotype. That's why I've really made a point of collecting primary source material. I try to include people of different backgrounds. I like to include working-class people and educated people, both men and women, and younger people and older people. I try to include as wide a variety as I can. People seem to like my analysis of the dialects, and those who know phonetics like the fact that I include phonetic symbols. Another thing I do is make a lot of suggestions for other source material such as films and recordings, local radio stations, YouTube, NPR, and PBS archives, things that I have come across in my own searches, and websites where they could go to get more listening material. There's a lot out there. In terms of my actual coaching, I don't take any single approach, except perhaps to start from where the actor is. I like to encourage actors to think about the fact that their face and mouth and the whole vocal apparatus feels different and moves differently with each unique accent.

Saklad: How would you describe the current state of affairs of actor training in voice and speech?

Lane-Plescia: Nowadays I only deal with the actors I work with in dialect coaching. At Juilliard, for example, I don't teach them voice and speech. I only do dialect work, and I often find that actors either didn't have any dialect training—they may have come out of school with a degree in theatre and have never had a voice and speech class—or I find that the training was not intense enough or that they let go of it.

Saklad: Do you find there are trends in the layperson's voice and speech that affect the training of today's student actors?

Lane-Plescia: It seems to be "fashionable," especially in women, to talk with a gravelly voice. It's pseudosexy, or it's laid back, or it's "cool," and it's bad for their voices. A girl that I worked with recently had no idea that she was doing it. When I pointed it out to her, she was horrified that she was consistently going off her support at the end of her phrases, which meant she wasn't going to be able to project safely if she kept doing that. So I find that troublesome, and the whole area of diction is getting worse and worse. The phonetician Peter Trudgill said—and this was quite a long time ago—that in twenty-five years from whenever he was writing, the *l* in words like *milk* will be gone. The word will be pronounced "miook."

Saklad: What unique role does voice and speech training play in performance training?

Lane-Plescia: Well, the most obvious one, of course, is it prepares an actor for the stage. I think it's important. I wish people had it in their lives.

Saklad: Where does vocal presence come from, and is it teachable?

Lane-Plescia: It can come from a person's character and it's also teachable. There are some people who seem to be born with it, but I definitely think it's teachable, and I'll tell you why. This goes way back to when I was studying with Iris Warren. There was a girl, a student in my class, whose name was Beverly. She was an American and had come over to study in England. Beverly was extremely soft spoken. In our voice class with Iris, she discovered she had a gigantic voice. In fact, when Iris left my program and went to teach full time at another school, Beverly went with her. She knew when she was on to a good thing. It was a miracle, really. Yes, definitely teachable, but I'm not sure that everyone can teach it.

Saklad: I've always wanted to know why some actors delight in dialect work while others struggle.

Lane-Plescia: The people who delight in it have a naturally good ear. Usually I'll ask people if they sing. There is a correlation between the musical ear and the dialect ear. People who love dialects often play with them in their everyday lives. They may like to talk funny and assume different accents. If you look at acting as a form of play, then dialect is just another aspect of that playfulness. I think some people struggle with it because they don't think they'll be able to do it. An actor once said to me, "If you want to be an actor, you have to be prepared to have your pants fall down in public." I love that expression. The idea of putting yourself out there and you could be making a fool of yourself. Then you introduce another thing that isn't really in your repertoire, and that also makes you feel distant from what you're doing—which I think dialects do initially, especially for some people. The actor is metaphorically being asked to use a foreign language, and they're afraid that that language is going to make it impossible for them to deal with creating a character and interacting with a sense of truth. I think that's why they initially struggle. Then there really is the question of how good the ear is. I believe that for most people the ear can be trained to be better, which happened to me with my own phonetic training.

Practical Considerations

Saklad: Do you think students should study multiple approaches to the work?

Lane-Plescia: When I'm teaching at Juilliard they have other dialect classes, not just mine. One of my focuses in working with them, because they've had phonetics, is to say, "Now you need to find your own way of working." Exposure to a variety of approaches is great, because the process can be an amalgam of many different ideas.

Saklad: What does the body need to produce optimal vocal work, and what types of body work do you use?

Lane-Plescia: Physical training is terribly important. Yoga is very good for the body, for stretching, for relaxing, and for breathing. I think work that extends the body is important, that enhances the body's capacity. Getting the body flexible, strong, and responsive; and getting the body and voice to work together, are all important. This has been the underlying principle of the major voice teachers of recent years: Cicely Berry, Kristin Linklater, Patsy Rodenburg; and it was certainly part of Iris Warren's work. Before that, it tended to be all about a "beautiful" voice and perfect diction. But I don't think anybody has come up with the absolute final formula for body work for the actor. There are many options.

Saklad: Do you think an understanding of anatomy deepens a student's relationship to his or her voice?

Lane-Plescia: Yes, I do. I don't think the students need to be able to pass the medical exams, but I do think a basic understanding of it is important. A lot of people don't have the faintest idea what their vocal cords look like. They often imagine them as cords stretched across the throat, rather like violin strings—quite a different concept from the reality, which is that they are simply the top of the larynx or voice box. When you understand this, you have more idea of how important the relationship of the head, neck, and body is to voice production. I was very happy that I had pretty intensive training in that respect as a student. I had to understand how it all worked. Then we know what's there and we can use imagery, which is much more important for people working on their breathing. Visualizing it through images is more effective than thinking about it anatomically. It's much better to imagine the ribs floating up and down than to think about moving your intercostal muscles. But it's still good to know how it all works.

Saklad: How do you address breath work?

Lane-Plescia: After Iris Warren left our program, we had another voice teacher whose teaching was much more in the classic English style of voice teaching. She focused on technique and not how we were feeling from moment to moment. She taught us about rib reserve breathing. It's like almost a dirty word now, but I still use it. Once you've learned it, it's in you whether you like it or not. Occasionally over the years, I would introduce students to it just to let them experience what it was. As far as working with the breath, one needs to make sure that students understand the importance of breath work. For quite a long time I worked with the nontheatre voice. I was a consultant, and I taught a class called "Your Vocal Image." It was for people who wanted to improve their voices, mostly in order to improve their work effectiveness. And because it was so specifically about how your voice presents you to the world, I had to try and lay down much the same approach as I would with actors, but in a single workshop! You always have to go back to the breath, because so many people hold their breath without even realizing it, which is, quite obviously, not a good thing

Saklad: What does it mean to support the voice?

Lane-Plescia: It's what we've been talking about, isn't it? To support the voice is to have the breath in the right place to support whatever voice needs one has. When there's no support or when the support gives out, you get the phenomenon I described at the beginning of the interview with people who have vocal fry and strain. Most actors that I work with don't do it because they have already discovered that it doesn't work onstage. If they do it, they generally don't get work in the theatre.

Saklad: How do you approach tonality, resonance, and vocal qualities?

Lane-Plescia: My big thing was expanding the pitch range of the voice. One of my ways of doing that was to assign students text to work on that was very demanding in terms of the emotional range. This was really when I was working at North Carolina, and was working with people for an extended period of time—at least two years or sometimes three. It took that long for students doing exercises all the time to extend their range and find different kinds of resonances.

Saklad: Do you teach Standard Speech, and if so, what is its value to the student?

Lane-Plescia: I believe Standard American Speech only exists in people's minds. So no, I don't teach Standard American and I never have, because I don't really understand what it's for. People keep trying to explain it to me and give me the phonetics, but I still stand firm that nobody speaks like that. The students at Juilliard used to be taught a Mid-Atlantic sound that was probably how some people spoke thirty years ago, but it's totally irrelevant now. I used to feel very satisfied with the fact that in England we did have a Standard Speech, until I realized that that wasn't true either. Especially now that I know that what was considered to be RP (Received Pronunciation) was also an invented dialect that somebody decided to codify as "proper speak." It was basically the speech standard of people in the upper classes, and it was very important in England for people who had regional accents to learn to speak RP for their various professions. You could not be in certain professions if you did not speak RP until maybe forty years ago. Now not many people speak RP as I knew it, as we learned phonetically when I was in drama school.

Saklad: You have a Standard British CD, don't you?

Lane-Plescia: Yes, and it also has other accents that I don't think of as standard. I now teach something called Classic Stage British. Masterpiece Theatre presented *The Forsyte Saga* a few years ago; that would be a Classic Stage British. So I don't teach Standard Speech. I'm not sure there's ever been one in American. In England there's no standard anymore. Everyone does their own thing. I teach Classic Standard British because when Americans see an Oscar Wilde play or *Pygmalion*, they expect to hear very clear diction, and they expect the actors to speak in the RP that I still use.

Saklad: Do you see scientific and/or technological advances influencing your work or the work at large?

Lane-Plescia: Technological advances certainly influence my work with dialect. Obviously, it's much easier for people to get dialect material through the Internet, which is why I'm working on creating Internet downloads of my dialect work instead of actual CDs. When people have an audition tomorrow, they can't wait for the mail. Then there are all the smallish items you can carry around that become your portable dialect coach. You can carry dialect recordings on your iPod and not have to lug cumbersome equipment around and all the new small instruments for recording. Those are technological advances that are extremely useful in dialect work.

Moving Into the Future

Saklad: What advice would you give to voice and speech teachers at the beginning of their careers?

Lane-Plescia: Learn from your students. In other words, we're back to the concept of listening. And also be patient.

Saklad: What voice and speech advice would you give to performance students on the brink of their performance careers?

Lane-Plescia: Do the same as Olivier. Work on your voice, then work on your voice, then work on your voice...

Saklad: Have you witnessed much of an evolution in how voice and speech and dialects in particular are taught?

Lane-Plescia: Yes I have, and the fact that I had this training at the very beginning with Iris Warren has really given me a sense of continuity in that. This is very different from the other training I had as a student, which was much more a training of the externals. Lots of diction exercises, rib reserve breathing, and learning to speak about twelve lines of

Shakespeare on one breath! But that was fifty years ago now. The initial training that I had with Iris is very close to the best kind of work that's being done today. A lot of other things have changed. The focus of the work has changed from in the past when one needed to attain a goal that came from without, as compared to today when the goal is to develop and release the expressive self that lies within. I'm pretty sure that's what Iris was doing, and it's what the best vocal people are doing today. Instead of pursuing "the voice beautiful," you're going to find the best of your own voice. That's what drives most of the vocal teaching today.

Saklad: And that was not the case certainly in years gone by?

Lane-Plescia: No, it was not the case even with some of my teachers afterwards. One of the things Kristin said was that the voice isn't always going to be beautiful, because sometimes what it's saying isn't going to be beautiful. The voice has to be able to express terrible things, and a beautiful voice isn't always going to serve the text. The aesthetic is not governed by a particular sound but by the freedom of the instrument and the actor's expressiveness. And Kristin, of course, was important in bringing this forward because she was trained by Iris Warren very intensively. I definitely see the through-line. Something was going on at that time in England that caused people to move in that direction. I don't really know what it was, but it seemed to be a revolt against the old classical-training discipline, with its emphasis on hyperdiction and superbreath—the twelve lines of Shakespeare on one breath that I referred to before. Cicely Berry was a pioneer of the new movement in voice training, as was Litz Pisk in movement. I'm sure it was happening elsewhere too, but it took time before it became widely accepted. As I say, after Iris Warren left my training program, we definitely went back to more conventional voice work.

Saklad: What do you think the future holds for voice and speech training?

Lane-Plescia: I hope we're going where we'll be able to counteract what's going on with the general population regarding the voice.

Saklad: Can we salvage the *l* and the terminal *t*?

Lane-Plescia: I think we should try. I used to tell my students when I was teaching this kind of thing, "You people are the guardians of language. Writers and poets and actors are the guardians of language. If you abandon your speech, in a way you're abandoning language." We don't want to end up with actors who sound overstated, but it would be lovely if they could still maintain clarity against all that's going on.

Saklad: What impact do you hope your work will have on vocal training at large, Gillian?

Lane-Plescia: I hope the work will help actors to develop their dialects. It's always been rather satisfying to me when people have said that the work that they did on their voice with me has helped them with their careers. That's what I hope it will continue to do.

Kristin Linklater

Kristin Linklater has worked as a vocal coach at Stratford Ontario, the Guthrie Theatre, the first Lincoln Center Repertory Company, the Open Theatre, the Negro Ensemble, and the Manhattan Project. In 1978 she cofounded Shakespeare and Company with Tina Packer. In 1990 she began teaching at Emerson College. She is now a professor of theatre arts at Columbia University. Kristin has lectured and has given workshops in the US, the UK, Europe, and Russia. She is the author of *Freeing the Natural Voice* and *Freeing Shakespeare's Voice*.

Background

Nancy Saklad: Kristin, what was it like to work with the legendary voice teacher Iris Warren?

Kristin Linklater: I was very young when I started working with her. I was studying at the London Academy of Music and Dramatic Art when I was seventeen, so I had no idea what I was getting into. I just did whatever I was told, and we all were fairly lighthearted about it. Iris would teach us twice a week. She was a rather formidable woman. She had not worked in the theatre herself, and had never been an actor, but taught privately at the Wigmore Studios, where she taught a lot of the leading actors of the time who were performing in the West End. Then she was persuaded to teach at LAMDA by the principal at the time, Michael MacOwan, who was an inspired teacher and director. He always said that when he directed on the West End stage, there was something really interesting about some of the actors with whom he worked. It had something to do with the truthfulness of their voices, their connection with themselves. Those words were not used much in London in the 1950s. He gradually realized that they were the actors that had been working with Iris Warren. So he persuaded her—and it took a lot to persuade her. She'd never taught before in a drama school. She taught the progression of exercises that we learned in a rather parrot fashion. We'd have twenty minutes of warm-up every day, and we'd run through the exercises without knowing really what they were for, except that they covered the whole range of the voice. She was rather distant, very formal, and then after I left LAMDA, I got a letter from Michael MacCowan suggesting that I come to train with her as a teacher, because he had thought that I had qualities that were those of a teacher. I was twenty-one and I was flattered. I had no idea. People who look at my professional life tend to ask when I decided to be a voice teacher. I never decided to be a voice teacher. I never had any inclinations in that way, but I was pointed in that direction. I sat in on most of Iris's classes. I had ten private classes with her, and I learned to teach on the job. She had an instinct, an intuition, and a sense of what was emotionally truthful. That was a vocabulary of work that was unknown in those days, particularly in the voice world. We didn't talk about truth much. Over here there was emotional veracity at the Actor's Studio, but not so much in England in that time. But Iris had a vocabulary of working from the inside out—working from the touch of sound that is the center of you, and from that she elicited amazingly open, spontaneous, and honest performances.

Saklad: And it seems to be the center of your work now.

Linklater: Oh, I inherited that progression of exercises that she taught us. We did it without any thought in those days. Then I gradually discovered what it was. I don't think she could have described it in anatomical or voice science terms. We didn't have that vocabulary. We worked absolutely from what we saw or what we felt or what we touched, and it didn't have any academic or scholastic background. It was entirely human.

Saklad: Were there other mentors for you, Kristin?

Linklater: At that time at LAMDA, Michael MacOwan, whom you'll not hear much about, was an extraordinary teacher—a man of enormous enthusiasm and a Shakespeare worshipper. He taught me an enormous amount about Shakespeare and also about presence and openness. Bertram Joseph, who was the Shakespeare teacher at LAMDA, was also extremely influential. His books are still in print, I think. He came out of an academic background, but he had an amazing feeling for how to speak Shakespeare that came entirely from observing the imagery and allowing it to play on your voice. And of course, that's become the heart of what I do with Shakespeare.

Saklad: You've vocal coached for a number of highly acclaimed theatres: Stratford Ontario, the Guthrie, and Shakespeare and Company. Who are some of the directors you worked with, and how has their work impacted your own?

Linklater: The first big professional production that I worked on was *King Lear* at Stratford Ontario in the mid-1960s. Michael Langham directed it. I was twenty-seven years old and had just come out of a drama school. I was thrust right into the middle of this extremely potent professional company with extremely powerful and talented actors. I was scheduled into their rehearsal to work with every single one of them from the top to the bottom. Gradually I learned more about what I was listening for in the text. Michael Langham's ear on the text was impeccable, and I got a lot of Shakespeare training there in terms of the voice and also presence. It was a great training to work with Tyrone Guthrie, too, at the Guthrie Theatre. I learned a great deal about the practical and highest artistic demands of professional theatre from some of those directors: Guthrie, Langham, and John Hirsch. I was such an innocent, though. When I came to New York and was working at the newly created Lincoln Center Repertory Company, I had no idea that sitting in on Elia Kazan's rehearsals was anything particularly interesting or special. I had no idea that sitting in on Harold Clurman's rehearsals was something I should remember or make little notes on for the future. I didn't know who they were, but I worked with some amazing people, looking back on it—Joe Chaikin, too. I arrived in the US in 1963. So the time that I was in New York, twelve years through the '60s and the '70s, was the golden age of experimental theatre—of subsidized theatre. The Ford Foundation was pouring millions of dollars into the arts. It was a glorious time to be in theatre.

The Voice and Speech World of Today

Saklad: What features would you say distinguish your work in the field?

Linklater: One feature is the precision, the detail, and the real discipline of adopting, practicing, and developing the techniques that are personalization techniques, "emotio-techniques," as I sometimes call them. The methodology is very exact and very demanding. Anybody that really does the work gets something on a deep level and on a subtle level of personal expressiveness. That I think is particular. Another feature that is something I bring with a solidity of experience is the commitment to the belief in the emotional basis for intelligent understanding of a text, and certainly of Shakespeare. I can get people to that place where they free themselves emotionally in a speech and can keep thinking at the same time. The form and content balance out; therefore, the delivery is unique and very alive. Whereas a lot of my colleagues are very good at and very interested in the text work—because it's very interesting—I deal with the causal stuff more, with the basic voice and the belief that the text comes alive in this act of releasing one's self. I do text work, but I don't put all my eggs in the text basket. I put most of my eggs in the breath and impulse basket.

Saklad: What aspects of the work most inspire you?

Linklater: I get fanatical from month to month about different things within the work I do. It can be the spine one month, and then there's all this controversy about core muscles. I can get fanatically excited about that argument. I am fascinated by anatomy and how a lot of information is coming over the Ethernet about how wrong it is to try and isolate any muscle in order to strengthen it. The body doesn't work like that. There's evidence that all that Pilates core work is not really good for the body. It's not how the body likes to work at all, and of course for breathing it's disastrous. They've coopted the word *core* and have turned it into "huge amount of muscle support." But the true core is the whole psoas system and its connection with the whole viscero-sensory motor system. The body works best holistically with a global sense of itself. So I get excited about that. I'm always dreaming up new things vis-à-vis the students that I'm working with. The minutia of Shakespeare is really what gives me the most pleasure, as in, "How do you deliver this argument? How do you do a parenthesis? How do you do a parenthesis within a parenthesis?" The joy of Shakespeare's text is awakening those parts of the student actor's brain—that "Aha!"

Saklad: What myths about voice and speech training abound, and how can we demystify them?

Linklater: One of the things we need to be careful about is not working so much with the ear, listening to a result. It's tough, but I think you have to reeducate the connection between thought and the neuroanatomy, and then trust the thought. That's what good actors do anyway. The trouble with us teachers is that we think we have to teach everybody everything. We really don't. You have to get them oiled up and then get them out of their way. If they're talented, their systems know what to do.

Saklad: How would you describe the current state of affairs of American actor training in voice and speech?

Linklater: Healthy—healthier in this country than in the UK, to be so bold. Things change all the time. I just don't think the UK is at a terribly interesting stage at the moment. Then, there's too much emphasis on voice science and not enough focus on artistic voice. In this country, on the other hand, there are drama departments all over the country that hire voice teachers and speech teachers. There's good knowledge on Shakespeare and how to speak it in this country. There are a huge number of Shakespeare companies—summer and year round. That's very healthy.

Saklad: What do you think are the greatest voice and speech obstacles that the student actor faces?

Linklater: iPods, texting where all the vowels have been killed, and robotic voices in technology. I think there's an enormous technological impact on the way that people speak. There isn't enough oral nourishment for the students' ears. On the other hand, when they speak poetry it's like food. The color comes into their cheeks.

Saklad: Do you think that voice and speech training plays a unique role in actor training?

Linklater: Oh yes, it's central to it. The interesting thing is that voice and speech was all there was until the 1920s and '30s, and in England it was really until the '40s and '50s. At the big drama schools in England, which were started at the turn of the century—RADA, Central, Webber Douglas, LAMDA—actor training was voice, speech, elocution, poetry speaking, and then you got up and did plays. You learned how to walk around and not knock over the furniture, and you would send your pear-shaped vowels to the wall. Voice was the center of the training. Then along comes Stanislavsky. The Moscow Arts Theatre came to New York during the '20s. Before that, elocution was huge. There were hundreds of elocution schools around the country. People would go and learn to speak properly, and then they'd start acting. They weren't taught acting. You learned acting by apprenticing with older actors and working your way up to it. The Moscow Arts Theatre came into existence, and Stanislavsky came up with ideas and theories and practical exercises. Then in the US, the Group Theatre emerged, and from that seminal work came Stella Adler and Lee Strasberg and the Actors Studio, and suddenly we have this thing called acting. The whole idea of acting being at the center of training is rather recent. Here, it's been difficult to get the voice and speech back into some central position, but I think it's getting there.

Saklad: Where does vocal presence come from, and is it teachable?

Linklater: Let's start from an idea. If you hold your breath, you're absent. So the basis of vocal presence is to actually be breathing in the moment. From there you have to have done some work on your voice, but then it's a question of being there, knowing what you want to say, and saying it freely. I think that's vocal presence, if you want to use those words. Presence is presence. The voice should reveal the presence of the person. We should hear the presence of the person through the voice. I don't trust someone who says, "Here is my voice. Listen to how musical it is. Listen to how well placed it is." I don't trust a well-placed, well-modulated voice, because it's been trained to be a pleasant mask. The goal of training to free the natural voice is to get the voice to be transparent—transparently revealing the thoughts and feelings of the person speaking.

Practical Considerations

Saklad: Do you think students benefit from studying multiple approaches to the work?

Linklater: No, because we don't have enough time. I have a lot of time to teach here at Columbia, and it still is not enough. There's no value in learning a lot of different approaches to breathing. Stick with one and go in depth. That's enough for the body/mind to explore.

Saklad: How do you approach breath work?

Linklater: Experientially. First, we become aware of the organic movement of the diaphragm in everyday natural breathing and its relationship with emotion. Then we explore the body/mind connection through the psoas system to the pelvic floor by way of lumbar spine and sacrum. These are the breathing muscles that pick up instinct and intuition. Finally, we develop the elasticity and openness of the ribcage in order to maximize breath capacity. We open up the whole organic breathing mechanism to the galvanizing triggers of impulse.

Saklad: What does it mean to support the voice?

Linklater: What it means to support the voice is to have done your work, which is to get yourself all connected up—impulse, breath, no pushing in the external musculature, an awareness of resonators so that you've got your whole range. You free your voice first, and then you don't have to support your voice. You have to think clearly, and you have to have a strong desire to speak. Once you've freed your voice, then all your attention needs to go to what you want to say. So you don't support your voice with anything but strong intention, lively impulses, appropriate emotional input, and by the content of what you want to say. The support for the voice is the content of what you want to say. You do not have to support your voice with conscious musculature application. In fact, you compromise the integrity of the neuroanatomy of the voice if you try to consciously do what is already extremely well organized on the involuntary level. Then people ask about singing, and I say it's the same for singing. I've just been talking to a man who's the vocal coach for City Opera. He's been a singing teacher for decades, and now he's also an Alexander teacher, and he is more fanatical than I am. Even for opera, you do not need to support with conscious breath control. For opera or for any vocalizing, if you add external muscular support, your voice is diminished.

Saklad: What role does listening play in voice work?

Linklater: Oh, an enormous one. As children we learn language in the first place through the ear. What I hear is what triggers what I want to say. Now there's an inner ear and an outer ear, and the inner ear is listening to me while the outer ear is listening to you. This circulation of energies is what enlivens the voice and gives it plenty of nourishment. My latest little fanatical game is an exercise we do where you're swinging your arms and your knees are bouncing and the sound is coming up vertically from underneath the ground through your body, then laterally out of your arms at the same time. We usually do this with arpeggios for loosening and strengthening the voice. Then you do it facing someone. The energy of thought is vertical, lateral, and also sagittal. Now when you think about Shakespeare, my students will say, "How do you deal with objectives and playing actions and intentions in Shakespeare?" and I say, "Look, the trouble with Shakespeare is you can't put everything under the impetus of playing an objective, because quite often what the character is doing is letting off steam, or exploring a philosophical idea." So you've got the listening in the scene, and the intention to affect the other person, which is the sagittal energy. You have lateral energy, which is going out to the whole story. You have vertical energy, which is suddenly saying, "I'm going to talk about the entire chain of being," or "What a bastard it is to be a bastard." That's the listening in. You're listening in to your own need and then you're listening out to what you need to say to the other and what the other needs to say to you.

Saklad: Your book *Freeing the Natural Voice* is both practical and profound. How long would it take someone to complete the sequence that's laid out in the book?

Linklater: It takes sixty hours, and then you need to go back and do it again and again. What you're doing is reconditioning the way you think, the way you breathe, the way you are, the way you listen, and the way you express yourself. You'll get some results, though, from doing it superficially. It's like vocal yoga; you can go back to the beginning again and again and it gradually shifts the way that your brain/body works.

Saklad: How would you describe the relationship between emotion and voice and speech work?

Linklater: It's essential. Emotion is running in us all the time. We don't express it all the time, but we are made of emotion and thought and experience and the senses. You only have to look to babies to see what the natural emotion is doing to make voice. That's the original desire—the desire to have this emotional sense come from inside to outside and with need. There's real need in it. The raw and extreme sources of voice are emotional. Most of us have been through an education that divides and separates the natural brain from the experiential body, even though now we know that Descartes was wrong. It is not, "I think, therefore I am." It's, "I am, therefore I think." The schools separate the brain from the body. What you learn is very focused in one part of the brain, and it's the rational part. What gets restored during this kind of work is an emotional source, which is your life, your liveliness, what makes you vital.

Saklad: Louis Colaianni does a lovely rendition of your exercise "zoo-woh-shaw" with the phonetic pillows. Have you seen it?

Linklater: Of course.

Saklad: What was your inspiration for this exercise?

Linklater: Zoo-woh-shaw? I was doing some lo-o-ong workshop in New York with Shakespeare and Company, and everyone was in their heads, and I went on, as I always do, about the Elizabethans and how they experienced language in their bodies, and I realized you can't force people to get language from their heads to their bodies. So I thought, better go back to the absolute concept of words, the vowels and consonants. That'll get them into their bodies. I had worked in drama school with something called the vowel resonance scale, which takes into account the intrinsic resonance of vowels. D. W. Aiken developed it in the 1920s as the most economical way in which vowels get formed. We learned them as part of speech through Iris Warren. So it was the lip vowels, then the tongue vowels. We learned to run the vowels sitting in chairs, doing it "right," and I realized that it was still all up in the head. Once we started with the vowels down in the body, I realized that's where they really lived, and they needed consonants to carry them out of the body, because that's what the consonants do really. They help to expel the vowels from the body. I just intuitively came up with those consonants—zoo-woh-shaw, etc.—but it's all been developed experientially. You can feel them. Each has its resonating home in the body.

Moving into the Future

Saklad: Have you witnessed much of an evolution of voice and speech training over the course of your career?

Linklater: I think the work's getting much more real. There's so much new information coming in from voice science, anatomical science, and also the fact that you can see things better than you did before. Though I find that a lot of that doesn't really help much. There's both a good and bad side. You can see how things work—which muscles are working. The trouble is, you see some muscles working through sound imaging and you think, "Okay, that's how it works. I'll do that." No, as soon as you start consciously working those involuntary muscles it's no longer how it works. I find there's a lot more psychological understanding now. There's also a lot more understanding of trauma in the body, and a lot of us work with people that have had very troubling childhoods. I think we can recognize that, certainly more than when I was starting out. It's good. I feel fairly hopeful about it.

Saklad: Finally, Kristin, what impact do you hope your work will have on vocal training at large?

Linklater: I hope my work will keep it honest. Keep it honest and on purpose. The purpose of what we're doing is to make acting as good as it can possibly be. I'm really interested in the art of the voice and its contribution to the art of the theatre.

Natsuko Ohama

Master voice teacher Natsuko Ohama trained under the legendary Kristin Linklater at the Working Theatre in New York. A founding member and permanent faculty of Shakespeare and Company, Lenox, MA; and senior artist at Pan Asian Rep., NY, she has taught at numerous institutions, including the Stratford Festival, CalArts, Columbia University, the Sundance Institute, New Actors Workshop, and NYU, and was the director of training at the National Arts Center in Ottawa. Presently she heads the voice progression in the masters program at the University of Southern California. A Drama Desk–nominated actress, she has portrayed roles ranging from Juliet to Lady Macbeth, from Hamlet to Prospero (Los Angeles Women's Shakespeare Company), from action films *Speed* to the cult series *Forever Knight* and *American Playhouse* on PBS. She has been seen on screen recently in *Pirates of the Caribbean 2*, on television in *Nip/Tuck*, and onstage in *Dogeaters* as Imelda Marcos at the Kirk Douglas Theatre.

Photo by Christine Pan

Background

Nancy Saklad: I know Kristin Linklater is one of your mentors, Natsuko. How has her work inspired your own?

Natsuko Ohama: Her work and the opportunity to work with her have been my major inspiration. Who she is inspires me. The incisive intelligence, imagination, courage in teaching, curiosity in learning, humor, temperament, intuition, and vision that is hers rarely come together in one person. When I went to the Working Theatre in the '70s I really went to work with Joseph Chaikin. I had never heard of Kristin Linklater or Peter Kass. When I got there, I saw how extraordinary she was in terms of her ability to teach work that was useful and practical. She works without fear, and investigates both the acting process and the way we communicate. She was, and is, an extraordinary teacher. So it doesn't matter if you are a physicist or a chimney sweep, if you're a great human being, you're going to be inspiring. Kristin is an extraordinary human being.

Saklad: Were there other mentors?

Ohama: Yes, Peter Kass, who was a brilliant acting teacher. He just died last year. He was the greatest acting teacher I've ever encountered. Peter taught at NYU for many years. Olympia Dukakis, Ron Van Lieu, and John Cazale were students of his. Then there was A. J. Lawrance, who was a high-school teacher who completely transformed all the kids in my class. He taught English and theatre. Now I come from the middle of the prairies. There is nothing out there, so this teacher introduced us to performance, to theatre, and to writing. In high school we were doing plays written by Leonard Cohen, D. H. Lawrence, and Samuel Beckett, and we wrote our own work. He played a great role in the way we saw the world. Also Trish Arnold, master movement teacher and major influence on the voice work and, phantasmagorically, Fred Astaire and Francis Bacon.

Saklad: You were a founding member of Shakespeare and Company. Does your work there continue?

Ohama: I am a permanent faculty member of Shakespeare and Company. I have not taught there in years, but I love that theatre profoundly. Much of my formative work took place there in the organization's early years. In fact, I was accidentally Shakespeare and Company's first voice teacher. In those first seasons I played Juliet, and the voice work was a great exploration. We worked outside doing warm-ups on the grass. During the early winter workshops, we trained on a level I don't think we will ever see again. The intensity of the early Shakespeare and Company years was the most fertile world one could imagine for the vocal training. The love, hate, anger, fear, joy, jealousy, chores, rehearsals, luxury, penury, sexuality, discipline, pleasures, countryside, personalities, animals, children, performances, training, romances, creativity, fighting, hilarity, friendship, community...I taught in all the workshops for the first ten years, I think, and Tina Packer, founder of the company, is a huge influence and force of nature.

The Voice and Speech World of Today

Saklad: What features would you say distinguish your work in the field?

Ohama: My strong suits are imagination, personalization, clarity of thought, and intuition...and the work is very personal.

Saklad: How would you describe the current state of affairs of actor training in voice and speech?

Ohama: It's very good. We don't do apprentice programs anymore as we used to do. We don't learn through watching great actors. Instead we train. Voice and speech training is relatively young, and I think it's good.

Saklad: What are the greatest voice and speech obstacles that the student actor faces?

Ohama: The greatest obstacle is the students' fear of what people think of them.

Saklad: How do you help the actor get past the fear and self-consciousness?

Ohama: I enter the arena with them at a particularly challenging moment, and then I do whatever I need to do in order to get them to "go there." Through example I try to open them to the place where they can break through whatever it is that's inhibiting them in that experience. I'm an actor, and I operate from my instinct and the spontaneity of the moment. So if the student is doing something and I perceive what that something is, I go in there with them and I follow my instinct. This is what I learned from Kristin.

Saklad: There's something about the moment that's precious and requires a variety of tools and responses that can happen only in the moment.

Ohama: That's right. It's about being present. If you're present then they have to be present. You have to draw them into being present. That's all.

Saklad: Do you come across trends in the layperson's voice and speech that affect the training of today's student actors?

Ohama: No, not really. Trends evolve and we have our prejudices against them. It doesn't bother me.

Saklad: Do you think voice and speech training plays a unique role in performance training?

Ohama: No, I don't. The training is always about acting. We only separate the roles of voice, movement, and acting as a practical aspect of training. For me, acting is a complete way of being, and we only separate out an element of it and call it the voice in order to manage it. The work is always framed by the acting process. So is it unique? Yes, but not separable from the rest of the work.

Saklad: Where does vocal presence come from, and is it teachable?

Ohama: Vocal presence originates in the individual but can be helped to be revealed.

Practical Considerations

Saklad: Do you find students benefit by studying multiple approaches to the work?

Ohama: After a certain point yes, if there is need. Voice teachers make too much of a fuss about how important we are. Actors should be able to do whatever they want. There are phases, of course, when students are transformed by voice work. They describe it like that. It's a good thing for them to be overtaken by the work. But in the end, it's not about voice. It's about being a human being. I think too much of acting work tends to be about the voice. You just want the actor to be able to come into the arena bringing him- or herself.

Saklad: What does the body need to produce optimal vocal work?

Ohama: Courage and desire. We see it all the time. We see it in people with all kinds of issues—terrible spine or physical injuries. If they have desire and courage, none of that matters.

Saklad: Does an understanding of anatomy deepen the student's relationship to his or her voice?

Ohama: After a certain level of experience, yes it does. You really want to keep the experience in the body. With actor training any knowledge that you get, especially about anatomy and how the body works, is great, but it probably shouldn't come very early, because it can be limiting.

Saklad: Do you find an imagistic understanding of the voice to be helpful?

Ohama: Yes, without a doubt. I use too many to mention, but I would say many of the images are created in the moment, out of the immediate circumstances and what is needed. I use the images to illuminate and provoke an experience for the actors—as the muse strikes.

Saklad: How do you address breath work?

Ohama: As naturally as possible. I focus on connection, flexibility, freedom, and strength. The difficult part is consciously letting the autonomic process do most of the work, which is a conundrum.

Saklad: What does it mean to support the voice?

Ohama: Having the physical, mental, and emotional ability and connection to sustain the required demand. The breath is supported by the actor's mental, physical, and emotional energy, which carries out spoken thought. The body has to be in a certain state of strength and power, but really it's the intention that's going to carry it out in the long run. A lot of voice students tend to think support is about breath capacity and muscles, when in fact you have to have the intention behind it and practice behind the intention.

Saklad: Would you describe how you approach range in tonality, resonance, and vocal qualities?

Ohama: I use Kristin's resonating ladder and the progression of these exercises to continue to strengthen and explore different resonating areas. When you're a student, it's important to drill the exercises over and over. You have to be able to feel the sound. You have to do it along with connecting to your breath, feeling it in your body, and using images that help. So in terms of exploring all of those different things, do the basic vocal progression.

Saklad: What role does listening play in voice and speech work?

Ohama: Listening is the other half of breath. It is reception. Listening, as Evelyn Glennie the Scottish percussionist might say, is not the same as hearing. It happens with the whole body. It lives in the world of the senses, and for me, the core experience is with breath. Listening is the other half of everything. It's a perception. I can draw a parallel to breathing: breath comes in, breath goes out. So we speak, we listen. Lately I've been focusing a lot more on the reception of breath, because the outgoing breath, which carries sound, is where everybody puts focus. In truth, it's the breath coming in where we listen. The listening experience occurs when we take something in, when it's given to us and when we receive it. Sound is processed through our being, and if we so choose, it is given back in communication. So I think listening is tremendously important; it's the other half. It is hard to describe. The ancient Greeks described all the senses as touch, so maybe I should leave it to them!

Saklad: You recently became certified in Louis Colaianni's *The Joy of Phonetics*. What drew you to this work?

Ohama: I am a huge fan of Louis Colaianni. I have known him for many years, and he is an original. He is brilliant, and his phonetic pillows are incredibly useful for speech and dialect training. They make the learning fast, indelible, fun, and profound. The phonetic pillows are the best way I have encountered of learning phonetics. You try to explain it to people who don't know about the pillows, and it just sounds a bit crazy. They are a wonderful kinesthetic tool for embodying all of the IPA sounds. I've taught some BFA classes, and one of the students came to me afterwards and said she had struggled to learn phonetics for an entire year. With Louis's pillows, she and the rest of the class learned the IPA in a week! The students retain it because the work is so visceral and imaginative.

Saklad: How do you help your students connect imagery and the text?

Ohama: Lightly. Humorously. Willfully. Wishfully. Demandingly. Cajolingly. Mockingly. I use Kristin's sound and movement work, and it is very difficult to teach because it is advanced work. Sound evoking movement, image evoking sound. There's a certain level of doing sound and movement where you have to will the students into it, and again, that's where Kristin is brilliant. The crystal-clear thinking that she applies to language to get the actors to hook up their imagination to an experience is stunning. I could watch her do it all the time, because she simply wills the students and they do extraordinary things. Every time I enter into the world of sound and movement I always have tremendous anxiety, because there's a certain kind of bullshit element to it if one doesn't do it well. To really teach it is to enter into the arena like a matador and say, "I'm going in here, and every fiber of my mental ability and my language is going to be used to make them make this connection. And I'll do anything to accomplish that."

Saklad: How would you describe the relationship between emotion and voice and speech work?

Ohama: I don't think they have a relationship. They are one.

Saklad: Do you devote time to teaching vocal characterization?

Ohama: Yes I do. We do personal resonance explorations, "feeling things out," imaginative searching, coming from character inspirations. We also do donor work—record people and interview them for accents. I send the students out to research. They listen and record. Character work is usually done once the students have completed their basic voice work. Then they do some movement, imaginative work on text. In the second year we start working with the phonetic pillows, which moves into dialect. We also work on different resonators, trying to get into those difficult resonating places. The quest is how to stretch the essence of yourself into different pockets of your being.

Saklad: How do you see scientific and/or technological advances, within or without the field, influencing your work or the work at large?

Ohama: I find the major use of this kind of knowledge for me is that it spurs my imagination and inspiration, particularly in sound and movement work, and helps the abstract nature of images to evoke experience in the body.

Moving into the Future

Saklad: Have you witnessed much of an evolution in voice and speech training over the course of your lifetime?

Ohama: For me personally, yes. I trained doing mainly articulation exercises as a young actor. Kristin Linklater's work was a revelation for me that was much more involved than lips, tongue, and throat.

Saklad: What advice would you give to voice and speech teachers at the beginning of their teaching careers?

Ohama: Listen and breathe. Have a heart. Enjoy yourself.

Saklad: What advice would you give to students at the brink of their professional careers?

Ohama: Have a creative appetite. Love what you do. Be fearless and live.

Saklad: Natsuko, what impact do you hope your work will have on vocal training at large?

Ohama: I want actors to be human beings. They are the soul of humanity. They are our only hope really. What I do is to try to make them recognize that, remember it, stand by it, and be alive as human beings, in all phases of whatever that means.

Saklad: Would you explain what you mean by "be alive as human beings?"

Ohama: Thinking back to my early days with Shakespeare and Company, there was so much emotional contrast in the living of the joy and the angst and the love and the hate and the fear and the courage. That's what I'm talking about. We tend to not want to live in all those possible worlds. And so, to have the strength to embrace that type of living, to truly live within it, that would be my hope to give to those with whom I work—to encourage the actors to embrace that without fear.

Bonnie Raphael

Since 1997, Bonnie Raphael has been a full professor in the department of dramatic art at the University of North Carolina at Chapel Hill, where she headed the professional actor (MFA) training program from 1997 until 2005. She teaches voice, speech, dialects, and text analysis, and she serves as resident coach to the Equity theatre on campus, Playmakers' Repertory Company (LORT). For eleven years before coming to Chapel Hill, Dr. Raphael coached productions for the American Repertory Theatre and taught at its Institute for Advanced Theatre Training at Harvard. She has taught for over thirty-five years at educational institutions including Northwestern University, the University of Virginia, the National Theatre Institute in Denver, and elsewhere; and has coached more than 250 productions, working with directors such as Jerry Zaks, Garland Wright, Andrei Serban, Robert Brustein, Robert Wilson, and Anne Bogart; and with actors including F. Murray Abraham, Christopher Lloyd, Cherry Jones, Annette Bening, and Anna Deveare Smith. She has coached professionally at theatres throughout the United States, including the Guthrie Theater, the Oregon Shakespeare Festival, and the American Players' Theatre.

Photo by Peter Wishnok

Background

Nancy Saklad: Who were your mentors, Bonnie?

Bonnie Raphael: Arthur Lessac, Kristin Linklater, Dorothy Mennen, Cicely Berry, and Dr. Wilbur James Gould.

Saklad: Your background is rather unique. You trained in both theatre and speech pathology.

Raphael: I was very lucky that I had the desire to be a theatre voice specialist at the same time the field was growing in the United States. I ended up in the PhD program at Michigan State University in the late 1960s, because it was the only school I could find in the entire country that would let me combine voice science and theatre. Michigan State was very flexible and let me complete concentrations in psychology, speech pathology, and dramatic literature. I wrote a dissertation located in two different departments that were willing to let me cross those lines. My dissertation was a descriptive study of the relationship between the demands of characterization and functional voice problems in the male actor. Today there are programs of study where you can do this, but I couldn't find any at the time.

Saklad: Would you describe how your expertise with speech pathology mixes and mingles with your coaching and your teaching?

Raphael: I consider myself a screener; I often hear a potential pathology and refer an actor for further testing. I can interface easily with both doctors and speech and language pathologists, because I speak and understand their language. My speech sciences background also helps me be an advocate for the actor with the director for his or her vocal health. I spend a lot of time educating actors and directors about better vocal choices, you know, making what I call a "sustainable choice," one that is good for the longevity of the actor's instrument.

Saklad: What about the work most inspires you?

Raphael: I love the midwifing. I'm an Equity actress, but I discovered early on that I really enjoy rehearsals more than performances. I enjoy the birthing. I enjoy the labor pains. I enjoy seeing people overcome particular problems and find solutions that never would have been thought of. So I love the challenges and adventure of every new production I work on.

Saklad: Is there an achievement of which you are most proud?

Raphael: I'm very proud of the Voice and Speech Trainers Association (VASTA.)

Saklad: You're one of the founders, aren't you?

Raphael: Yes I am, along with Dorothy Mennen, Carol Pendergrast, Mary Corrigan, and Lucille Rubin.

The Voice and Speech World of Today

Saklad: How would you describe the current state of affairs in actor training in voice and speech?

Raphael: Actor training gets better and better due to the really good graduate programs, but I think there are far too many programs giving degrees to too many people for the market. On the positive side, I find voice work is being incorporated more in acting programs. Another positive: VASTA has established a set of criteria for promotion and tenure, and the Voice Foundation—which is an international foundation of voice specialists, all of whom treat professional voice users—has a bigger presence of speech and voice people than it ever has before.

Saklad: What would you say are the greatest voice and speech obstacles that the student actor faces?

Raphael: We all have an inherent desire to be comfortable. We seek homeostasis, and anything that disturbs it is off-putting, especially if the actor has received praise and even some success based on his or her vocal idiosyncrasies. People who have a particular kind of voice achieve some success on that basis, so why should they change it? We're teaching an aesthetic. We're also teaching the students that comfort is not as interesting as range or even the unknown. Doing the same thing over and over again and getting cast repeatedly for those idiosyncratic qualities is nowhere near as interesting as pushing the envelope. Another obstacle is fear of incompetence, and it is a real obstacle to growth. Another big obstacle is the "I want it now" mentality. This values *product* to the detriment of *process*. Skill acquisition takes time and repetition. It's unrealistic to dictate how much time it will take any given person to accomplish any given skill. Some people get it right away and some people never get it.

Saklad: What features distinguish your work in the field?

Raphael: I don't consider myself much of an original thinker. I think my greatest strength is as a synthesizer. I have studied the work of many other people, and I have a capacity to call up the right exercise at the right moment, whether that exercise arose out of a book I read or speech-pathology training or Arthur Lessac's work or Patsy Rodenburg's work. I synthesize and adapt people's work on a daily basis. I'm also a bulldog; I persist and I don't give up easily. I'm collegial. I'm very good at integrating seemingly different systems, and I adapt easily to a variety of situations.

Saklad: Do you think voice and speech training plays a unique role in performance training?

Raphael: People who lack training have basically one quality to sell. What training can do is give the actor a wider range of options so he or she is not totally identified with one sound. There is a difference between a transformer and a performer. A lot of film actors are performers. We go to see them for their particular quality. We think the quality is attractive. The movie itself may be less important than the fact that Hugh Grant or Tom Cruise or Julia Roberts is in it. But there are other actors who are transformers. They can change their affect so they're castable in very diverse roles, like Dustin Hoffman playing *Midnight Cowboy, Tootsie,* and *Death of a Salesman.* Or Meryl Streep doing *Mama Mia* or *Doubt* or playing Julia Child. Good voice and speech training provides the actor with an array of options.

Saklad: Where does vocal presence come from, and is it teachable?

Raphael: Vocal presence is connected to the ability to be present; it is the ability to see, hear, smell, and touch in the presence of other people rather than operating on automatic pilot. I don't know if it's teachable. What I do know *is* teachable is avoiding a lack of presence. If we can teach our students to stop apologizing for taking up *x* amount of space in the universe or stop criticizing themselves for being anything less than perfect, if we can eliminate those negative aspects, I think that allows a greater vocal presence to emerge.

Saklad: Vocally, what do you fine appealing in an actor? Which well-known actors possess these qualities?

Raphael: I like transparency. I like the actor who can be a vessel for the material without distortion and without limiting the material. I love when I watch a truly wonderful performance and only in retrospect do I notice that the actor was using his or her voice very well. I love Helen Mirren. I love the way she can transform. Daniel Day Lewis, Christopher

Plummer...I like all those actors who are perhaps not as famous as the biggest "stars" because they are transformers.

Practical Considerations

Saklad: Your own voice and speech training is quite diverse. Do you think students benefit by studying multiple approaches to the work?

Raphael: That's a double-edged sword. I like being a mutt. I had Lessac training from Arthur Lessac. I had Linklater training from Kristin Linklater. I've studied with the Roy Hart people and Cicely Berry, and for me, it works. There's a danger, however, of cafeteria education—I'll have a little of this and a little of that—but nothing is substantive. Nothing is really internalized and synthesized. There's always the potential that the student will become a jack-of-all-trades and a master of none.

Saklad: I know your own study includes training in Alexander and Feldenkrais. What does the body need to produce optimal vocal work?

Raphael: Integration is so important. I lament the fact that actors go into one classroom for Alexander class and another for dance and another for voice production and yet another room for speech, and so forth. In my opinion an important part of voice, speech, movement, and acting training has got to incorporate synthesis. If you look closely at my career, you'll see that in my teaching, I've never been part of a bigger voice team. I like doing it all, and while I may not do as good a job as a whole voice department, I like giving the actor a sense of the whole rather than pieces. One of my beliefs is that it is the acting that drives the work, even when we're doing the most technical exercise. It still has to be about acting, so the tools complement each other. The Alexander and the Feldenkrais work are very good for giving the actor a sense of internal space, of *expanding* into what is called for rather than contracting into it. He or she will have greater flexibility—not only physical flexibility but mental flexibility—as a result of being in better touch with his or her instrument. The body likes to feel a sense of its wholeness. If we can help actors synthesize different aspects of their training, we're putting them on the right path.

Saklad: Does an understanding of anatomy deepen the student's relationship to his or her voice?

Raphael: To a certain extent, yes. For one of the classes I offer the first-year MFA students, I bring in the ENT doctor from the medical school and the speech pathologist to talk about anatomy and physiology and voice care. When the actors see how tiny the vocal cords are and how they function and what they look like, it is a revelation for them. In women the vocal folds are about the diameter of a nickel, and in the typical male they're about the diameter of a quarter. That's a tiny little instrument! So then, when I'm teaching breathing and I ask them, if they were playing that musical instrument, how strongly would they have to blow into it? The answer is—it's not about a hurricane; it's about a gentle, steady breeze. Some knowledge of anatomy is good, but to a certain extent too much knowledge can result in people talking about voice rather than doing it. So I integrate this information on what I would call "a need to know" basis.

Saklad: Do you find an imagistic understanding of the voice to be helpful as well?

Raphael: Absolutely. This is essential. Instead of describing physiologically what's happening to the vocal cords and the false vocal folds and the resonating areas and on and on, I find it's much, much more fun for the actor to use images. I use the image of a dinosaur tail growing out of the actor's tailbone, which allows the weight of the tail to gently release the lower third of the actor's spine, for example. In this way the actor doesn't feel he or she has to force the release of the tailbone. The image facilitates the release. I talk about the breath being the horse and the voice being the rider, so the voice rides out on the breath.

Saklad: How do you address breath work?

Raphael: It's much more important to get actors to breathe than to determine exactly the location of that breath or how they're breathing. I spend a lot of time asking actors if they are holding the breath. I assign homework asking actors to count how many times they've held their breath in the last twenty-four hours, and they're amazed at how frequently they do. Then we concentrate on undoing that habit.

Saklad: What does it mean to you to support the voice?

Raphael: Support is the dynamic relationship between the exhaled breath and the voice. It's dynamic, because as the exhalation proceeds, the relationship between that exhalation and the resistance of the vocal folds changes. I usually teach a support sequence, part of which is just getting the lips to flip like a horse sound. And then I tell actors, "You don't need any more air than that to support your speaking voice. You need the steadiness of a breeze, but you don't need more air than that."

Saklad: How do you approach tonality, resonance, and vocal qualities?

Raphael: In this first year of training, which is Linklater based, we work on freeing up the tensions that get in the speaker's way, and getting the breath to support the voice. After that I teach a resonating ladder: finding vibration in the chest resonator, then moving into the mouth resonator, then into the teeth resonator and up into the sinuses and the nasal area and the skull. After combining the resonators into mixed voice, I do a lot of range exercises. In the second year, which is Lessac based, I teach his tonal exercise "the-Y-buzz" and "the + Y" at the beginning and open that into regular speaking, carrying over as much diluted tone as possible. This involves opening up the back of the mouth, near the throat, and releasing vibrations on /ee/ and /ay/ right onto the alveolar ridge. Then I spend time on "the Call," and then there's an exercise where the actors go through their range using Call and eventually dilute back into their own speaking voice, and I consider that very important. It is easier to demonstrate than to describe, but the result is a very natural but more focused and forward version of the conversational speaking voice. Arthur's resonance work is so wonderful. I watched a documentary years ago where Arthur is working with profoundly deaf people at the Rochester School for the Deaf. These people had never heard a human voice. In the past, training for the deaf had been very heavily speech oriented. The goal had been to achieve articulated sound so the words could be understood by the listener. But therapists weren't paying much attention to the sound of the voice. Consequently, many deaf people were very nasal, or their voices were very breathy or high in pitch, because they didn't have a means of gauging what was happening anatomically with the voice. And when Lessac taught them how to feel tone on the hard palate, he normalized a whole lot of voices in the duration of one class. Because his tone work is kinesthetically based, the deaf speakers found a reliable way to monitor their sound without hearing.

Saklad: What role do you think listening plays in voice and speech work?

Raphael: That really depends on the teacher and on the system you're using. What many people don't realize is that listening is as individualized and unique as voice production. We take for granted that we all sound different when we talk. We listen differently as well. We should not assume that good listening is universal. For example, if you were to use all the phonemic substitutions that one should use for a particular dialect, but you don't deal with the intonation or the melody of the dialect, it just doesn't sound right. Yet a lot of people are much better at hearing sound substitutions than they are at melody. So they need to be taught not only to listen for a substitution but also to hear the melody of the dialect to do it well. We don't do that automatically. For those who do, we say they have a better ear. Listening is an acquired and teachable skill.

Saklad: Do you teach the IPA?

Raphael: I do. I teach it in the second year of training as the first unit of dialect work.

Saklad: How would you describe the relationship between emotion and voice and speech work?

Raphael: On the one hand, the Linklater work is very important because we have emotionally edited ourselves for so long. At an early age we have learned to stifle our emotions, or we might get punished for misbehaving. The emotion remains, but we choose to edit or repress it. So the voice work is about learning to make sound and feel at the same time. Many of us have been conditioned to talk less the more we feel, so regaining the capacity to talk and feel at the same time is very important. On the other hand, actors need to remember that the audience is the receiver, not themselves. It's not about how much they're feeling; it's about how much they're communicating so the audience can feel. They're acting better when they're serving as a vessel for the emotion so the audience can understand not only what they're feeling, but why. George C. Scott talks about the fact that he doesn't want to see the explosion. He wants to hear the hiss. I love that analogy.

Saklad: How do you approach the teaching of range?

Raphael: I use the Linklater resonating ladder and get the pitch to move around. I also love the Lessac work, because you're not learning through imitation, and you're not learning what is "the right" thing to do. You're learning your voice and its range. And of course imagery and the "magic if" are always important.

Saklad: How do you see scientific and/or technological advances within or without the field influencing your work or the work at large?

Raphael: The International Dialects of English Archives (IDEA) has changed the way a lot of people are teaching dialects. Dialect research is so much more accessible than it used to be. The way we record and transmit information now digitally and MP3 files and iPods has also made the teaching of dialects a lot more accessible. Incorporating scientific advances into my work has given actors greater vocal longevity. I teach them preventative work. Whether it's warm-ups or warm-downs, or sustainable choices, the objective is that they will have a forty-year career instead of a quick ascendance and a rapid decay.

Moving into the Future

Saklad: What advice would you give to voice and speech teachers at the beginning of their teaching careers?

Raphael: Get a good solid foundation and don't think of your training as being over. Continue through VASTA or the Voice Foundation or singing lessons or workshops. Never stop training.

Saklad: What advice would you give to performance students on the brink of their professional careers?

Raphael: Again, never stop training. There was a time in Laurence Olivier's life when he chose not to work for about ten years. He got a very bad case of stage fright because he was getting so many good reviews that he knew they couldn't get any better. He talks about this in one of his autobiographies. Anytime he got onstage he was terrified that this was going to be the beginning of the descent. So he stopped stage acting for a long time. To keep himself in shape, he would either learn a sonnet a day or he'd review a Shakespearean role every week. I think the lesson here is very clear; never stop training.

Saklad: Have you witnessed much of an evolution in voice and speech training over the course of your career?

Raphael: Yes, absolutely. I've been doing this for over forty years now, and the work has changed radically and wonderfully, from a British-derived ear training and meeting a speech standard that's set across the ocean, to a way of working that allows the individual to realize his or her full potential and finding out who he or she is, rather than being told, "You're this type, you're that type; this is what you should be doing." The former approach can be soul killing.

Saklad: What do you think the future holds for voice and speech training?

Raphael: I think there's a great deal of potential out there in terms of expanding possibilities, in terms of synthesizing work from a lot of different sources, and in terms of building a better mousetrap. Contributors from medicine, from voice science, from brain research, from linguistics, from singing, from other cultures, from gender studies can open up many brave new worlds.

Saklad: Bonnie, what impact do you hope your work will have on vocal training at large?

Raphael: I hope that people—including voice coaches—embrace the concept of the voice coach as a midwife. I hope we can embrace the potential for midwifing a birth that belongs to the actor and not to us. I want to continue to see the actor's eyes light up or the director's eyes light up with possibility of things they just hadn't considered. And really, the pinnacle is process, not product. I know that product is important, and I too judge my colleagues and my contemporaries by their product. I don't care who teaches what. The question is does the person sound different at the end of training, or is the director happier with the actor that I've coached than he or she was at the beginning of rehearsals. I know product is important, but one of my chief wishes is that we can get the actor and the director and the producers, God help us, more interested in process.

Patsy Rodenburg

Patsy Rodenburg has been the director of voice at the Guildhall School of Music and Drama in London for the past twenty-six years and until recently was at the Royal National Theatre for sixteen years. She trained in voice studies at the Central School of Speech and Drama and has worked regularly with the best-known actors of the British Theatre. She was previously in residence with the Royal Shakespeare Company for nine years and also worked at a number of London and other great world theatres. Patsy has also been a major voice for penal reform, taking Shakespeare into prisons. She is the author of a number of highly regarded books, including *The Right to Speak* and *The Need for Words*.

Photo by Clive Totman

Background

Nancy Saklad: Who were your mentors, Patsy?

Patsy Rodenburg: I've been very lucky to have been taught by lots of teachers, not only in voice and speech, but brilliant teachers of philosophy and brilliant acting teachers. I started with voice because I had problems speaking as a child, and I was sent to an elocution teacher, which was very confusing. Years later I was at the Central School of Speech and Drama, where I studied with a fantastic teacher, Margot Braund, and I had connections with Gwyneth Thurban, who didn't teach me but mentored me. I had great teachers of philosophy as a child. I went to a very old-fashioned school, and I was taught philosophy at the age of nine. They always helped me make connections. It's not done anymore—blue-stockinged women, wonderful, classical teachers. I had no literary connection at home. No one in my family was very interested in literature or communication. My mother enjoyed poetry but didn't have any artistic connections at all. So Central was very important to me.

Saklad: Were there other influences?

Rodenburg: While I was at Central I needed to make money, and I found myself teaching in prisons, and that was an epiphany on many levels. One was that I felt that I could teach, because I was teaching very difficult people, and I could engage them. But I also had the epiphany of, "Oh my goodness, they have lost their voice. There by the grace of God go I." And it seemed very simplistic at the time, but the idea was that if I was stopped by the police, I could speak and a lot of these people that I was working with couldn't, and so I was teaching them basic reading, writing, and communication skills. Then I was very lucky to get my first voice teaching job. I was working with a woman whose name was Sheila Moriarity. Sheila was a classical singer and teacher, and I apprenticed with her for about five-and-a-half years. She taught the traditional old-school approach. I sought that out because at Central during the early '70s, the old classical vocal techniques, such as rib reserve, and the very traditional ways of teaching voice had been thrown out. That work took me into the Royal Opera House, working with singers, students, and actors in a very formal way. So I was actually being introduced to voice work that had died out in most places, which was really useful for me.

Saklad: How so?

Rodenburg: Well, I've spent my life trying to see the good in all forms of voice work, and the old, traditional ways were being lost to a certain extent. By the time I got to the Royal Shakespeare Company, where I started to work with Cicely Berry, the traditional training was very useful, because I was working with actors who were in their sixties, seventies, eighties, and I understood their training—the positives of the traditional ways of rib reserve, and of the "voice beautiful." We don't sound like that anymore, but that work was very pragmatic, very craft based and has a lot of repetition. Then of course, Cicely is so brilliant at text work. She communicated the notion that form, content, sound, and sense release meaning. So I have spent a lot of my life marrying the two: the voice work—the very athletic voice work—and the very powerful support systems with text work—the two rivers. All that awareness had been built into me in my early-to-mid twenties.

The Voice and Speech World of Today

Saklad: What features would you say distinguish your work in the field?

Rodenburg: Do you know something? I think I do work which I don't think of as mine. It's a sort of universal work. When you're working on somebody's body and breath, there are things that unite all of us, and you just try to help that person. People say "Rodenburg technique." Well I don't know what Rodenburg technique is, because when you're working with someone, all you're trying to do is find any door to get them into the room that they need to go into—any door that will release them. I'm very interested in the fact that most of the work is about energy—energy of the body, of the breath, of the voice, of the word, of power, of the impact of the word on the world and in the world. I suppose if I did have a way of working, I'd say I'm very craft based on one level. I believe very much that actors need technique. They need to know the work so well that they forget it. I find that I can only do that with an actor or whomever I'm working with by teaching them craft, which means repetition...and it seems to work. So I'm very pragmatic. I also think I can make people feel secure enough to go into very imaginative places, to release into imaginative places. So on one hand, I'm a pragmatist that uses a lot of craft. On the other hand, I think it's important to teach with unconditional love. We can't judge. I've been very angry in my life about the number of people that I've met that have had such terrible things said about their voices that they can hardly speak. I suppose another thing that I feel strongly about is that it's my job to teach young actors as if they're going to be lead actors. Now the fates will take over, and that will happen or it won't, but the actors must be strengthened and extended—not only in their bodies, but in their minds and their hearts—so they can take on the leading roles, and I just try to find the right thing for the right moment. The main thing is I want to release, empower, and help people communicate in a more effective way.

Saklad: How would you describe the current state of affairs of American actor training in voice and speech, as compared to your work in Britain?

Rodenburg: In America I have a sense of tremendous hunger for the work but more fear about it than in Britain. Maybe the actors feel they're not good enough to speak Shakespeare or they're not good enough to use their voices. At the Guilford School in London, movement, breath, voice, speech, and text are all linked. There is no dividing line. I strongly suspect that in some teaching here, those connections are not being made. I personally made those connections in the '70s partly because I was at Central and Cicely's influence was there, but also Gwyneth and Litz Pisk, who was a great theatre movement person, was there. So it's always been very apparent to me that the body leads into the breath, leads into the voice, into speech, into text. It's a whole practice. I love American actors. I love their energy; I love their curiosity. I think it's very hard for them because the system of theatre in the US is so dissipated. There's not enough subsidized theatre, so actors here have to do a lot of training in isolation. They don't get involved with a company where their work can be developed. It's a great thing, if you go work with a major company as a young actor, to actually be in a room with Judi Dench using her voice so you train by osmosis. British actors tend to train, and then they don't do a lot of classes afterwards because they've been trained in a very consistent way. They've done thousands of hours of voice work by the time they finish training. They've had the work imbedded. Very important. I don't think you can train a voice in a couple hours a week.

Saklad: What do you consider the greatest voice and speech obstacles the student actor faces?

Rodenburg: Well of course, fear. That is at the root of all of it, isn't it? There's an idea out there that truth in acting is mumbling. We all know that's not the case. We live in a society that is very frightened of passion. In order to use your voice, you have to connect to your heart. You have to connect to your breath, which is part of your heart and your feelings. You can stretch the range of a voice. We all know that range is about passion of either the heart or the head, the reflection of the voice and the mani-festation of the voice. But if you stretch the actors' range out, do they dare use it? The main thing is most of them don't use their voices. They don't sing in the morning. I went to school and I used to sing every morning. My voice was being used. Suddenly, we need more hours in voice work and training than fifteen years ago, because the reduction of the human voice in Western urban society is very profound. So the work changes, the world changes, and you adapt. I'm going to be political... I think there's a great stifling of voices. Thank God for Barack Obama, because at least he stands up and speaks with passion and clarity and authenticity. And I'm always an optimist, so I believe we might be on a new wave.

Saklad: Do you think voice and speech training plays a unique role in performance training?

Rodenburg: Well of course I do. On the simplest level, the playwright wants the words communicated. I've been very lucky in life. I've worked with most leading British and American playwrights—you know, Harold Pinter, David Hare, Arthur Miller—and I've never had a playwright say to me, "Make them more naturalistic." Great writing is not random, and it requires oxygen, it requires breath, it requires athleticism, and number one, we have to communicate to the audience. If you haven't warmed your voice up and you stand up in front of two hundred people—let alone 1,000 or 1,500—if you haven't done the basic voice work, whatever you are doing as an actor is not going to read. Speaking is about need. The English language is very rich in that sound equals sense. If you can't feel the diction and word in your mouth, you don't release a certain part of the meaning of the word.

Saklad: Where does vocal presence come from, and is it teachable?

Rodenburg: I think it is teachable. We're all born present, and most of us are born with amazing voices. I don't think of myself as teaching presence of voice. I think of myself as seeking the lost voice and the lost presence with the student. All we have to do is look at babies and see them completely and utterly present. Then you hear them cry. The voice goes on and on. It's full of range, and it never tires. The work is about rediscovering something with which we entered into the world. Once rediscovered it can be enhanced.

Saklad: You are an incredibly insightful and accomplished text coach of Shakespeare. Where does your keen sense of humanity come from?

Rodenburg: We're lucky to be loved unconditionally. That gives us a jolly good start in understanding humanity. I had a very powerful working-class grandmother who had a very tough life, and I was very close to her.

My mother was working class and had a very tough life in many ways. Maybe I was educated with more upper-class people, and I never felt I belonged really. So when I look at the nurse in Romeo and Juliet and see actors mocking her or laughing at her, I find it offensive, because that's my grandmother. I think you just have to look at what I call the evidence of the text. Shakespeare is full of humanity. That's why I want to spend my time with him. We see actors play Goneril as if she's an evil woman. I don't agree with what she does, but if you read the play you realize it's a terrible burden not to be loved by your father. "By day and night he wrongs me. Every hour he flashes into one great…"— Shakespeare can't resist saying Goneril does some terrible things, but the kingdom should be hers. I'm not an academic. I just get my hands on a play, and I look at what's there, and I try to figure out what the human condition is. You know, I think I learned a lot of humanity from my experience in prisons, because I could have judged them, and it just felt wrong. I've been amazingly lucky. I've taught in Africa and India and all over the world, and all you see is the sameness of us, and that's all that Shakespeare sees.

Saklad: What is most recent in your work?

Rodenburg: I've just been filming these DVDs on Shakespeare, which follow my book *Speaking Shakespeare*. I've made eighty hours of DVD, consisting of very basic techniques in working on Shakespeare, and I think that's going to be very good. I'm very happy with that. I've been doing a lot of work on leadership in the corporate world using Shakespeare, but also challenging leaders to use their power well. But also, saying that if you have power you do have to use it, which is the double whammy in Shakespeare. And that's been incredibly successful.

Practical Considerations

Saklad: Do you think students benefit by studying multiple approaches to the work?

Rodenburg: The broad answer is yes, but you have to have a foundation before you know what you're doing. The way I think about it is that if my students have a strong enough grounding, they can do anything, go anywhere, and take and leave whatever they need. I think if we are too eclectic in the initial stages of training, we won't have the hours to do it all. I think we have to imbed certain fundamental principles, and then they can try all sorts of things after that.

Saklad: What does the body need to produce optimal vocal work?

Rodenburg: It needs very strong breath support. It needs freedom. You can't get that if your shoulders, your upper chest, and your spine are tight. You need to have your feet on the floor with your knees unlocked. You need to be centered and yet ready. You need the breath to be there. You need the voice to be open and free, and then you might get it. It generally takes about two years.

Saklad: How do you address breath work?

Rodenburg: Well it's very, very important, isn't it? I always say it's the first thing you do and it's the last. I work on releasing tensions in the breath, strengthening the ribcage, including the back of the ribcage, and getting the breath deep into the body. I work on feeling the support system, feeling the readiness in the breath. I work—this is old-fashioned—on building up athleticism in the breath, be it capacity and freedom of breath, a released breath, but also a powerful breath. I don't really expect a student to be fully connected to his or her breath for about eighteen months.

Saklad: Would you talk a little bit about breath support?

Rodenburg: I like the word because it creates the sense of a column of air. If I were to push a wall down—I push against the wall, and my breath has to go deep, and I have to feel that power, and I push the wall down with my power. It's the same in the martial arts. It's the same when you play a sport. The breath comes in, you feel that moment of suspension in the breath, and you go. And like everything I teach, you do the work so you can forget it. Now I learned the word *support* from singers. But I like it. It seems to work. And I know it's a controversial word with a lot of people.

Saklad: What role does listening play in voice and speech work?

Rodenburg: Well it's essential. You have to teach people to listen. The teacher has to listen very carefully on so many levels. The actor has to listen to the other actor. They have to listen to the audience. The teacher needs to be able to listen to what's going on, although you actually have to watch very well, as well. The ear, like every other part, needs to be trained. If I take a weekend off and I start teaching, I can generally hear up to about sixty people in the room individually. But if I have two days off, it takes about twenty-five minutes before my ear comes in again. I'm very aware of that. It's a point of attention and attentiveness. Listening is vital.

Saklad: How would you describe the relationship between emotion and voice and speech work?

Rodenburg: Well, it's interesting that when we describe our emotions and then we look at the words we use, we find that they're physical. "I'm depressed." "I'm elated." "I'm disturbed." Emotion in the body starts in the breath, and we cannot feel unless we breathe. So breathing is fundamental. I don't think this is scientific, but I strongly suspect we hold our deep, less pleasant emotions down in our lower abdominal area, and if we don't want to feel those things, then we don't breathe down there. So when you teach someone to breathe and they breathe down there, they touch those things, and those less pleasant emotions are going to come up.

Saklad: How do you see scientific and/or technological advances influencing your work or the work at large?

Rodenburg: They're very important. I've done a lot of collaborating with scientists. I have to say that what has been quite pleasing is that many of the things we felt were instinctive, science is now proving.

Saklad: Have you witnessed much of an evolution in voice and speech training over the course of your career?

Rodenburg: Oh yes. There's a much greater awareness of the need for the work, of the world needing the work more too. When I started in theatre there was something called the "silent space," but now there's no silence anymore. In stage lighting, we're so highly technical that every instrument has a little fan that whisks around, and the hydraulic systems of theatres are churning around at so many decibels interfering with the actor's voice. So the demands on the actors' voices are increasing. The actor has to be more skilled vocally these days. All these things require greater skill. Authenticity of dialects requires greater skill—and we have to teach those skills; the demands are out there. A great training also trains for the theatre that you believe in, not only the theatre that exists. That means that we have to do a lot more ensemble work, because the ensembles aren't out there. There are some, but there are not as many as before. Science has helped us. We have to look at certain vocal qualities that are being encouraged, and might not be that healthy. We have a lot more knowledge about connections in the body. We have to be very alert to the cultural differences. There's tremendous diversity and more coming in. London is the most diverse city in the world. In my time you didn't see black leading actors. You had to train black actors to be classical actors in order for the theatre to accept that they could play those roles. That happened in the '70s, and I'm very proud that I was part of that. I think the education system today is set up so that young people expect to be taught at; there's no dialogue. You have to actually ask them to answer you back, to have dialogue, to have debate. As I said earlier, there's a stifling of passion that we have to work on. We need passionate, authentic speakers. We need to teach our children about language, about, and voice teachers are very well equipped to do that.

Saklad: You have inspired a generation of performers and teachers. What advice would you give to voice and speech teachers at the beginning of their teaching careers?

Rodenburg: Stay open to your students. Go out and work with anybody. If a theatre company needs a workout or warm-up and they haven't got any money, go out and do it. Learn your craft. Learn your trade. The adventure of actually working with people is how you're going to get very good. And don't be frightened if an exercise doesn't work; try another one. I think a lot of young teachers are trying to do too much in a class. If you've got an hour-and-half class and you profoundly achieved one or two things, you're doing very well. Teach people how to work; don't try to entertain them. And don't worry about being liked. It's impossible. And this is very important. I've always worked with nonactors, not only in prisons but anybody—teachers, anybody—and I really urge young voice teachers not to just to feel that their life is in theatre or film. In fact, we need this work on the planet very much. I felt very strongly in my twenties that I could help people communicate. The theatre knew something that everybody needed to know, which was how to communicate with passion, with clarity, and with vigor.

Saklad: What do you think the future holds for voice and speech training?

Rodenburg: Well, I'm optimistic. I think the training is going to be needed. I just think the only danger is if we restrict ourselves. There are many, many doors into the same room. We have to behave to each other well. You know, we are educators; we are dealing with very powerful things—the body and the breath and the voice—very profound, potent things. We don't own the work; the work is given to us, and there's a huge amount of work out there. It's very important work, not only in theatre but for the planet. We just have to want to improve communication on the planet, and whatever road that means, you take it.

Saklad: And finally, Patsy, what impact do you hope your own work will have on vocal training at large?

Rodenburg: I hope to take away some of the mystery. I often felt when I was training that voice work was some holy of holies that a few people were invited into and others weren't—students I mean. "You can do it, and you can't." I feel I've helped say that this is important work in a particular way. I hope I have encouraged people to speak passionately from their hearts with empathy, and be thrilled by exciting thoughts. So rowing against the tide, the tide of cynicism, the tide of mockery, the tide of sarcasm, and maybe one's being ridiculed, but that's what I believe, and I believe that the human spirit yearns to express itself with passion and clarity, with power and variety.

Susan Sweeney

Susan Sweeney has been a voice/speech/ text/dialects coach to professional theatres for the past thirty years, among them the Guthrie Theatre, Milwaukee Repertory Theatre, Madison Repertory Theatre, Skylight Opera Theatre, Philadelphia Drama Guild, Walnut Street Theatre, Baltimore Center Stage, Virginia Stage Company, and the Colorado, Illinois, Utah, Sedona, and Oregon Shakespeare Festivals. In 2006, she coached dialects for Francesca Zambello's production of *Show Boat* at Royal Albert Hall in London. For the past nine years, she has served as head of voice and text for American Players Theatre. She was on the faculty of the Professional Theatre Training Program at the University of Wisconsin–Milwaukee from 1981–89, and then moved with the program to University of Delaware, where she taught until joining the faculty of the department of theatre and drama at the University of Wisconsin–Madison in 2003.

Photo by Zane Williams

Background

Nancy Saklad: You studied with Edith Skinner. What was it like to work with her, Susan, and what was her primary focus?

Susan Sweeney: She was a force of nature, extremely demanding and definitively precise. I worked with her near the end of her life. In fact, Edith died while I was managing a workshop in Milwaukee for her and taking care of her needs during the workshop. I was the beneficiary of remarkable anecdotes that she shared with me about her childhood and her life as a teacher and coach. From Edith I learned precision and rigor, the dramatic and emotional richness of following the form of the writing, and how to interpret from those forms. I learned about the evocativeness of the orchestra of vowel, diphthong, and consonant sounds as they come together and interact, and the rhythmic magic of long and short sounds in spoken English. Those were very deep lessons for me. I learned a lot of mechanics from Edith that I've used for all these years.

Saklad: You also trained with Kristin Linklater, Arthur Lessac, Patsy Rodenburg, the Roy Hart Theatre, and then studied Feldenkrais method and Bioenergetics too. What impact did the variety of this work have on your own?

Sweeney: Each of those training experiences came at moments when I needed some insight or a new way of experiencing what I thought I knew about the voice from years as a singing actor. The Lessac work was my very first experience of theatre voice training. That work deepened my experience of the physical nature of breath and resonance. Lessac resonance work is truly wonderful for actors. The work with Kristin was during an early Shakespeare and Company workshop, at a very early point in my teaching career. From that work came a clearer sense of opening physically to making sound, as well as a brand-new picture of what a vocal process for the speaking actor might entail. The Linklater work was also my first experience of playing imaginatively with the voice through movement. I took a long workshop with Patsy Rodenburg in London in the middle of my career, which came at a moment when I needed to remember how practical the work can be. Patsy's work is so detailed and no nonsense. I needed to get back to a kind of basic bedrock and trust my own instincts about teaching, and that happened there. The Roy Hart Theatre Extended Voice work is ongoing work that I've done for about twenty years in workshops both in the US and France. The work has expanded my notions of what the human voice is capable of. It deepens the connections between body, voice, and imagination, and has become a perfect balancer to the more technical facets of voice, speech, text, and dialects training, which I also value. Once an actor feels how far it's possible for the voice to go, he or she never works in the same way again. It doesn't matter whether he or she is working on skills acquisition or improvisation. The Roy Hart work presents the notion of vast possibilities for both the voice and the human spirit.

Saklad: Have there been any other influences that have guided your work?

Sweeney: I'm one of those people of a certain age who grew up sitting around the large radio set with my family listening to radio broadcasts, and the kind of specificity and expressiveness of those actors and the places they took my imagination had an enormous effect on me, and to this day, I listen more muscularly than I see. I've also been a singer for a long time, so music has affected me. That relationship to music started very early, and it figures strongly in the work I do with students and actors. And then, I must acknowledge Bonnie Raphael, who was the mother to so many of us at the beginning when we were just becoming teachers and vocal coaches in the professional theatre; she was a bridge of an extraordinary kind. Both Bonnie and Jan Gist have been my invaluable sounding boards and inspirations over the years. We've taught and coached side by side on occasion and have worked through many ideas together.

The Voice and Speech World of Today

Saklad: What would you say are some of the distinguishing features of your work as an educator in the field?

Sweeney: A flexible, brave, expressive voice is the great engine of the live theatre. The human voice is the great storyteller. So actors can work their entire lives on their voices—getting the voice more embodied; letting the imagination loose; developing more range, tonal expressiveness, rhythmic possibilities, an easier access to dialects; becoming more responsive to language and poetic thought, the vitality of arguments and ideas. I ask, "What if the audience closes their eyes? Is the play still happening?" What does it take for an actor to become so expressive, so evocative, that the play can be heard as vividly as it is seen?

Saklad: How would you describe the current state of affairs in actor training in voice and speech?

Sweeney: Working in professional theatre, the major thing I notice is that the aesthetic for acting on the stage has shifted, which affects how the voice gets used. There is now a much greater insistence on just-like-real-life verisimilitude, and it often is not all that different from the kind of energy and focus required for film acting, which can so easily pull the vocal and physical energy back into the body and down. It does not require the audience to listen. It flattens expressiveness, vividness, and the range that was once expected of the theatrical voice. I hear fewer voices with real presence. And I hear a lot of throat acting that seems to be passing for emotion.

Saklad: Where does vocal presence come from, and is it teachable?

Sweeney: Vocal and physical presence come from how energy is used. Do speakers actually vibrate or excite the space around them, or is the energy held back? Presence requires a willingness on the part of the individual to move the energy outward, as well as a willingness to be noticed, to be received, to be related to, to change the space, to be vibrantly alive, to take a place in the world and stand there in it. And I do think it can be taught, even though some people are just born with this vibrancy.

Saklad: Do you think voice and speech training plays a unique role in performance training? And if so, what is the role?

Sweeney: Absolutely. It provides a place where actors can come and find themselves again. The work of a voice class is the portal into the full scope of human expression. Actors must be extraordinarily vibrant human beings who know themselves, and others, deeply. Actors who develop these skills have the means to trigger becoming an entirely different human being. The voice and the body can so quickly be the doorway into transformation.

Practical Considerations

Saklad: You studied multiple approaches. Do you think students benefit by studying multiple approaches to the work?

Sweeney: Yes, because there's no one approach that addresses the needs of every kind of actor or every kind of dramatic material. The ability to work with many different approaches allows one to tailor coaching to meet individual needs.

Saklad: What does the body need to produce optimal vocal work?

Sweeney: Vitality, suppleness, strength and endurance; breath, openness, awareness, economy, control and specificity; the ability to mimic, rhythmic sensitivity, and responsiveness. What I tried to do over the years was find body work that facilitates the development of these qualities. I use Feldenkrais to open the breath and to teach physical specificity, economy, and awareness. Feldenkrais opens the pelvis, the lower back, and the shoulder girdle like nothing else I have experienced. It also discourages the habit of using more effort than is necessary. The few Bioenergetics exercises I use do a very good job of opening head-to-toe energy flow and getting the breath to move very deeply into the body. I use yoga exercises to expand the breath line and to encourage suppleness of muscle. I use a handful of Qigong exercises to teach simple focused attention, grounded-ness, dropped-in breath, and a sense of flow. Qigong can also help release determinedly tight shoulders, lower backs, and necks. I also use the hard foam-rolls that physical therapists use, which open the ribs and help align the spine.

Saklad: Does an understanding of anatomy deepen the student's relationship to his or her voice?

Sweeney: I think so, and especially in the sense of being able to appreciate the brilliant design of the body and its basic mechanics. But I have found that too much clinical detail can distract and worry some students. I'm fortunate to have the benefit of being able to take the MFA actors to the voice clinic right here at the university, which specializes in the performing voice. The clinic therapists scope the actors, which gives them the opportunity to see their own anatomical structures in the act of producing sound.

Saklad: Do you find an imagistic understanding of the voice to be helpful, and if so, what images do you use and how?

Sweeney: Images come up in the process of doing exercises, and I don't tend to use the same images all the time. I often ask the actors to describe in their own images what it feels like to do a particular activity or exercise.

Saklad: How do you address breath work?

Sweeney: Students are directly affected by how quickly technology moves them ahead, how much noise they contend with every day, and how physically tight and/or collapsed they are in reaction to the way they live. It's hard for them to pay attention. When they can't pay attention, they are ungrounded. I have noticed more and more that when I ask the students to close their eyes and feel the sensation of their bare feet on the floor, a common response is that they are unable to feel their feet in contact with the floor. They have no sensation! As this has happened, I have begun using more exercises from Feldenkrais, yoga, Qigong, Bioenergetics, and other physical practices that move energy down and ask the mover to breathe with the whole body, while following a slow movement to its conclusion (and not forcing past the end of that movement), returning from that movement back into neutral. Starting with these exercises allows the students to notice breath working freely and expansively as they move. Once that has happened, it's possible to begin investigating the more specialized breathing practices needed by the performing voice: making space in the mouth and pharynx; opening the ribs, the belly, and the back; developing capacity; controlling release; engaging support; shaping breath for the idea; and so forth.

Saklad: What does it mean to you to support the voice?

Sweeney: Well technically, it means relaxing the muscles of the laryngeal cavity—the neck, the jaw, the tongue, and pharynx—while the muscles of the abdomen, the lower ribs, the back, and—depending on the degree of vocal power needed—even the glutes and thighs, are being used to maintain, increase, or decrease the pressure of the air column below the glottis. The voice riding on that column of air is steadied by the pressure that is maintained in the lower sections of the body. Basically, supporting the voice means using what was designed to do the job of support instead of the ineffectual, disorganized substitutes of the neck and the throat and the shoulders.

Saklad: Would you describe how you approach range and tonality, resonance, and vocal qualities?

Sweeney: I use the Roy Hart Extended Voice Work to provoke a muscular experience of these things. The games, exercises, and working around the piano ask the actors to imaginatively explore archetypal images or characters in intense dramatic circumstances. Changes in tonality and resonance quality happen as a result of the use of the imagination. The students get very excited doing that work, and in any work that follows, they are less satisfied with anything flat.

Saklad: What role does listening play in voice and speech work?

Sweeney: Listening is being open and present. Listening is what provokes thought and the in-breath. There is no possibility of acting specifically without listening. It's so obvious to all of us, especially when you listen to a classical play and an actor is playing in a scene "by himself." Without listening there's no give and take in the language or the sound of the voices, no development of idea or argument. Nobody is triggering anyone else. The actors are not hearing the setups, so they're emphasizing too many words, as though there's been no antecedent for the idea. On another note, I don't think actors can be excellent actors without being excellent mimics, and there's no mimicry without listening, taking in, opening oneself to another. Also, there's an invaluable thing that a good actor does while onstage, which involves listening to the audience, sensing what's going on with them. It's almost as if there's another track of awareness with these actors. They're completely present to what they're playing onstage, but another track of attention allows them to adjust according to what they're sensing out there. That's a kind of deep listening that I think is important. Developing listening is also tied to taking in a variety of kinds of models. Student actors should listen to a full range of musical styles to broaden their palette of rhythmic and dynamic possibilities. Taking in a new kind of music infuses them imaginatively. It's difficult for an actor to feel the rhythms of poetry and long thoughts and to inhabit the language of those kinds of plays, if all they have experienced in their bodies and psyches is the thumping, unvarying regularity of hip-hop and rock music.

Saklad: You've worked extensively as a vocal coach, text coach, and dialects coach in acclaimed theatres all across the country. What would you say are the most important ingredients in coaching the classics?

Sweeney: One of them is just exactly the same thing that I suspect all of us work on in every coaching situation: being the audience's agent in the play's happening expressively, vividly, clearly, compellingly, rhythmically. Voice coaches have to have the ability to listen to a play that they have heard for weeks as though for the very first time. Does the language belong to the actor, or is it being worn like a nice period costume to which the actor has little relationship? Good coaching is also supporting actors in giving good, healthy voice to these plays. There's often a great deal of spit-and-shout effort in the performance of Shakespeare. The coach needs to help the actor transform that generalized effort into specific, purposeful expressiveness.

Saklad: What do you do as the vocal coach if the actor does not own the language?

Sweeney: Well, we would go back into the studio and work on specificity. "Why do you need those forty-five lines, since basically it's the same idea said in several different ways? What has not happened yet that necessitates continuing to speak? Why the metaphor here, the series of questions there, the repeated phrase? Let's physicalize this series of images. Let's find the energy to drive through this long arc of thought. Let's turn off the lights and reach through the darkness with the sounds of these words." I do whatever it takes to awaken the connections.

Saklad: What's the relationship between emotion and voice and speech work?

Sweeney: Well, emotion for me is a byproduct of breathing, being truly present, meaning what you're saying, listening to what others are saying, and thereby being captured by the moment that's unfolding. The actor can then be acted upon—caught by surprise—by language and moment. This is to say that one is not working on it directly. In my experience, working directly on emotion almost always results in shallower and less specific expression, and I believe it very often eliminates the possibility of the audience feeling anything at all.

Saklad: What are some of the ways you begin working on Shakespeare?

Sweeney: You've got to know exactly what is being said. In addition to engaging in precise glossary work, the actor should be able to paraphrase the text in the grammar of the playwright. This is the all-important intellectual element of Shakespeare. The actor must be able to actually think these ideas, just the way they're written, and the audience must be able to have an experience of the actor thinking, reasoning, and working it all out. I tell students to make sure they've got some "daydream time" to just lie down or take a walk and say those words over and over, looking for those moments of "aha!" when something from the text suddenly becomes real and available to the mind and the imagination. Then figure out what the language is doing. What is the specific nature of that short thought, that long thought, the repetitions, the expletives, the alliterations, the oaths, the metaphors, the lists, the antitheses, and so forth. What specifically is happening at that verse line-ending? How is the argument getting made, and in how many different ways? Why are there so many words given to proving a point? Finally, it's important to play with all of it physically, even to the point of doing a cartoon physical rendering of the text. In this way, a line such as "And madly play with my forefathers' joints" becomes connected to an imaginative muscle memory, and the actor can live inside that language.

Saklad: How do you see scientific and/or technological advances influencing your work or the work at large?

Sweeney: I am incredibly grateful for the efficiency the computer has brought, because now it is so easy to do the preliminary work with both directors and actors long distance before we even get into rehearsals. It's a piece of cake to locate a dialect sample and send a link to it. I can send my students a YouTube sample or a Google link as the example of something that came up in class or rehearsal. I'm appreciative of these advances because they allow us so many more layers of participation and detail. As I mentioned before though, the speed at which technology is moving us along can challenge the young student actor in very big ways. Making the best use of technology without sacrificing health and presence, that's often the teaching now.

Moving into the Future

Saklad: How would you describe the evolution of voice and speech training that has happened in your lifetime?

Sweeney: When I started teaching voice, there were certainly a lot fewer of us teacher-coaches around. At that time there was a healthy regional repertory theatre-circuit that needed actors with substantial skills training in order to handle the classic repertoire and then university-conservatory training programs sprang up in response to that need. That created a demand for skillful teachers, and our ranks swelled. At that point VASTA came into being, and there was a community of practitioners who could meet and share their ideas and practices. That was the early part of my career. Today there's a much reduced demand for actors, which is now playing out in the tenuous survival of many university theatre programs. There's been so much knowledge shared over the years since I was a young teacher—the incredible variety of body work that has proved valuable in the voice classroom, vastly different from a time when elocution was the primary focus of voice training. Networking between teachers and coaches, and scholars and voice scientists, is very lively. I find it painful now to see our graduating actors having such difficulty finding ways to practice professionally and develop themselves as artists in the current theatre scene, which seems to be shrinking daily. It also concerns me that there seems to be less demand for actors who have physical and vocal technique—actors who are able to transform by using skillful manipulation of physical and vocal choices. The current inclination towards cinematic realism in rehearsal and onstage often makes theatrical energy and theatrical transformation unnecessary. I don't know if that answers the question in full, but I think it's the context in which the teaching of voice happens now, which prompts the question: what are we creating actors to do?

Saklad: How your own work has evolved?

Sweeney: I used to teach speech and text work, primarily, with IPA narrow transcription and the older Standard Stage-Speech model. I still use that narrow IPA, because I think it's a very useful tool for ear training and distinguishing the kind of detail and consistency that good dialect work requires. But I teach Standard American Stage Speech as one of many dialects now, because that's the use that it has in the profession. I think that is a natural development, since everything changes over time. I still believe that actors who have that dialect as one of many options have gained something very useful. The work they've done to obtain that dialect makes them more knowledgeable, more versatile, and more articulate. I've always felt that working on Standard American is an experience of using one of the broadest collections of American sounds, many of which later turn up in other dialects and accents. But perhaps the deepest piece of my evolution is that I've arrived at a place where all facets of voice and speech are full-body physical acts, which was not the case for me during the first third of my teaching career.

Saklad: What advice would you give to voice and speech teachers at the beginning of their teaching careers?

Sweeney: Work with as many vocal and physical practices as you can, because they will make you more responsive to how varied learning and work styles of different students can be. Find out what really matters to you and also where your particular gifts and aptitudes lie. Work with as many different directors as possible. Keep working on yourself and let your students know that you are. Develop excellent skills and be a good model of everything you teach. Listen well—and manage your facial expressions as you listen. Demand that your students practice daily. And maintain your sense of humor and know when to let go.

Saklad: What advice would you give to students on the brink of their professional careers regarding voice?

Sweeney: Live a healthy life, because this is the only voice you've got, and it needs supportive habits. Keep practicing. Maintain a healthful meditative body practice in your life, especially if you're a weightlifter. Take singing lessons. Read books aloud for the blind and for other people and for yourselves. Continue the practice of vocal physical warm-ups and cool downs. Take care of your hearing by not cranking up your iPod. When you're out of work, develop a great role you would love to do someday. Read poetry and great literature. Go to museums. Listen to all kinds of music. Keep learning and challenging yourself.

Saklad: Susan, what impact do you hope your work will have on vocal training at large?

Sweeney: I think in the face of this deteriorating cultural attention span, deteriorating focus on listening, and deteriorating verbalness, what we do becomes more necessary with every year. So we want to keep being the forces that call for breath and articulateness and full expressive humanity. I think Roy Hart said it very well: "The human voice is the muscle of the soul." What we are teaching and coaching lies at the heart of what it is to be passionately alive and human.

Philip Thompson

Philip Thompson is currently an associate professor of drama at the University of California, Irvine. He teaches voice and speech in addition to heading the MFA program in acting. He frequently teaches with Catherine Fitzmaurice as a master teacher of Fitzmaurice Voicework®, and with Dudley Knight through their innovative approach to speech and dialects. He is the past president of the Voice and Speech Trainers Association (VASTA). For the last decade, he has worked professionally as a voice, speech, and text coach for numerous theatres, such as the Denver Center Theatre Company, Pasadena Playhouse, Opera Pacific, and the Alabama Shakespeare Festival. In addition, he has developed long-term relationships with three Tony Award–winning theatres: the Cincinnati Playhouse in the Park, South Coast Repertory, and the Utah Shakespearean Festival.

Photo by Tira Palmquist

Background

Nancy Saklad: What drew you to voice work, Phil?

Philip Thompson: There was a lot in my background that had some linguistic variety to it. I grew up in Iowa. My mother is from South Dakota, not very different, but my father is Irish and was born in China. One branch of cousins are African Americans living in Chicago, and I hung out with them a lot. Then I lived for six months in London as a child. My uncle is a linguist and a paleographer studying ancient Chinese texts. So I have a lot of background and experience in the way language changes, and that probably predisposed me to be interested in it. Then I had Dudley Knight as my teacher. That was incredible and opened my mind. This was when I was an MFA student in acting at UC Irvine (1986–89). Dudley was my teacher for voice and speech, and I couldn't begin to measure how great an influence he has been on me as a teacher, as a role model, and when I returned to teach at UC Irvine, as an incredibly generous colleague and friend.

Saklad: Have there been others that have influenced your work?

Thompson: Robert Cohen, who, although not a voice teacher, is definitely a text work person. He introduced the idea that my intellect could give me access to text in a way that also allowed my emotional life to enter, and I realized that I had a real affinity for Shakespeare. The next mentor was Jerzy Grotowski. I only spent a few weeks working with him, but he was pretty important. He told me—and this was a very accurate assessment— he said, "Philip, right now you are young. Your teachers probably like you, but your body is already speeding toward annihilation. So you must work." And it was true! He set about to achieve extremely rigorous goals. Catherine Fitzmaurice was another big influence. She really made me look at the work I was doing and rethink it, which is always valuable. We all specialize a little bit, but Catherine comes to me and engages me in the certification teaching for really everything, and that's encouraged me to be a generalist in voice. Patsy Rodenburg came in to talk for a few days at Ohio State in 1994. She was talking about accent on the English stage, and she said, "Most people at the National speak RP, like I'm speaking now." And my measure for RP was distinctly different from what hers was—which I would say was in the Estuary camp. (She might disagree with that.) So her framing that for me really let me realize I had to go back to the drawing board and not take for granted the things that I knew about accent.

The Voice and Speech World of Today

Saklad: Would you describe the features that distinguish your work in the field?

Thompson: I'm the past president of VASTA, so I'm very much committed to and engaged in serving the profession. I'm also a protégée twice: I am Dudley's and Catherine's protégée. This is presumptuous of me, but I see it as my mission to continue their work on into the future as far as I can manage it. My place in the professional world is also as a voice and speech coach. I've been coaching for a long time, and I'm trying to do more work now in training new voice coaches.

Saklad: How would you describe the current state of affairs of actor training in voice and speech?

Thompson: I am incredibly optimistic, again because of VASTA. VASTA was instrumental in establishing voice teaching as a profession. We're also on the start of something that's a long time coming and revolutionary in the voice and speech profession. For a few years now, VASTA has had a diversity committee. In doing this we've had to do a couple of things: We recognize that bringing people into the voice profession involves getting people when they're young, and that means looking around at the people we're training and saying, "I choose to train you, and I'm not just choosing to train people who are like me." We've a very traditional group, because we are concerned with craft. I hear people talk all the time about, "How terrible it is, the kids of today. They spend all their time on the computer and they don't have a vigorous connection to language." I disagree. There's a generation of kids that we like to think of in our ivory tower as ill equipped. They're equipped with things that we're not equipped to perceive. We teachers are big enough and strong enough and broad enough to keep one foot in what we know and what we believe is beautiful and righteous and helpful and artistically correct, and we can also reach across the divide and be brave enough to be naïve and learn what our students are saying. If we don't, we're going to have to give up Shakespeare because we're all going to die, and if we *don't* reach out across that boundary to our students, they'll never trust us to learn what we know.

Saklad: What unique role does voice and speech training play within performance training?

Thompson: You can touch people really quickly and deeply. You can get right up next to somebody, their humanity and their performance, and you can do it in a way that isn't obtrusive, that is really beautiful. We walk right up to the boundary of physical resistance to an emotional life, and we invite students to cross that boundary, and we can do it in a way that is unrelated to a specific role, unrelated even to the actor's identity as an actor, and we can help the student to make tremendous change. I do think that we are the guardians to the sea change, the subtle transfiguration, the transmogrification of our actors' beings, their bodies, their selves, in a way that isn't directly about any of their specific acting skills. There's one last little detail that makes us unique, and that is we have so many different angles from which we can go at the work. We do voice work. We do breath work. We do posture work. We do rhythm work. We do text work. We do accent work. We address the performance in so many different ways, and in spite of the fact that theatre comes from the Greek word *to see*, opsis is the least important aspect of theatre. Spectacle isn't it. We go to hear a play. The essential ingredient of plays is people talking to each other.

Saklad: Where does vocal presence come from, and is it teachable?

Thompson: Presence comes from people, and we're in real danger if we see this particular quality or that particular quality as the equivalent of vocal presence; we're in a little bit of danger of imposing an outer shell on an actor. This, by the way, has been a fundamental divide in acting theory and is certainly a fundamental divide in voice training: Do we let the actor's self shine through, or do we offer skills? Do you let things happen, or do you do things? I think you do both. By inviting actors to experience the freedom of their breath, to discover where they're bracing, we're giving them a lot of freedom to not block. So we let actors shine. We let them grow into themselves, and that is the core of vocal presence and presence. Now there's another thing that we do. We help actors work muscles of strength, clarity of thought, and skill in negotiating the complexities of archaic text, so we also give actors tools for sharp engagement with the world, and that's necessary. We can do all the letting go we want to, but if we don't find a way to engage with other people with the text then we won't be present—or we'll be present to ourselves and not to our audience, and that's a failure.

Practical Considerations

Saklad: Do you think performance students benefit from studying multiple approaches to the work?

Thompson: Absolutely. This is one of the things that is so remarkable about Catherine's work and her certification. People come in with other ideas, and the ideas are folded in with the rest, and there's an open dialogue between approaches.

Saklad: What does the body need to produce optimal vocal work, and what types of body work do you use?

Thompson: The body needs freedom, alignment, and strength. Another way of thinking about alignment and strength is isolation of muscular activity. I use Fitzmaurice Destructuring, and I use a hodgepodge of physical interventions that I have stolen from Alexander, Feldenkrais, and a variety of other sources.

Saklad: Does an understanding of anatomy or the use of imagery deepen a student's understanding of his or her voice?

Thompson: I think the answer has to be yes to both for the reasons that I was just saying. Imagery is incredibly important. You do have to think an image so that the resultant action doesn't have unnecessary interference from your volitional musculature. A great source for this sort of thinking is Eugen Herrigel's *Zen in the Art of Archery*, and the key part of that that I'm sure a lot of people latch onto is, "Don't shoot the arrow, the arrow shoots itself," which seems very mystical, but the author goes on to investigate why that idea of letting the arrow shoot itself is important. It's because if you decide to let go of the arrow, you will unconsciously add a little pressure that will jiggle the arrow, and it won't hit the target. So we could say, "Don't shoot the actor, the actor shoots himself," or, "Don't shoot the impulse, the impulse shoots itself." An image is an organizing principle that is entirely appropriate for a human being to engage in that creates a physical result that we could record and specify. I'm a very, very materialistic person—not in the sense of liking fast cars, but in believing that the world as we know it is the world of material, that there isn't magic in the world except for the magic of our imaginations. So we will often be more successful in creating the results we want by the use of imaginary constructs than we might be by pursuing those results directly, treating our bodies like marionettes.

Saklad: How do you address breath work?

Thompson: Using Catherine's model of Destructuring and Restructuring. Destructuring is a process of interfering with the interference that human beings put into their natural flow of breath. I've described the problem of breathing in performance as an uneasy truce between the need to respirate and the need to communicate, and that's tough. We're doing two different things with the same system, and we have to take turns, and then we have a whole emotional life that lives within our breath. Destructuring helps us to untangle that conflict, and Restructuring leads us to an effective but supple use of breath to "support" our expressions.

Saklad: What happens when there is no support?

Thompson: Well first, I should probably give a brief explanation of what happens when the voice is operating smoothly. Whenever we make a trill with our lips or with our vocal folds, we're relying on the Bernoulli effect. That is, essentially, that higher-speed air has lower pressure. The faster air moves, the lower its pressure, all else being equal. And so when we want to start making voice, our vocal folds close until pressure builds up and overcomes the force of that closure. Once the vocal folds are opened, the air starts moving again, and because it's moving, the air pressure drops. The vocal folds can then fall back together, stopping the air flow and starting the cycle over again. And that happens again and again and again, because each of these events creates the conditions under which the next event occurs. In order for that to work, there has to be a sweet spot of perfect balance between the flow of pressure and the elasticity or the strength of adduction of the vocal folds. So when there isn't enough air to make it vibrate, you end up recruiting other muscles to make that vibration happen; and because there isn't a lot of perceptual feedback, certainly in the intrinsic muscles of the larynx but in the whole neck itself, you end up doing more work than you have to do when you don't have enough air to speak on. The same thing is true if you're pushing too much air through. Then you have to brace against it, and you have these people who are like weightlifters who are squeezing their vocal folds together for that reason. For easy phonation to happen there has to be a balance. If you don't have enough support, then you end up working too hard to make that happen.

Saklad: You have a unique approach to accent work. Would you talk a little bit about that?

Thompson: The approach is something that, as I mentioned before, I've come to with my work with Dudley, but I think the story that talks about the inception of these ideas is the one to help clarify what the ideas are. In graduate school I learned about accents, and I read the books that one reads. The approach I used was one of "substitutions"—a simple list of sounds that were noticeably different in the target accent. The methodology was out there in Jerry Blunt's book and other books and it all made sense to me. Then I went off to work on my own and was placed in a situation where I had to coach a Romanian dialect for *Mad Forest* that wasn't in any of the books. I had to find not only one Romanian accent but a whole variety of Romanian accents. So I did what probably many other people do: I found a Romanian and interviewed her and went right to work transcribing what I perceived as the accent features that I was hearing. But what I really did was listen to the sample enough times that I "felt it."

Saklad: Would you describe what you mean by "felt it"?

Thompson: I had internalized the accent in some actorly way. I was transcribing the substitutions, carefully analyzing not only what was on the tape, but what had already gone into my brain and into my body. I had taken on this accent, and I was writing down what I was experiencing. I realized at that point that I was not dealing with that in my teaching, that I had an ability as an accent performer that I wasn't yet teaching anybody how to do. That intuitive—and I'll now say physical grasp on what's going on with an accent is something that I took for granted, that many actors take for granted. Actors do all sorts of things that nobody told them how to do. And so I decided at that point that I needed to start teaching what was under the hood of my own accent ability, and I did this through a variety of approaches. I started to use computers a lot more to listen to sounds, to slow them down and so forth. I had been teaching for several years and developing these ideas on my own. Then, when I rejoined the faculty of UC Irvine and began to work closely with Dudley again, the both of us formulated this approach together, which is to discover the physical reality of the accent before using the descriptive vocabulary of phonetics. In this work, we're trying to help students attend carefully to what's going on in their mouths when they speak, and how an accent might flow naturally out of a particular configuration of the vocal tract. One of the problems that Dudley and I both see in accent work is that there's a little bit too much analysis of sound changes, which can lead an actor to simply execute mechanically changes in sound rather than experiencing the physical configuration that makes those changes useful, inevitable, or comfortable. That very much matches the process that I've described before of how we approach speech in general, which is to gain a physical understanding before going after the symbolic understanding. When Dudley and I met up in Chicago at a VASTA conference, I mentioned that I had this wonderful idea about oral posture. And he coincidently said, "I also feel that vocal track posture." Essentially we had come up with the same image, simultaneously and independently. Although I think you have to credit him since he was my teacher, so he probably inserted that seed in my head somewhere. So by thinking about what John Laver calls "The Settings of your Oral Posture"—Laver is an English linguist who writes about the settings of the vocal tract, where the tongue is, where the lips are—we find exactly the way we are describing oral posture.

Saklad: It sounds like you're going right to the physical root of the dialect.

Thompson: Exactly. If I'm really moving my lips forward, I'm going to feel something that's different from me, and my linguistic imagination will be drawn into that. I suppose that this is sort of a summary statement about a lot of what I think about voice work. We have to be incredibly intellectually rigorous and science based. By that I mean we really have to use terminology that has a specific meaning that we can all share and understand. We need to use logic and observation in a way that helps in the transmission of knowledge. We have to do that for the service of the magic and wonderment and emotional joy that is theatre making.

Saklad: How would you describe the role of listening in voice and speech work?

Thompson: Fundamental. There is no communication without listening. This manifests itself in every interaction we have as human beings. It manifests itself in how we are open to a text and to our fellow actors, allowing them to touch us and shift us and give us something that we are bringing to the table, but there's something more that I find, and most frequently, it's the quickest road to freeing up an actor's performance. Here's my big secret: *inhalation is acting too*. Actors so frequently try to put all their acting in the exhalation and then feel a little embarrassed that they have to take a breath. Breeeathe! There's a room full of air!

Saklad: You and Dudley Knight have been instrumental in the development of a unique, non-Skinnerian approach to speechwork. Would you describe some of the features of this work?

Thompson: I'll refer you to the Dudley's articles, also my article "Phonetics and Perception" in the *Voice and Speech Review*, Vol. 5, August 2007. At its core, we're rejecting a notion that speech can be "good" and replacing it with a notion that perhaps speech can be "good for something." We're rejecting the notion, too, that the first project of speech teaching is to eliminate the student's home accent, his or her personal identity, and replace it with a new accent that is, in our estimation, neutral.

Saklad: How would you describe the relationship between emotion and voice and speech work?

Thompson: Obviously emotion in life as in voice and speech needs to be respected, and it's absolutely true that working on voices exposes emotion, and the tools for freeing breath will generate emotional responses. I won't go into much detail as to how that occurs, but I think it's really important for a teacher to come back to the work. When an actor begins to weep, the teacher's project is still their breath, not what they're crying about. If they're angry, I don't care if they're angry about their mommy; I don't want to get into that conversation.

Saklad: How do you see scientific and technological advancements influencing your work or the work at large?

Thompson: I do try to read as much as I can about linguistics and voice science. But as I said earlier, science is useful to the point where it gives students a revelation that is able to be felt. I also use technology in the classroom quite a bit, primarily for the manipulation and playback of speech sounds.

Moving into the Future

Saklad: What advice would you give to voice and speech teachers at the beginning of their careers?

Thompson: You have to teach what's in front of you, and you also have to listen to your instinct. So as long as you are well prepared—you've learned everything and learned it well and you do a lesson plan—then you have to walk into the classroom and encounter who's there, what's happening, and really see the results of the exercise you're trying. Preparation is your friend, because then you know you can fill the time, but you have to move from there into listening to the students. I also have to say that if you're in an academic institution that deals with tenure, then you should definitely connect yourself to the Voice and Speech Trainers Association.

Saklad: What advice would you give to actors on the brink of their professional careers?

Thompson: They have to trust themselves in the same way that a teacher does, and they have to invest primarily in their own engagement as an artist and their engagement and passion with things outside of their primary art. We get so caught up in how to get the job, how to run the interview, and how to manage our careers—and that's incredibly important, but it's a hollow victory if you're not also feeding yourself as an actor. Your voice—that is to say, your *self*, what you have to express—is something worth cultivating.

Saklad: What do you think the future holds for voice and speech training?

Thompson: I made some references to this throughout. I think that a greater diversity and a real sea change in the way we think about our mission as voice teachers is underway. I think our profession as a profession is strengthening day by day, but I think the greatest challenge facing us now is integrating technology. Amplification is moving forward under its own power, and I don't think we can put the genie back in the bottle. We need to train actors so they can do both. We need them to be astute and sensitive to making a big sound in a big old space, and also adjusting themselves so that they can provide the material that will be best picked up by a microphone. It's more work to do, but it's vital, and that will probably lead to people saying, "Oh, I guess we don't need to mike this." That could happen in the future.

Saklad: What impact do you hope your work will have on vocal training at large, Phil?

Thompson: I do think that part of my reach is extended by VASTA. I really believe in VASTA's mission. The heart of who I am as a teacher is in the coming together of scientific rigor, I hope, and creative imagination. We go astray when we go too far down one road or another. I think we need to balance at the middle. So what I really hope is that I can bring some clarity and rigor to our understanding of how actors' voices work, but also apply that understanding in such a way that our students' creativity and autonomy are strengthened.

Andrew Wade

Andrew Wade was head of voice at the Royal Shakespeare Company from 1990–2003. He codirected and devised with Cicely Berry *Journeys, Words, Words, Words, More Words,* and *Lifespan*—a poetry and prose collection later developed into a theatrical program that was commissioned by the BBC World Service and won a bronze medal at the International Radio Festival in New York in 2000. Wade has travelled the world widely—lecturing, leading master classes and workshops, as well as coaching for theatre companies in over twenty countries. From 1993–97 he was external examiner for the postgraduate diploma in voice studies, and MA in voices studies, at the Central School of Speech and Drama. In 2002 he was made a fellow of the Rose Bruford College. Andrew was verse consultant on the film *Shakespeare in Love.*

Photo by Mike Haberman

Background

Nancy Saklad: Who are your mentors, Andrew?

Andrew Wade: Well in my professional life, without question it's Cicely Berry. To have had the opportunity to be a colleague and friend of hers for seventeen years at the RSC has been a huge gift.

Saklad: And were there any other influences that shaped your work?

Wade: As a child, my appetite was sparked by an inspirational drama teacher named Jean Harley, who lived in Lincolnshire in the flatlands of England. She happened to have a passion for Shakespeare. She gave me the experience of discovering the congenital role language plays in distinguishing oneself in society. Shakespeare allowed me—as a very quiet, inarticulate child—to understand that role. Looking back, I didn't realize at the time how important those years were. On the weekend, in the summer, I would be involved with poetry, performing Shakespeare outside in the grounds of a hotel in Stamford Lincolnshire. Those experiences were defining me, and I understood myself by having that language move through me.

The Voice and Speech World of Today

Saklad: What features distinguish your work in the field today?

Wade: I think the career that I've had has invited me to respond to the needs of the productions and to the needs of the directors, hopefully using sound principles of voice production grounded in disciplines of rhetoric. I'm reluctant to conform to a particular technique or a style, because it seems to me when I was at the RSC, or when I work at the Guthrie or at Oregon Shakespeare Festival—when I'm working with a cast of actors who range in age and who come from different backgrounds, some with training, some not—I really have to find a way to help the actors find what's appropriate for what they're doing without imposing technique on them. I have a viewpoint, which means that voice work to me is voice work for language. Over the years, through my own experience and voice exploration, I have formulated my own perceptions of language, but when working professionally, I have to respect that everyone accesses their voice and their connection to language in a different way from me or anyone else. It's really just a matter of keeping the work practical all the time. I have to keep reminding myself that voice work is not that complicated, and sometimes we voice people perhaps can overcomplicate it. I learned very early on that an experienced actor simply doing breathing work on the floor—feeling the ribs opening up and the diaphragm filling down, and so forth—is having an infinitely different experience from my own as a student actor. So it's not necessarily just what I'm coaching the actors to do. It's also giving those actors the opportunity to develop their own physical ability, while I remain constantly aware of what they're bringing. Often what we're doing is quite straightforward. When Cicely took me to meet her teacher Gwyneth Thurban, who used to run Central, she said amongst other things that she hadn't been able to sleep for the past two weeks, and then she got up and wrote down everything she knew about voice. (I believe she was in her nineties then, so that was quite an undertaking!) She produced four full pages of pencil-written notes, and then she looked very sternly at me and said, "Remember, Andrew, as you carry on working, in my lifetime there have been many different techniques of breathing...[pause]...but there is only *breathing*."

Saklad: That's a great story. How would you describe the current state of affairs of American actor training?

Wade: I'm grateful that most of my work now is in the United States, and I'm really enjoying it. I am working in a different culture and, in many ways, a different system than the one I grew up in and have spent most of my working life in. I can't help but compare. On the one hand, it would be too easy to say there are too many training programs. On the other hand, I think there may be too many people training. It seems that most everyone here in the US is an actor, and I don't get that in many other cultures. A lot more people seem to want to train as an actor. I'm also learning that a difference between the United States and Great Britain is that in the US, a theatre is more closely attached to a training program, such as the Guthrie Theatre's relationship with Juilliard and the University of Minnesota. That's not the case in my experience. I'm also finding that the idea of company work often seems to be talked about, craved, and practiced in training institutions. I sense that in the last year there was a change in the air in the actor's response to his or her confidence of language, and I wonder if that's to do with the fact that suddenly we have someone in charge of this country who is very verbally articulate. In working with actors on Shakespeare, I sense an appetite and a relish to work on being verbally articulate that hasn't been there in years. That translates into students in programs who have an excitement and vulnerability for Shakespeare that gladdens one's heart and makes one want to carry on. So I think the climate is particular. In professional companies, I'm also feeling a new and increasing respect for voice and language work. The whole idea of what rehearsal is, is changing in interesting ways. It's not just necessarily those four, five, or six weeks before opening. When I coached and co-directed *Hamlet* at the Guthrie, the actor playing Hamlet and I were both paid to work on that part over a year before we went into the main rehearsal process. That's very encouraging. I often resort to the French word at this point before rehearsal, *repetition*, to remind us all that by repeating something over and over, one will discover something. I think that underpins a lot of the work that I feel I'm invited to do in a rehearsal—to give people the opportunity to discover by repeating.

Saklad: What do you consider the greatest voice and speech obstacles that student actors face today?

Wade: The danger with a lot of voice and speech work today is that it appears to be about solving vocal problems. I learned very quickly from working with professional actors that that approach is no help at all. For better or for worse, they've got to be out there on that stage that night, and for better or worse they have already been hired. When I started teaching in the 1970s one of the first obstacles I encountered was how to actually help the student actors understand the need for voice and text work from an actor's point of view. I'd ask, "How could I help the actor meet the demands of this play in this space?" So I used to take them to a place called Speaker's Corner in Hyde Park in London and put them in a big space outside and let them experience debating in front of an audience. They would start to realize it's not about being inadequate. It's just that as an actor I may have demands put on me that my apparatus has not had to deal with in everyday life. I don't think that's any different today. Because in the end you're trying all the time, aren't you, to give the individuals an opportunity to take responsibility for their own work so that they know what's required and what they're working towards.

Saklad: So you're empowering them.

Wade: Yes, and in the end I suppose they become their own teacher. I think too often our societies today want to control people, by enforcing our own ideologies, which really disempowers them. I think perhaps the biggest challenge—and it's one I don't have the answer for, because we're working through it—is that in training we have to always be careful, don't we, that we're not just imposing on prior or present training. It is very clear that the actors are coming from very, very different experiences through their education. I think we're going through a period in Europe and in the United States where we're pushing people into a system that may not actually be responding to all the needs of these young people today. Too often do we adapt a didactic approach of "Simon says," where instructors expect the students to mimic their own methods. It's one language, but there's more than one way to speak it. There's a better way. I think that's the big challenge today.

Saklad: Do you think voice and speech training plays a unique role in actor training?

Wade: [laughs] Otherwise I'm wasting my life away! Yes. Do I think it plays a central role? I hope so. When training programs first started in Great Britain, they were led by voice and speech teachers. Then they became led by acting teachers. These days, they often have to be run by people who are not necessarily practitioners in theatre, but business or inspiring leaders in another way. The truth is that voice and speech can be trivialized, taking a back seat to what is more visually appealing or entertaining. Theatre is grounded in rhetoric—the art of speaking words to communicate life as we know it. So as a portion of the cake, our area, yes, is very important.

Saklad: Where does vocal presence come from, and is it teachable?

Wade: I suppose it comes down a lot to taste, taste for you the listener in many ways. So that's also a tricky one when we are instructors, when we are coaches, when we are teachers, isn't it. My particular taste for vocal presence is when that speaker is absolutely engaged with that particular language and passionately wanting to share that particular story through the playwright's words.

Saklad: You are an accomplished and insightful text coach of Shakespeare, Andrew. Where does your keen sense of humanity derive from?

Wade: If I am . . . it seems to be the only way that I am passionately fed as a person in my professional life. And I care. I care about verbal communication. I care about humanity in that way, I suppose.

Practical Considerations

Saklad: Do you think students benefit from studying multiple approaches?

Wade: That's a good question. I'm aware that in this country that seems to be a current wave of training—that an actor is given opportunities to experience this and that, through that person or this so-called technique, and it seems that the jigsaw pieces are put together either by themselves or in some better institutions through the guidance of tutors. I think of course we should all be open to as many different experiences as possible. I do think, however, that it needs to be within certain guidelines or the viewpoint of that institution, because in the end, I would like to believe that an actor leaves a training with a viewpoint of how to approach acting.

Saklad: What do you think the body needs to produce optimal vocal work?

Wade: Opportunities to practice—being put through the process of work repeatedly in order to reassure that the voice is absolutely an aspect of the whole body.

Saklad: How do you address breath work?

Wade: By getting people to breathe. There is only breathing. It's your energy, absolutely. It's a lifetime constant search. We all know that it's a much more complex situation when you're doing it. I learned very early on that accessing breath and sound without words is much easier than accessing it with words. I've learned over time that I need to involve words much earlier than I thought, because in the end the actor wants to speak words. I think if there were any simplistic development in my own work, I would say that I start with words and work outwards today rather than work up to words. You're then hopefully finding why you need the breathing work, because it serves something.

Saklad: What does it mean to support the voice?

Wade: I think for me it amounts to accessing the outgoing breath. If you are feeding the vocal folds with the appropriate stream of air—whether that's to do with you engaging certain external muscles—I think the central aspect that we're all looking for is the true feeding of that breath and producing a good clear sound, but also finding ways in which actors are able to access a deeper, fuller breath and do it enough times that they can feel a difference— if it does make a difference to their sound and connection to language.

Saklad: What role does listening play in the work?

Wade: It is *it*, period. And I think I would rest my case there. I'm aware that many of us as practitioners will talk about the need to be visually aware of what's going on with the actor. The whole idea of being able to truly listen is a particular challenge for us all today in our visually dominated society.

We resort quickly to saying, "I'm going to see a play" and don't say, "We're going to hear the play." So I feel that much of my work is about encouraging an audience to see with their ears as well as with their eyes. Listening is very, very important. It is a particular area where I feel the work craves attention today. In the workshop that I'm presently doing at Julliard, I want to help the actors hear the possibilities of the language rather than manipulate that language into a possibility or try to impose a certain way of doing it. Instead, I encourage them to actually sound it out—vocalize the thought, vocalize the meaning, taste the words. One of my favorite quotations from Oscar Wilde is, "How do I know what I think until I hear what I say?" I think a lot of the work is summed up in that way.

Saklad: How would you describe the connection between emotion and voice and speech work?

Wade: There seems to be so much investigation for an actor in this area that if I can make any contribution, it's to actually put people in situations where they discover that actual emotion comes out of action, comes out of speaking, as opposed to some other layer that is there. For example, in the first rehearsal (which I like to call the "word rehearsal") we had with the Julliard company the other day, we looked at the speech from Titus: "If there were reasons for these miseries—" and we were playing around with it and sounding it out, and I got the actors to read it all together, and one actor had to leave the circle. When she came back she said, "I'm so sorry but that was actually making me wretch. I was going to be sick." Well, the speech is about vomiting. She got very pale. Now I did not set out to do that, but many of them had quite a strong emotional reaction to that piece. That wasn't my desire. But on the other hand, it is part of it. That's the only way I can answer it. But yes, we worked on emotion. But that wasn't what I went in that room to do; that just happened because we were doing other things.

Saklad: There's a passage that you wrote once. I think it was in *The Vocal Vision* that I am quoting here. It's so perfectly crafted, and I quote, "The issue that we are what we speak must never cease to be a preoccupation." Then there's a little break in the text. "Precision of words is what fascinates me. It is the journey between finding the articulatory truth of someone else's shaped thought in a carefully worded line and finding the reference point to a truth of our own. There is a definition of self when you actually achieve this. Such precision creates an elation. It is never about a descriptive external impression, but about the absolute delight of the moment of the word." So beautifully stated. How might you start an actor in training on this journey?

Wade: I did a workshop the other week for an undergraduate group at NYU. It was their first year, and I'd been briefed that they were just beginners. They were very tentative, and I'm sure what was expected of me was to do a very basic voice class in terms of breathing, resonance, and so forth. I tried to go in to do that and I couldn't. I couldn't for various reasons. In the end I just took a very complex piece of Shakespeare, and we worked on that. What that group was observing may not be what they'll observe in twenty years' time, but it was relevant for them, and that was the starting point. I had to start with words and start opening up either listening to what they know about their relationship to words or giving them opportunities to start confronting that—to begin to either reinforce that speech or to dismiss it. They may surprise me; I may be wrong. But I think it's got to be about words.

Saklad: How do you see scientific and/or technological influences affecting voice and speech training?

Wade: Well, if it can validate what we see as common sense I'm delighted. When I was at the RSC we used to be part of a voice team working with an ENT consultant and speech therapist. That was often very important and useful for the actor. We all know that if a doctor tells us something, we believe it. So I think that can be very beneficial. It ultimately doesn't excite me to know about all those physical things. I remember going to a conference in London with Cis, and I sat there in my early years at the RSC, and these speech consultants were talking about subglottal pressure. I have to admit it took me ages before I realized they were talking about breath!

Moving into the Future

Saklad: What advice would you give to voice and speech teachers at the beginning of their professional career?

Wade: Don't try and teach like other people by whom you have been taught. In the end we can only teach from our own passion and our own strength and our own confidence. Then I would say, as we've touched on: be careful about getting locked into one particular technique, as opposed to finding a viewpoint for the work that may involve different so-called "book approaches." And then a third one, because it's important to lead for goodness sake: fly the flag for keeping words alive in a vibrant, exciting, dynamic way.

Saklad: What do you think the future holds for voice and speech training?

Wade: I feel very optimistic. I think that I tend to speak more from the professional side than I do from the institutional-training side. I feel that from actors, from directors, from the theatrical profession at large that there is acknowledgment and respect that our subject plays an increasingly vital and important role. I think you have to be very strong in yourself as a voice person to carry on struggling, because in the end it is about the challenge of struggling. I'm not quite sure we ourselves will know if we've actually quite achieved something in the broader society in terms of what we want voice actually to be about. I think people sometimes forget the actual purpose of theatre. It isn't to entertain. In fact that is just a byproduct. It is to shock, to embarrass, to encourage, to illuminate life. Whoever said "sticks and stones can break my bones, but words can never hurt me" has never felt a playbill.

Saklad: What impact do you hope your own work will have on vocal training at large, Andrew?

Wade: I would like my epitaph to be, "His ego was in his work, not in himself." I mean that one hopes that if one has made a contribution, that it is about trying to keep Shakespeare in particular, that verbal language alive and heard and accessible for us all. And to loop it back just to being political—again, I'm sure this is from the influence of being around Cis— but it seems to me that working sometimes in elitist theatre or a very particular area of society, one needs to keep oneself grounded. The work is about dealing with seemingly relevant things like a line ending or whatever or meter, when actually it's really about that political importance that perhaps we all might be able to get on better and understand each other if we were more curious and wanted to actually communicate with each other, because only by communicating will I understand, potentially, someone living in Iraq. So for me it's actually about that.

Robert Neff Williams

Robert Neff Williams is professor emeritus of the drama division of the Juilliard School, where he taught from 1970 to 2010, heading the voice and speech work from 1988 to '93. In charge of the speech division of the department of English and Comparative Literature at Columbia University until 1990, he was also head of voice for the original theatre division at Columbia's School of the Arts. He was chairman for ten years of the voice and speech section of the Neighborhood Playhouse School of the Theatre, and conducted actor training workshops for many of the major regional theatre programs, as well as his private two-year classes. Many Hallmark Hall of Fame television productions carried his credit as speech consultant, and in 1973 he held a Folger Shakespeare Library Fellowship. Mr. Williams has been voice and text consultant for many Broadway, off Broadway, and regional theatre productions. In New York City, he has had a continuing association with the Pearl Theatre and Theatre for a New Audience, receiving honors from both for lifetime achievements, and he was awarded an honorary doctorate in 2007 by the University of South Dakota, his alma mater.

Note: Robert's history as a voice, speech, and text coach and teacher is extraordinary. Since he is quite modest about his accomplishments, for this interview I invited his former student, current voice and speech teacher Shane Ann Younts, to join our conversation, in order to paint a generational picture of this iconic master teacher. Shane Ann was Robert's student in private group classes over twenty-five years ago, and she teaches voice and text work using his methods (specializing in the works of Shakespeare) in New York University's graduate acting department, where she is an associate arts professor and head of the voice/speech/text program. In addition she works professionally as voice/dialect coach for

Broadway and off Broadway theatres. She is the coauthor (with Louis Scheeder) of *All the Words on Stage, a Complete Pronunciation Dictionary for the Plays of William Shakespeare*.

Nancy Saklad: Who were some of your mentors, Robert?

Robert Neff Williams: Nadine Shepherdson, Gertrude Keller, Robert and Priscilla Bollard, Rita Morgenthau, Evangeline Machlin, Louise Gifford, and Edith Skinner.

Saklad: What is it that they did that inspired you in the work?

Williams: They set an example. Edith, for instance, was the *doyenne* of theatre speech. She was the person who began it all and whom everyone emulated.

Saklad: Did you work from her book *Speak with Distinction*?

Williams: No I didn't, because I have my own exercises.

Shane Ann Younts: A lot of your way of teaching speech was very similar to Edith's. The biggest difference was in the r-color because Edith didn't use r-color, right?

Williams: That's correct.

Younts: So her prescribed speech sounded a little British.

Saklad: And with your own work, did you use the r-coloring?

Williams: Yes, of course.

Younts: I remember one of the things that Robert always talked about was that he wanted American actors to sound American and not sound vaguely English or vaguely mid-Atlantic.

Saklad: When you think of all the different things that you do, and I've heard you do everything—

Williams: —what do you mean by "everything"?

Saklad: Voice, speech, text work, making the language clear, Shakespeare—

Younts: It might be easier to say what you don't do, Robert. Years ago when I was looking for a teacher, I could find a *voice* teacher, I could find a *speech* teacher. I didn't find anyone that we could call a *text* teacher. But the whole concept that these things might be linked—I never found until I found you. Today almost everyone, even if they say they're a voice teacher, also does speech. Or if they say they're a speech teacher, they'll do some kind of a voice warm-up. But when I was starting out, that was not the case. Edith was a speech teacher and she didn't do voice work. [To Saklad] This was very unusual for that time, what Robert did—the whole concept of putting voice, speech, and text together.

Williams: You can't separate them really.

Younts: Teachers do all the time.

Saklad: Why do you think you can't separate them, Robert?

Williams: Because the speaking becomes very artificial.

Younts: But I think what you do, Robert—at the time you started doing it—it was revolutionary in a way. One of the things you do is include the historic context of the play and details like how a person would hold his or her body or her fan or his cane, and which foot would be placed where, and so on.

Williams: Well you know, I do that because the young actors don't know any of that. Nobody teaches style anymore. So you have to do that or they're going to kind of shamble around.

Younts: [To Saklad] I remember watching him show a woman how to use a fan. It was for a restoration poem—how to use a fan and how to curtsy, because it's true the students don't know how to do that.

Saklad: I've also heard that you do a unique introduction to the work in the first two days of a rehearsal process. Would you describe it?

Williams: I bring in lots of pictures, images for the world of the play—pictures of the interiors and of the clothes, and pictures of famous actors—because the students don't really get any exposure to any of that.

Saklad: You don't hear about integrating the acting-style elements very often from the voice, text, and speech coach—more often, perhaps, from the director.

Younts: His process is a remarkable education that he gives the students. Before they ever even stand up and start doing the language, you can just see their imaginations are already in motion—"Oh I'd be wearing that," "Oh my hair would be styled like that," and so forth. I've watched his first presentations to a class a number of times; he has these huge notebooks filled with pictures and postcards—

Saklad: So it's a way into the style of the language, and your work gives life to the text in a way that is intimately tied to the acting of each particular play.

Williams: That's right.

Saklad: When you coach a play, how would you prioritize what you do?

Williams: First the actors must understand the text. If they understand what they're saying, it'll all be fine. But if they are a little vague, or they don't have any kind of reference points for the language, then the speaking of the text is going to be unclear and not very interesting.

Younts: I still remember when I was your student doing Julia's speech from *Two Gentlemen of Verona*. And when she has the letter all torn up, she has the line: "Be calm good wind, blow not a word away till I have found each letter," and Robert came over—I'm kneeling with the letter, and he's right there by me, and I didn't know it—I was going on with the speech, and he blew my letter all over the place. "Be calm good wind, blow not a word away, till I have found each letter in the letter" —I will never forget how that physical example clarified what I needed in a way that for me no explanation could ever clarify. My voice changes came out of what happened in that moment, so that the vibrancy of the language came to life and continued through to the end of the speech. That's part of his genius. He was the wind. So it's two things really: what the actor is saying and then the context—making it so specific that the student would never forget it.

Saklad: Robert, I have a passage from your work *Speech Practice Exercises* (2nd ed., 1982) that speaks to the properties of the work that Shane Ann describes:

> The actor's diction and voice should serve the language, ideas, emotions, style, and world of the play. It should not call attention to itself as voice and diction which is especially grand or awkward or

beautiful or unclear, or to the personal idiosyncrasies of the actor rather than those of the character being played.

Because the language of classic plays is normally what is termed "heightened" or "elevated text," it is more convoluted in form, and uses more elaborate and sometimes archaic words, than our current, everyday language. Therefore, above all, the actor's voice and speech must be flexible, varied, and expressive enough to convey every nuance and color and subtle shading of the words the character uses, whether in intellectual argument or emotional outburst. If the diction is slurred and careless, the words will be incomprehensible, and if the voice is dull and monotonous, the language will be flat and without vibrancy.

Saklad: So clear. When did you start teaching, Robert?

Younts: I would love to know the answer to that. When did you start?

Williams: Well at the end of the war, I was involved in the effort to place GIs in civilian training programs all over the world. And when it was my turn, I sent myself to the Guildhall School in London for six weeks. I studied with Sir Reginald Bassant, who said to me [stern voice]:"Mr. Williams, I want you to go home and think about your *diaphragm*." What I mainly did was to go to the theatre. It was lovely to be in London at that time. I saw Edith Evans, Laurence Olivier, Peggy Ashcroft, John Gielgud, and all the famous actors. I went back to the university after the war to visit people I knew there, and they asked me if I would stay and teach speech in the drama department. So I did. I didn't have anything to lose.

Saklad: Where was that, Robert?

Williams: The University of South Dakota. But then I decided very soon that there wasn't much scope at the university, and I had a choice of going to Northwestern where I had met Nadine Shepherdson earlier—she was a teacher of oral interpretation and a marvelous woman—or New York City. So I picked New York. I'd never been to New York, and I'd been to Northwestern. And I was invited to go to NYC to teach one or two courses at Columbia and do graduate work. But I started right off teaching full time because they were so overwhelmed with soldiers coming back from the war that they were in need of teachers.

Saklad: From whom did you learn how to teach speech?

Williams: Nobody, you just did it. I was also teaching at the Neighborhood Playhouse. I got that job through Bob Bollard, a wonderful guy, who was a singer as well as a teacher. Evangeline Machlin was the speech teacher at the playhouse who preceded me and hired me. She was British, and had very definite ideas about pronunciation and precision and so on. Rita Morgenthau was the head of the Neighborhood Playhouse until she retired in 1963. When she retired, I left.

Younts: But you were still teaching at Columbia at that same time?

Williams: Yes. And I had a number of interesting colleagues there: Gertrude Keller in theatre voice, Louise Gifford in movement and dance, and Mildred Daniel in speech and oral interpretation. Their work at the Columbia School of the Arts Theatre Division certainly was at the beginning of a kind of coherent actor preparation.

Younts: And you also did some coaching, didn't you, for individual plays and so on?

Williams: Yes, I did. The most notable one was probably with the Lunts—Alfred Lunt and Lynn Fontanne—in 1965. I was hired by Compass Productions to work with two other people who were in a Hallmark Hall of Fame television play they were in, *The Magnificent Yankee,* which is about a judge, Oliver Wendell Holmes, Jr. When everybody else went off to lunch, I would hide behind the scenery and spy on Alfred and Lynn. Alfred was an excellent cook, and he would bring a big basket covered with a red-and-white checked cloth and a bottle of wine sticking out one end and a long loaf of bread out the other. He would set up two chairs and a table, and they would sit down and have lunch. They were quite remarkable people. And I found out why they were so effective on the stage. It's because they worked everything out to a penny. I can remember Lynn Fontanne getting up and crossing the room and putting a chair *there* and saying, "Now, Alfred, do you think I should say the line when I get up, or on the way, or at the chair?" And they had a long discussion, you know? So that's why they were so good, because they worked everything out in detail. One time I was working with the other actors, and when they left and I turned around to go, Miss Fontanne swept up to me—she was the only woman I ever saw who could sweep in pants—and she said, "Mr. Williams!" and I thought, "Oh my God, there goes my job." So I said, "Yes?"

And she said, "Now in this line I have to say *vest*," and she said, "Wouldn't it be better if I said *weskit*?" And I thought, "Hmmmm," and I said, "Well, Miss Fontanne, as you know, Judge Holmes and his wife were Americans, and *weskit* is British." And she said, "You're quite right. I shall say *vest!*" And she swept away. Ahh, she was something.

Saklad: Did you do any other work in television?

Williams: I worked on a lot of the Hallmark plays, many of which were award-winning shows directed by George Schaefer. And I also worked on a number of other shows over the years, on Broadway, off Broadway, and all over the country. In 1988 I worked on *M. Butterfly* with B. D. Wong and John Lithgow. *The Autumn Garden* was a lovely Lillian Hellman play directed in 1951 by Harold Clurman with the Marches—Fredric March and Florence Eldridge—and a man named Colin Keith-Johnston. I've worked at many theatres doing warm-ups and classes for the whole company, and individual work with actors on the shows: the Milwaukee Repertory Theater, the Pacific Conservatory for the Performing Arts, the Guthrie, the Stratford Shakespeare Festival Theater in Connecticut, and the Stratford Festival in Ontario. In 1975 they set up a kind of "young company" and chose the people to be trained: Colm Feore, Lucy Peacock, and so on, and I enjoyed working with them. At the Great Lakes Shakespeare Festival in Ohio I conducted some extensive training for Vincent Dowling, and worked on their *Nicholas Nickleby* in 1982, a very successful show that was eight hours long and had nearly fifty actors in 300 roles. In the 1960s and '70s Vincent had been the head of the Abbey Theatre in Dublin where I also worked. They had never had any kind of voice training there when he brought me over.

Saklad: And you were doing private classes too, I believe.

Williams: During all that time after the playhouse, I was conducting private two-year classes, with a new one starting each year and overlapping with the previous group. There just seemed to be a demand for it, and word got around. I never had more than about a dozen in each group, because there wouldn't have been time for the kind of individual work we did. When I stopped doing private classes, I still did summer workshops coordinated by Jeffrey Horowitz at Theatre for a New Audience for six or seven years, focusing on various types of theatre: Greek drama, Shakespeare, Restoration/

18th century, special workshops on Moliere, Shaw, Noel Coward. I've also worked a lot for Theatre for a New Audience on specific shows, such as the 2009 *Othello* directed by Arin Arbus. And I've worked a great deal at the Pearl Theatre in NYC, including directing a couple of plays for them: Sheridan's *The Rivals* in 2003 and Shaw's *Misalliance* in 1996. I had met Joanne Camp in Washington when I was working on a play, and when she got established at the Pearl, she called and asked me if I would come downtown and work with their group. She and her husband, Shep Sobel, the artistic director, did classic plays there for over twenty-five years and they really worked on them in the best way. That is, they worked on the speech and on the language.

Saklad: So most of your work was coaching voice and text. And when did you move over to Juilliard?

Williams: I started at the Juilliard Drama Division when it was pretty much brand new, in about 1970. I knew a lot of marvelous people at Juilliard. Edith Skinner was the head of speech, first at Carnegie Mellon and then she came to Juilliard. Elizabeth Smith was the one who brought me there. Tim Monich, Marian Seldes, Ralph Zito—they were all excellent teachers.

Saklad: When you think about voice and speech training over the span of time from early in your career to now, do any specific changes come to mind?

Williams: I think the work develops, but I don't think there's a huge change somewhere along the line. Do you, Shane Ann?

Younts: Well, I think that's an interesting question. I would think from the time when you first started teaching, training has probably changed a lot. Robert is—and I know I keep coming back to this—as far as I know he was the only person I knew of to really combine voice and speech and text. Once you do that, you change everything, because then voice and speech work is going to get connected to the acting. Before that happened, there was the notion that the actor was training to have a "beautiful" voice. It didn't matter that it wasn't connected to anything truthful; it was resonant and buttery and lovely. So I think that's a big change.

Williams: I guess it probably is.

Saklad: I'd say it certainly is. You've been instrumental in the growth of the work of so many actors. What do you think the students today most need to hear or do?

Williams: They need to practice. A lot of them don't.

Saklad: I'm sure you are not alone in that sentiment. Shane Ann, Robert is very humble about speaking about his own work and accomplishments. What can you tell us about his work and how he has affected your work and the work of your students?

Younts: Well, Robert's effect on my own teaching in particular is extensive. From Robert I learned the importance of connecting all of the elements of the voice/speech work to text—all kinds of texts. He would use a few lines of a poem to work on breathing and resonance; a line of text to increase the vocal range of the voice; dramatic passages, which he wrote, to work on diction; and in the advanced part of the program, he used the texts of Shakespeare. The Shakespeare work was always acted—never just recited. He has an uncanny ability to take any monologue and make it clear to the actor so that the actor can make it clear for the audience. Sometimes it is just explaining the text in a way that you have never thought of before, and sometimes it is a visual or physical image that takes the actor to another level. Working on a monologue with Robert is like juggling; you have to do everything, and you have to do everything well. My students benefit from Robert, not only because they are learning his exercises, but because his example as a teacher is always in my thought. He is specific, patient, challenging, perceptive, knowledgeable, and expectant of progress. To be in Robert's class was to see and hear improvement in all of your fellow classmates. When I studied with him, he made a recording of us at our first class and then a recording of us speaking the same material at the last class. When the two tapes were played back, the changes in our voices and our speech were truly astonishing. It made such an impression on me that I do the same thing. I record my students at the first class and the last class. It's exciting to see that same look of astonishment on their faces when they hear the changes in their voices. It is also gratifying to know that Robert's work continues through my students. Some of my former students are now teaching—in NYU's undergraduate drama department, at the Yale School of Drama, and one of them is now my colleague in NYU's graduate acting program.

Saklad: Robert, what do you find most enjoyable about the work that you do?

Williams: Oh, the students. Watching them work and improve over four years.

Saklad: Do any notable students stand out in your mind over the last forty years?

Williams: Robin Williams, Chris Reeve, Laura Linney…I had all the students who came through Juilliard. Robin always had that ability improvise and be funny. Chris was a classic leading-man type. Robin was very generous, because after Chris broke his neck in that riding accident, Robin supported him—took care of him—for the rest of his life. Laura was a good actress from the very beginning, in addition to being thoughtful and pleasant. She did some excellent work at Juilliard. Her father is Romulus Linney, who is a very well-known playwright. And she has gone on to be a versatile actor and the spokesperson for Masterpiece Theater.

Saklad: Of all the things that you have done in your career, what is it that you tried to impress upon your students the most?

Williams: Well, I've tried to improve the quality of their voices and their understanding of language in general.

Saklad: Classical language?

Williams: Yes. I'm not interested in—you know…rock and roll plays!

Younts: So it's the material? And learning how to interpret the material?

Williams: Yes.

Saklad: What would be your advice for teachers and young students?

Williams: Read aloud. Repeat the same passage three times in a row. You will learn more about what you're saying, and it will get clearer.

Saklad: How would you describe the evolution in voice and speech training that's happened in your lifetime? Has voice and speech training changed?

Williams: Well, it's developed. There's more of it. And it's better. I think there are more people interested in it, better teachers—

Younts: Do they do something different than, say, what Nadine Shepherdson did?

Williams: They don't approach it in quite the same way, because she did something called oral interpretation, which grew out of elocution and oration. And that's fallen out of favor; that's no longer popular.

Saklad: What do you think the future holds for speech and voice training, Robert?

Williams: Well, we hope it will continue!

Saklad: Yes, we do. Thank you Robert, and thank you Shane Ann.

Afterword

Teaching—at its heart and at its best—begets evolution. This is certainly true of the teaching of voice and speech. New methods and new values in vocal training have surfaced in the past few decades. Many voice and speech teachers are moving away from a prescriptive means of teaching and towards developing the actor's sense of self-exploration, self-understanding, and ultimately, self-reliance. Much attention is being focused on freeing the actor's instrument. Teachers place tremendous importance on the understanding and integration of holistic approaches to the work. Colleagues and departments are discussing not only what is taught, but also *how* it is taught. Science has partnered with vocal training. Seeking the "right" sound has been replaced with pursuing a sound that is free, expressive, and safely produced. Teacher certification and designation programs have become popular. Participants leave knowing they have plumbed the depths of the material. Some teachers pride themselves on the eclecticism of the training they offer, while others remain true to the idea that one method best suits the student's needs. Certainly, some of the future of training lies in the hands of the students and how we rise to meet their needs. In light of how far the field has come in just half a century, it's hard to imagine what might be next.

A Vision for the Future

Vocal master and visionary teacher Arthur Lessac, who turned 100 years old during the writing of this book, has been known to say that one of the reasons he does voice work is because he views his work as a means to world peace. I have been repeatedly inspired by his message. I asked his close colleague Nancy Krebs to communicate his sentiment, and she described it to me this way:

> When we possess healthy posture, which will promote healthy breathing, we have the potential to produce healthy, focused tone (resonance) in our voices. This tone which if full of concentrated and dilute vibrations that feed and fuel the bones of the face and the head, will be transmitted throughout our sensate being and fill us

with a sense of well-being and 'peace.' Then this vibratory resonance can be transferred to another person when we are speaking—especially when we are using our Y-Buzz like focus to communicate. There is an emotional equilibrium created within when we use our Y-Buzz like focus—so we will exist as our own personal 'peaceful world', because our emotional experiencing system is affected positively when in this focus; and when communicating with others, we will be able to share our views without stridency or shouting—even when speaking on a subject that might be filled with passion. This emotional climate filled with Y-Buzz like focus creates harmony between people in our immediate environment—creating peace between 'worlds', rather than inflame or incite a negative emotional response, and by extension, in the larger environment as more people learn how to use this training.

Initially perplexed by this notion, I imagined that I was listening to the voice of Dame Judi Dench or Meryl Streep or James Earl Jones or Daniel Day Lewis (and the list goes on), and I was instantly transported. I am persuaded by each of these distinguished actors to follow along on whatever imaginative journey they will take me. The voice can make apparent the life within—the thoughts, feelings, and desire of the speaker, but it is training that develops the persuasiveness, the expressiveness, and the eloquence of the voice.

The voice is the expresser of senses, the delineator of thought, the embracer of other people.

—Louis Colaianni

Appendix

Teacher Certification Programs

Type of Certification:

MFA in Voice Pedagogy at the American Repertory Theatre/Institute for Advanced Theatre Training at Harvard University

Taught by: Nancy Houfek and the faculty of the American Repertory Theater/Institute for Advanced Theater Training at Harvard University

Location: Cambridge, MA

Duration of study: Two and a-half years

Contact: Julia Smeliansky, Administrative Director
Julia_Smeliansky@harvard.edu
www.amrep.org

Type of Certification:

Colaianni Speech and the Joy of Phonetics

Taught by: Louis Colaianni

Location: New York , NY

Duration of study: Fifty to 100 private sessions, frequent workshops with trainee group, classroom observation

Contact: Louis Colaianni
louiscolaianni@gmail.com
(816) 419-6915
www.louiscolaianni.com

Type of Certification:

Certification Program for Associate Teachers of Fitzmaurice Voicework®

Taught by: Catherine Fitzmaurice, with lead trainer Saul Kotzubei, other master and associate teachers of Fitzmaurice Voicework®, and specialty guest artists that have included Richard Armstrong (Roy Hart), Nancy Krebs (Lessac Master Teacher), Elizabeth Bergmann (chair of dance, Harvard University), and Jae Gruenke (Feldenkrais)

Location/s: New York, NY and Los Angeles CA; (London, UK in preparation)

Duration of study: Two month-long sessions in the same month in two consecutive years. Prerequisites include one to three years of previous study of Fitzmaurice Voicework®, in college, workshops, private classes, or private study

Contact: Program Coordinator
Fitzmaurice Workshops
info@fitzmauricevoice.com
www.fitzmauricevoice.com

Types of Certification:

Certification to be a Lessac Practitioner

Certification to be a Lessac Certified Trainer

Taught by: Lessac master teachers

Location: DePauw University, Greencastle, IN

Duration of study: For Practitioner: Time varies from one year to two years

For Certified Trainer: Time varies from four years to five years

Contact: Barry Kur
bxk1@psu.edu
(814) 863 1453
www.lessacinstitute.com

Types of Certification:

Linklater Teacher Training to Become a Designated Linklater Teacher

Taught by: Trainees are assigned a senior Designated Linklater Teacher.

Location: Designation training is held in the US, Germany, Mexico, and London

Duration of study: About three years

Contact: Andrea Haring, Coordinator of Linklater Teacher Training
aharingvoice@aol.com
mail@thelinklatercenter.com
www.mail.thelinklatercenter.com

Bibliography

Acker, Barbara and Marion Hampton, eds. *The Vocal Vision: Views on Voice By 24 Leading Teachers, Coaches & Directors.* New York: Applause, 1997.

Ayers, Alfred. *Acting and Actors: Elocution and Elocutionists: A Book About Theatre Folk and Theatre Art.* New York: D. Appleton and Company, 1903.

Berry, Cicely. *From Word to Play: A Handbook for Directors.* Theatre Communications Group, 2008.

Berry, Cicely. *Voice and the Actor.* New York: Macmillan Publishing Company, 1973.

Boston, Jane and Rena Cook, eds. *Breath in Action: The Art of Breath in Vocal and Holistic Practice.* London and Philadelphia: Jessica Kingsley Publishers, 2009.

Clurman, Harold. *The Fervent Years: the Group Theatre & the 30's.* New York: Da Capo Press, 1975.

Colaianni, Louis. *The Joy of Phonetics and Accents.* Kansas City: Joy Press, 1994.

Curry, Samuel S. Foundations of Expression. Boston: The Expression Company, 1920.

Curry, Samuel S. *Mind and Voice.* Boston: The Expression Company, 1919.

Damousi, Joy and Desley Deacon, eds. *Talking and Listening in the Age of Modernity: Essays on the History of Sound.* Canberra, Australia: ANU E Press, 2007.

Delaumosne, L'Abbe. *The Delsarte System.* Frances A. Shaw, trans. 4th ed. New York: Edgar S. Werner Wehman Bros., 1893.

James, William and Carl Lange. *The Emotions.* New York: Hafner Publishing Co., 1967.

Lessac, Arthur. *Body Wisdom: The Use and Training of the Human Body.* San Bernadino: L.I.P.C.O., 1990.

Lessac, Arthur. *The Use and Training of the Human Voice: A Practical Approach to Speech and Voice Dynamics.* New York: Drama Publishers, 1967.

Linklater, Kristin. *Freeing the Natural Voice.* New York: Drama Publishers, 1976.

Linklater, Kristin. *Freeing Shakespeare's Voice: The Actor's Guide to Talking the Text.* New York: Theatre Communications Group, 1992.

Murdoch, James Edward, William Russell, and George James Webb. *Orthophony: or Vocal Culture in Elocution; A Manual of Elementary Exercises. Adapted to Dr. Rush's "Philosophy of the Human Voice," and Designed as an Introduction to "Russell's American Elocutionist."* Boston: William D. Ticknor and Co., 1845.

Northrop, Henry D. *Delsartre Manual of Oratory.* Cincinnati: W. H. Ferguson Company, 1895.

Rodenburg, Patsy. *The Need for Words.* New York: Routledge, 1993.

Rodenburg, Patsy. *The Right to Speak*. New York: Routledge, 1992.

Rush, James. *The Philosophy of the Human Voice: Embracing Its Physiological History: Together With a System of Principles, By Which Criticism in the Art of Elocution May be Rendered Intelligible, and Instruction, Definite and Comprehensive*. 4th ed. Philadelphia: Lippincott, Grambo, & Co., 1855.

Russell, William. *The American Elocutionist; Lessons in Enunciation, 'Exercises in Elocution', and 'Rudiments of Gesture'*. 4th ed. Boston: Jenks and Palmer, 1846.

Russell, William. *Orthophony; or the Cultivation of the Voice in Elocution*. Boston: James R. Osgood and Company, 1846.

Smith, Wendy. *Real Life Drama: the Group Theatre and America, 1931–1940*. New York: Alfred A. Knopf, 1990.

Stanislavsky, Constantine. *My Life in Art*. New York: Routledge, 1987.

Stebbins, Genevieve. *The Delsarte System of Dramatic Expression*. 6th ed. New York: Edgar Werner Publishing and Supply Co., 1902.

Taverner, Graham, F. *Reasonable Elocution: A Text-book for Schools, Colleges, Clergymen, Lawyers, Actors etc.* New York and Chicago: A. S. Barnes and Company, 1874.

Withers-Wilson, Nan. *Vocal Direction for the Theatre*. New York: Drama Book Publishers, 1993.

Zorn, John. *The Essential Delsartre*. Metuchen, NJ: Scarecrow Press, Inc., 1968.

Index

Roy Hart Theatre, 17, 18, 22, 232
Rubin, Lucille, 13, 106, 212
Rush, James, 2–3
    Philosophy of the Human Voice, The, 3
Russell, William, 2, 3

Satir, Virginia, 35
Schaefer, George, 269
School of Elocution and Expression (see
    School of Expression)
School of Expression, 5
science/technology, effect of, 1, 12, 31, 35,
    47, 56, 66–67, 83, 89, 101–2, 132, 143,
    148–149, 154, 189, 197, 209, 219, 228,
    235, 239, 241, 245, 249, 251, 252, 260
scientific approaches, 4–5, 12, 35, 63, 64,
    66–67, 86, 89, 101–2, 103, 111, 120,
    135–36, 137, 143, 147, 148, 154, 197,
    202, 212, 219, 220, 228, 229, 240,
    250–51, 252, 260, 275
Scheeder, Louis, 264
    *All the Words on Stage, a Complete
    Pronunciation Dictionary for the
    Plays of William Shakespeare* (with
    Younts, Shane Ann), 264
Scott, George C., 118–19, 218
Seattle Rep., 69
Sedona Shakespeare Festival, 231
Seldes, Marian, 270
Serban, Andrei, 211
Seyd, Richard, 158
Shakespeare, William (see also individual
    companies and chapters on Cicely
    Berry, Louis Colaianni, Kristin
    Linklater, Patsy Rodenburg, Susan
    Sweeney, Andrew Wade, and Robert
    Neff Williams), 12, 29–30, 35, 51,
    57–58, 65, 72, 78, 94, 106–7, 115–16,
    118, 126, 132, 133, 190, 195, 196–97,
    200, 219, 221, 224, 225–26, 238, 244,
    245, 253–54, 255, 257, 260, 261, 263,
    271
    Hamlet, 29, 49, 142, 203, 255
    Henry V, 53
    King Lear, 49, 195, 226

Macbeth, 203
Midsummer Night's Dream, A, 54, 107
Othello, 270
Romeo and Juliet, 36, 51, 203, 204, 226
Tempest, The, 203
Titus Andronicus, 259
Twelfth Night, 32
Two Gentlemen of Verona, 266
Winter's Tale, The, 50
Shakespeare and Company, 39, 40, 76, 115,
    119, 193, 201, 203, 204, 210, 232
Shakespeare Festival of St. Louis, 69
Shakespeare in Love, 253
Shakespeare Theatre Company
    (Washington, DC), 105
Shapiro, Mel, 39
Shaw, George Bernard, 1, 107, 270
    Pygmalion, 1
    Misalliance, 270
Shepherdson, Nadine, 264, 267, 273
Sheridan, Richard Brinsley, 270
    Rivals, The, 270
Show Boat, 231
Silverman, Stanley, 41
Simon, David, 170
Sitwell, Edith, 93
Skinner, Edith, 7, 10–11, 15, 32, 40, 74,
    105–6, 112–13, 125, 126, 131, 134,
    150–53, 231–32, 250, 270
    Speak with Distinction, 7, 151, 264
Skylight Opera Theatre, 264
Smith College, 115
Smith, Anna Deveare, 211
Smith, Elizabeth, 270
Sobel, Shep, 270
Sothern, E. H., 2, 3, 4
South Coast Repertory, 243
Speaker's Corner, 256
Speed, 203
Stanford University, 125
Stanislavsky, Constantin, 6–7, 52, 117, 198
Steiner, Rudolph, 10, 70, 77
    "Eurhythmy", 10, 77
Stern, Marcus, 126
Strasberg, Lee, 7, 8, 11